W9-AVG-176

ŚTUDIES IN EASTERN CHANT
Volume Three

STUDIES IN EASTERN CHANT

General Editors

EGON WELLESZ
and
MILOŠ VELIMIROVIĆ

VOLUME III

Edited by
MILOŠ VELIMIROVIĆ

London
OXFORD UNIVERSITY PRESS
NEW YORK   TORONTO
1973

Oxford University Press, Ely House, London W.1

GLASGOW NEW YORK TORONTO MELBOURNE WELLINGTON
CAPE TOWN IBADAN NAIROBI DAR ES SALAAM LUSAKA ADDIS ABABA DELHI
BOMBAY CALCUTTA MADRAS KARACHI LAHORE DACCA
KUALA LUMPUR SINGAPORE HONG KONG TOKYO

ISBN 0 19 316320 9

© Oxford University Press 1973

*Printed in Great Britain
by Billing & Sons Limited, Guildford and London*

Preface

WITH the appearance of this volume, relatively shortly after the publication of Volume II in 1971, the editors hope to come closer to the realization of the original intention of making the STUDIES IN EASTERN CHANT a bi-annual publication. At the time of this writing the contributions for Volume IV are being edited and will be submitted to the Press shortly.

Starting with this volume the STUDIES IN EASTERN CHANT will henceforth include publications of articles in other Western European languages besides English. Potential contributors and collaborators are herewith invited to observe the deadlines for submission of articles which are set for the month of April of every second year. Thus, articles to be considered for Volume V should be sent not later than April 1974, and for Volume VI by April of 1976. All correspondence should be addressed to the undersigned.

Miloš Velimirović
University of Wisconsin
Madison, Wisconsin 53706, USA

May 1972

The Editors wish to express their gratitude to the British Academy for the generous grants which assisted the publication of this volume.

Contents

vii

List of Plates

(facing pages 88 and 89)

I

Dalia Cohen

JERUSALEM, ISRAEL

Theory and Practice in Liturgical Music of Christian Arabs in Israel

DIFFERENT types of music can be defined by characteristic sets of rules. These rules may be elucidated by examining four possible areas of study:

1) theoretical generalizations as formulated by theoreticians;
2) written music, which involves notation characteristic of a particular time and place;[1]
3) conventions among performers of music as embodied in a kind of 'verbal theory';
4) live music as it is actually performed.

One would expect the last of these to represent the primary source from which rules can be formulated, but unfortunately the actual practice is not available in many cases (e.g. music of the past), frequently presents great difficulties and inconveniences in research, and in general is a very neglected area.

Sometimes our information relates only to some (and perhaps even only one) of these four areas. Occasionally, this single area will be that of current practice. In such an instance it is necessary to try to discover the latent set of rules on which the music is based, without any known assisting rules.

The rules obtained from the different areas do not necessarily agree with each other. There are cases in which the different formulations are so close as to be almost indistinguishable, at least among the last three areas. This situation applies, for

---

[1] Actually every type of musical notation, any written designation of music contains within it some theory, defined to a greater or lesser degree.

example, to a large part of Western music where it may be sufficient to study the music from scores and theory, with no necessity for live performance.[2]

On the other hand, there are cases in which there are disagreements. Sometimes there is even a gap between the set of rules enunciated by the performers and that really contained in the music they perform.

The interrelation between practice and theory of all kinds changes continually in different places and periods. Until recently, there have been no attempts to explain what determines these relationships, to decide by what musical components the gap between practice and theory is expressed, why this gap is large or small, or why it changes from one culture to another and from one period to another. Moreover, there has not even been an attempt to define most of these connections. In particular, the large field of musical practice has not yet been investigated. As to the past, the information on this aspect (even in Europe, at least until the appearance of modern musical notation) is almost nil.

At present, there is a general agreement that music theory always crystallizes from live music. However, theoreticians sometimes deal with theory as if it were a separate subject independent of live music, exaggerating the discussion of rules to such an extent that the connection between these rules and the music itself is flimsy, and at times doubtful. It is thus important to ask to what extent theory reflects live music and how much a particular theory can tell us about the music with which it is concerned. Moreover, it is interesting to understand the meaning of theory from its relationship to practice.

In the present discussion, we shall examine the relationship between practice and theory as revealed in the hymns of the neo-Byzantine rite as sung by the Orthodox and the Greek

[2] It is worth noting that if we are looking for underlying laws in elements not written in the notation, such as fine changes in intonation, shades of sounds, or even tempo and volume, it is necessary to distinguish between the three possibilities mentioned above for Western music as well. The underlying laws of live music must not be derived from notation only, but from live performance as well. For this purpose electronic devices are generally needed. On experiments in this area see: C. E. Seashore, *Psychology of Music* (New York and London, 1938), pp. 21-32. C. Shackford, 'Some Aspects of Perception', *Journal of Music Theory*, 2 (1962), pp. 67-90. P. C. Boumsliter, 'Extended Reference: An Unrecognized Dynamic in Melody', *Journal of Music Theory*, 7 (1963), pp. 3-22.

Catholic Arabs in Israel.[3] Both of these churches have some connections with centres of liturgical studies outside Israel, which, for example, serve as places of study for some of the priests.[4] These centres are:

[3] This examination is part of a more comprehensive study presented by the author as a doctoral dissertation to the Hebrew University of Jerusalem in 1967, under the supervision of Professors A. Ringer and S. Morag. Most of the experimental work was done in 1964-5 and does not deal with the changes which occurred afterwards in the group examined. Thus the data presented here concern only Christian Arabs living in the State of Israel. As a matter of fact, a superficial survey of that part of the group which had been under Jordanian rule suggests that there is no additional material (except that found in the Old City of Jerusalem, an entity unto itself both ethnically and culturally) likely to alter essentially the conclusions of this study. No other work has been done on the specific musical material discussed here (except for the general description of this music by J. B. Rebours). However, a few research studies have been made on the live music of groups in the region, similar to a certain extent to the group examined by the author. These studies also touched on the problem of the comparison of theory and practice. See: J. Jeanin and J. Puyade, *Mélodies Liturgiques Syriennes et Chaldéenes* (Paris, 1924), Vol. I—Introduction Musicale; Vol. II—Introduction Liturgique et Recueil de Melodies, J. Parisot, 'Rapport sur une Mission Scientifique en Turquie d'Asie', *Nouvelles Archives des Missions Scientifiques et Littéraires* (Paris, 1900), pp. 169-244, A. Z. Idelsohn, *The History of Hebrew Music* (Devir, Tel-Aviv, and Berlin, 1924) (in Hebrew), R. Lachman, *Jewish Cantillation and Songs in the Isle of Djerba* (Jerusalem, 1940), H. Hussman, 'Die Tonarten der chaldäischen Breviergesang', *Orientalia Christiana Periodica*, xxxv (Rome, 1969), pp. 215-48, A. Z. Idelsohn, 'Arab Music', *Thesaurus of Hebrew Oriental Melodies* (in Hebrew), iv (Jerusalem–Berlin, 1923), pp. 44-91 (pp. 52-112 in German edition).

[4] The Christians in Israel are divided into different denominations, sects, and countries of origin. Almost all those belonging to the two denominations examined are Arabs. The situation of the priesthood in the two denominations is very instructive. Most of the Greek–Catholic priests are Arabs, graduates of the Theological Seminary of St. Anne in Jerusalem, or of Dir al-muhallas in Lebanon. Recently, a Greek–Catholic High School was established in Nazareth, as a school preparing for the Theological Seminary. This institution has become a focal point for youths chosen from many villages and has become a factor in strengthening religious activity. On the other hand, most of the Orthodox priests are Greek. The majority of them are graduates of the Theological Seminary of St. Demetrius in the Old City of Jerusalem. (The custom is to send eleven to thirteen-year-old boys to this Seminary from Greece; they are the source of future priests in Israel.) The Greek priests in Israel are obliged to remain celibate whereas the few Arab Orthodox priests are obliged to marry before receiving a post. Thus the higher echelons of the priesthood are retained by the Greeks. The Arab Orthodox priests usually serve in the places of their birth. Their general educational level is very low, though they sometimes travel to the Old City of Jerusalem for a month or two for a 'refresher course'. Their musical knowledge is almost nonexistent, and they have no experience of Western or Byzantine notation.

This gap between the Catholic and the Orthodox priests, however, has almost entirely disappeared in several places. In a number of Catholic villages, local priests are also found who received all their training only in the church or at

1) the Greek Catholic Seminary at Dir al-Muhallas in Lebanon;
2) the Greek Catholic Seminary of St. Anne in Jerusalem;
3) the Seminary of St. Demetrius in the Old City of Jerusalem.

The music examined is a blend of local oral tradition and neo-Byzantine written tradition. The local tradition is also influenced by folk-song. The majority of Arab singers who participate in the singing of liturgical hymns in church also sing folk-songs at ceremonies and celebrations, and some of them even play instruments. At any rate, almost all of them listen with great enthusiasm to Arab music of all kinds on the radio.

The type of music examined was vocal music in which the performance is still an inseparable, integral part of the composition. This implies that during the performance, the singer almost always makes impromptu additions of his own. Thus the same song is sung in a different manner by different performers. Therefore, for an examination of this kind of music, it is necessary to analyse the practice in all its variations.[5] The Arabs whose singing was investigated could be treated as an entity and the elements of musical expression common to the group as a whole could be clarified. On the other hand, the group was sufficiently large so that one could divide it into subgroups according to the manner of performance and could probe how different factors influenced this. In this connection, the following questions can be raised:

1) what is the influence of theoretical knowledge and study from books, i.e. what musical characteristics distinguish the performance of the same song by singers who are conscious of their knowledge and who are self-critical of their singing, from the performance of those who lack any knowledge, who do not consider song as a composition

---

home. The office of the priesthood in these villages, as in several Orthodox villages, is inherited. Thus from the point of view of knowledge, of cultural isolation, and of method of passing on tradition, there is no difference between these Catholic priests and most of the Arab–Orthodox priests.

[5] The problem of performance in oriental music is, to this author, of prime importance. Ignoring this problem and analysing only one example of each song (as has been done by all the scholars who dealt with practice) distorts the reality.

made up of different components but rather as a natural language;

2) what is the influence of the modern Arabic music blaring from every radio and of the playing of instrumental music.

Our findings suggest that the practice examined is strongly affected by:

A) the neo-Byzantine musical theory accepted in the centres mentioned previously;

B) the musical material actually used today in these centres. The major part of this material has been transcribed into conventional Western notation;

C) the system of *maqamat* in both theory and practice. This is for two reasons: first, the neo-Byzantine theory which became consolidated at the beginning of the nineteenth century was influenced by the system of the *maqamat*;[6] secondly, the Israeli Arab folk-song, which was found in the present study (see below) to have an important influence on the liturgical song, is also in the *maqamat* framework.

The comparison of practice and theory is complicated not only because of the intermingling of various streams of influences, but also because theoretical frameworks are not always directly related to the practice examined. The complications and difficulties in the comparison attempted here are probably due to five factors:

1) the relation between the neo-Byzantine theory which crystallized in Greece and Turkey, and the practice of the Israeli Arabs, is rather indirect;

2) both theory and practice were influenced by the *maqamat* system, to a greater or lesser extent. However, each was influenced in a different manner;

3) theory does not deal with all the components present in live music. Some cannot be dealt with since they are directly bound to the manner of performance; that is to

---

[6] Convincing evidence of this has already been given by H. J. W. Tillyard, *Byzantine Music and Hymnography* (London, 1923), pp. 63-4. '*Maqamat*' is the plural of '*maqam*'. Details of this concept will be given later.

say, there is a kind of 'filter' in theory which allows only particular matters to be treated;

4) theoretical concepts tend to be rigid and somewhat sterile;

5) practice varies with performance.

Nevertheless, these difficulties do not exempt us from attempting to compare practice and theory.

External Influences on Practice

A. *Neo-Byzantine Theory.* This theory of music is accepted in the centres of study mentioned above.

Byzantine liturgical music never lost its functional role, and underwent many changes and developments. At the beginning of the nineteenth century, theories of this music were evolved. These theories are broad and detailed, and deal with the actual musical material, in contrast to Byzantine theories of the Middle Ages which were mainly speculations with little if any connection with the music as practised. These theories were summarized by Chrysantus in his book *The Great Musical Theory* (1832). Later, several changes in the theory were introduced, but the conceptual foundations remained the same. At the Patriarchal Conference in Constantinople, in 1881, some changes in the theory of music were accepted. These two theories remain dominant until the present day.[7]

The neo-Byzantine theory deals only with *vocal* music, and is unique in that it deals also with the problems of exact intonation, an exactness presumed to be discernible within the range of normal sensitivity of hearing. The smallest unit of difference in pitch in this theory is one-sixth of one-half of a well-tempered tone, i.e. about fifteen cents. In contrast, other theories which dealt with exact intonation were derived by various mathematical calculations from instrumental music.

---

[7] The main source of our knowledge of the theory of Chrysanthos is J. B. Rebours *Traité de Psaltique. Théorie et Pratique du Chant dans l'Église Grecque* (Jerusalem, 1906). Rebours was assisted to a great extent by the text of Couturier, who was a professor in the Seminary of St. Anne in the Old City of Jerusalem. This theory was concisely described by Tillyard (op. cit., pp. 60-8), and Raes *Introductio in Liturgiam Orientalem* [Rome, 1947], pp. 251-61). The sources of our knowledge of the later theory are the book by Margaziothis, *The Theory of Byzantine Music* (in Greek) (Athens, 1958), and C. Vrionidis, *The Byzantine Chant* (New York, 1959).

The neo-Byzantine theory deals mainly with the following elements:

  1) The scales, defined by three factors:
      a) the size of the interval of the second in each scale;[8]
      b) the organizations of the seconds in the scale in groups of pentachords, tetrachords, or trichords;[9]
      c) chromatic changes and modulations.

---

[8] According to Chrysanthos, the ratio between the sizes of the seconds is expressed conveniently if the octave is divided into sixty-eight parts. Then one type of second contains twelve parts, another one nine parts, and still another seven parts. This means that if the first large second is called a whole tone, the second second will be a three-quarter tone, and the third second a little more than a semitone. The comparison of this scale with the well-tempered scale shows that:

  —the size of a whole well-tempered tone is equal to eleven and one-third parts (each part being equal to one-sixty-eighth of an octave);
  —the size of half of a well-tempered tone is equal to five and two-thirds parts.

This means that in the neo-Byzantine scale, the size of a large second is slightly larger than a well-tempered tone, and that the fourth in this scale is not 'pure' (the size of the perfect fourth is twenty-eight and one-third units; in the above-mentioned system, however, fractions of units do not exist).

In order to overcome these 'defects', a 'correction' to the method was suggested in 1881. According to the revised system, the octave is divided into seventy-two parts. The size of the large second (twelve parts) is exactly equal to a well-tempered tone. A similar example of a change in theory is the decision to organize the profusion of different seconds in the Arabic *maqamat* into a tempered division of the octave into twenty-four parts. It would be interesting to know if this change in theory points to a change in the music itself, or is due to Western influence.

[9] In the neo-Byzantine theory according to Chrysanthos, there are three basic methods for organizing the scale, and each organization has its own name:

  a) the organization by *conjunct* pentachords is called diatonic;
  b)   ,,   ,,   ,,   ,,   tetrachords   ,,   enharmonic;
  c)   ,,   ,,   ,,   ,,   trichords   ,,   chromatic.

There are, however, in addition to these basic methods, exceptions which do not conform to this organization.

The diatonic scale is made up of three basic seconds only, as mentioned previously, and is organized in identical pentachords. The enharmonic scale has two possible forms. One resembles the basic organization for it is organized into identical tetrachords made up of three basic seconds. In the second possibility, the scale consists of seconds with other sizes. The chromatic scale has two possible forms:

  1) made up of the three basic seconds only, and organized into two types of trichords which change alternately;
  2) made up of other seconds, and organized into identical pentachords.

The later theory differs mainly in that here the diatonic scale is made up of disjunct tetrachords. There are several other details in this theory which are controversial. In both theories, there are discrepancies with neo-Byzantine music.

2) The central notes in the melody.

3) The melismatic or syllabic quality of the melody.

4) The mode, defined by the three factors mentioned above, interrelated in a specific manner.

B. *Written Collections of Hymns.* The musical material in actual use today in the main seminaries and monasteries is written, for the most part, in conventional Western notation. The main reason for this is the desire to extend the knowledge of this music, since the number of people who know Byzantine notation is constantly decreasing, at least in comparison with those who know Western notation. Another reason is that modern notation provides a more convenient representation of recent changes in this music, especially with the addition of harmony. The problem of transcribing oriental music into Western notation is well known to all those dealing with it. In the introduction to his book *Syllitourgikon*, Couturier writes,[10] 'This music in European notation cannot, understandably, convey all the fine nuances of Eastern song, nevertheless . . .' and indeed, most of the transcriptions are oversimplified. Despite this the collections permit the study of present usage in the seminaries. This may include, for example, information about modes and their definitions by central notes, and the distribution of specific melodies.

The best known collections (in which the neo-Byzantine theory is dominant to a greater or lesser degree) are:

For example: according to both neo-Byzantine theories, the scale of mode I is diatonic from D–D, and the main central notes are D and G. From this we see that the organization into conjunct pentachords is meaningless for the neo-Byzantine musical material. This system is an unsuccessful attempt at copying the Western system. The second system of organization into disjunct tetrachords is also unsatisfactory. It is probably more suited to the Byzantine musical material of the Middle Ages, in which A is an important central note of mode I. For this material, Strunk's suggested organization A – D – G ⌣ A – D – G is suitable, but it is unsuitable for neo-Byzantine melodies of mode I in which G functions as an axis. It seems to us that if there is meaning to the organization of the scale, then the system of conjunct tetrachords D – G – C is more suitable here. This discussion does not concern the exact intonation suggested for the scale. A connection between intonation and organization within the scale is not necessary.

[10] See *Syllitourgikon* (arr. Couturier), (Jerusalem, 1924).

1) *Melodecte*.[11] A collection of more than three hundred and fifty chants for service 'hours' (the 'office') on different days, as sung in the Greek Catholic Seminary of St. Anne in Jerusalem. This collection is a type of 'horologion' organized for festivals and special occasions in the liturgical year.

2) *Syllitourgikon*.[12] A collection which contains the liturgy of St. John Chrysostom, the liturgy of St. Basil, *Apolytikia*, the cycle of eight 'Resurrection Hymns' for Sundays, hymns to saints, and hymns for great festivals and important days. The melodies are written in both Byzantine and Western notation. Sometimes several alternative melodies are offered for the same hymn. For the regular responses of the congregation, three melodies are usually suggested for each response. For most of the hymns, however, only one melody is given. (In his introduction, Couturier writes, 'I did not believe it necessary to quote several melodies for . . . I have transcribed the simplest, but experienced singers are always permitted to change the tone and the melody in keeping with the proper gravity [seriousness] of the religious song.')

3) *Al-Taranim al-Taqsiyya al-Bizantiyya* (in Arabic),[13] 'The Melodies of the Byzantine Rite', contains only the best known melodies of the liturgy; that is to say, for those portions which may be sung in any one of the modes, only the accepted ones were chosen.

4) *Byzantine Liturgy*.[14] This is a collection of chants for the liturgy, harmonized in four voices! Some of the chants were written by Greek composers of this century.

In these four collections, ostensibly containing the same songs with identical words and melodies, there is not a single case in which a specific melody appears in the same version in every book. Even the names of the notes are not always identical. In the *Syllitourgikon* the basic scale is from D to D. Thus, the 'tonic' of the melodies in mode I is D; that of the melodies in mode III F, and so on. In the *Melodecte* and the Lebanese book

---

[11] *Mélodecte*, composés et annotés par le Père Antoine Sayegh (Jerusalem, 1956).
[12] See footnote 8 above.
[13] Published in Dir al-muhallas, Lebanon, 1963.
[14] See T. Georgiou, *Byzantine Liturgy* (in Greek) (Athens, 1951).

there is a kind of transposition one tone upward. The basic scale is from E to E' with F sharp. In the Greek book there are several transpositions resulting from harmonic considerations or from taking into account the tessitura of the voice. In the following discussion, we shall use the names of the notes as employed in the *Syllitourgikon*.[15]

Great stress is placed on the modes in these collections. They are defined mainly by the scale (its intonation defined only to an accuracy of semitones because this is the maximum accuracy attainable in the Western system of notation), the central notes, the musical motifs, and the tessitura. However, the degree of definition of the different modes is not equal. For example, mode III is defined only vaguely from the standpoint of motifs and central notes, but mainly from the standpoint of the scale and the finalis. Mode IV appears in the books in several forms with respect to scales, tessitura, ambitus, and finalis. Mode I appears in only one, unified manner. In all the collections it has the same scale, the same central notes, motifs, and tessitura.

The collections described above represent a mid-point between theory and practice. On the one hand, to a certain extent they reflect the conventions formulated in a particular centre; but this reflection has limitations because of the system of notation. On the other hand, they contain many concealed directions as to what should be performed. The musical education of many priests in Israel was based on the material in these collections.

C. *The Maqam System.* It has already been mentioned that the neo-Byzantine music was influenced by the Turkish-Arabic music, and that the neo-Byzantine theory was influenced by the *maqam* system. This fact pertains to the music that existed in important centres such as Constantinople, and to a certain extent mainland Greece. It may be assumed that this influence

[15] The choice of notes for the musical annotation of collections of melodies organized in modes, can be made according to different assumptions. For each of the methods of notation, there are advantages and disadvantages (as already remarked by R. Lachman, op. cit., pp. 17-18). In our study, notation of music is only of partial value as a source of information. The complementary recording is the graph. Since we were sure that the comparison of intonation would not be neglected, in our choice of names of notes we considered only the comparison between practice and theory. In writing down from performance, we select the names of notes according to tones suitable, more or less, to theory.

was felt at the periphery as well, i.e. at places far from the creative centres (at just such a place this present work was done). Almost nothing, however, was written on this subject. Arabic folk-song, also within the framework of the *maqamat*, is another source of influence on the liturgical music examined in this work. It is important, therefore, to clarify the significance of the *maqamat* framework, both in theory and in practice.

The *maqam* is one of the best known forms of organization of notes in Arabic music, both instrumental and vocal. Another type of organization (for vocal music only) is the grouping of songs similar in verbal metre, content, and melody. These different groups are called by different names (such as 'shruki', 'Migana', etc.), whose origin is usually impossible to reconstruct (although there are various stories on the subject). This organization is much later than that of the *maqamat*, and as yet it is not known whether there is a relationship between the two, and if so, what it is.[16] While this latter organization is more restricted to a certain locality, the concept of *maqam* (already mentioned in the writings of the Arabic theoreticians of the Middle Ages) spread to all the Arab countries (though under different names, and not in a uniform defined form) and became almost a synonym for the organization of Arabic music.

Ostensibly, there is quite a large gap between practice and theory in Arabic music. In his article 'Arabic Music' Idelsohn writes: 'In this music, theory had no value. Theory is entirely disconnected from practice. This theory was a sort of objective in itself and all its energy was directed to hair-splitting debates and sharp conjectures completely unfounded in music as practiced.'[17] Baron R. d'Erlanger, the well-known scholar of Arabic music, accuses the theoreticians of betraying their task: 'Is it not strange that this art [Arabic music] is neglected by its founders, has been betrayed at all times by its theoreticians (those most capable people), in order to guard the purity of the theory and to protect it from the damaging effects of

[16] It is interesting that this organization is almost entirely ignored in the literature. In Israel, a comprehensive research study is presently being made on Arabic folk music, by Ruth Katz and this writer. One of the aims is to clarify the meaning of this organization and the relationship between it and the *maqam*.

[17] See A. Z. Idelsohn, 'Arab Music', *Thesaurus of Hebrew Oriental Melodies* (in Hebrew), Vol. iv (Jerusalem–Berlin, 1923), p. 44.

meeting oral tradition? ... In vain may we search in the theories for explanations of phenomena we meet in live music.'[18]

In the 'golden era' of Moslem culture, this gap was almost deliberate. Theorizing was an occupation enjoying high esteem, whereas practice was considered of lesser value and of no importance for the speculations of theoreticians. True, there were also Arabic manuscripts which included important information on musical life and practice; these writings, however, were considered by the theoreticians as strictly 'literary' creations.

At the same time, it seems that in reality there did exist a relation between practice and theory. The Arabic theoreticians (in contrast to the Greek and Latin ones), after paying lip service to the accepted opinion described above, received inspiration from, and even based their theories to a certain extent on music as practised. The very fact that the description of the scales is based on concepts derived from the actual playing of string instruments, proves the relation between practice and theory.[19] The theoreticians wanted to give a completely speculative character to their writings, making it now difficult to determine the exact contribution of practice to the theoretical framework. Comparison of theories of theoreticians from different periods and places, shows many variations in the terminology of theoretical conception, and in the determination of intervals, scales, and rhythms. It is likely that these variations are also evidence of different local developments in practice.[20] The most complete systematization in the field of theory was established by Safi-al-Din in the thirteenth century (his importance as an authority was so great that he has been called the 'Arabic Zarlino').[21] Even in his writings, however, no clear

[18] See Baron R. d'Erlanger, *La Musique Arabe*, Tome V (Paris, 1949), p. xi.

[19] The representation of the different scales in this manner is given by H. G. Farmer, 'The Music of Islam', *The New Oxford History of Music*, i (London, 1957), pp. 456-64; and by Idelsohn, op. cit., p. 45. This prominent relation is what brought d'Erlanger to the conclusion that 'all those artificial tones' which are so typical and important in the East were introduced only by instruments, since the human voice can by nature produce only notes in the 'natural' scale (see d'Erlanger, op. cit., p. 4). A similar conclusion was reached by Lachman.

[20] Apparently the clarification of the relations between practice and theory for Arabic music of the Middle Ages is far from final. This is also the opinion of Amnon Shiloah, the specialist in Arabic music of the Middle Ages at the Hebrew University of Jerusalem.

[21] See Farmer, op. cit., pp. 462-5.

or detailed definitions of the *maqam* are to be found. One gains the impression that the *maqam* is not only a scale, but also a framework determined by both melody and rhythm (he calls this framework a 'tariq', i.e. a route; of course, the conventions connected with the *maqam* and performance were of no interest to him!). Most of his attention is paid to the simplest theoretical element, the scale. It is instructive that the scale element is treated in terms of smaller units, usually tetrachords, so that the scale resulted from a combination of smaller units in different ways. This resembles what takes place in practice. On the other hand, the theoretical treatment of the rhythmic modes is independent of that of the scales, and the relationship between the two is not clear.

Until the beginning of the present century, Turkey was the main centre of the art of Arabic music and theory. Today there are major centres for Arabic music in Damascus, Beirut, and especially Cairo. In these centres, many variations of theory have developed, just as in the Middle Ages.[22] At the famous Conference for Arabic Music which took place in Cairo in 1932,[23] an attempt was made at an agreed definition of the intonation of the various tones (at the same time establishing a tempered scale divided into twenty-four equal parts), the scales of the *maqamat*,[24] and the rhythmic modes. As yet, however, there is no one definitive system, in the arrangement of the intonation of the tones, in the scales of the *maqamat*, or in the connections between them. This lack of unity is apparently a typically Eastern characteristic. Different groupings of the *maqamat* into 'families' of close kinship are possible,[25] but it is not yet clear which kind of organization best reflects practice.

[22] The systems which developed in various places, and the division of the octave into twenty-four tones, are explained by d'Erlanger (op. cit., pp. 21-41), and by Idelsohn (op. cit., pp. 45-9). A comparative table (in cents) for part of the different systems of intonation is presented by d'Erlanger (op. cit., p. 47).

[23] See d'Erlanger (op. cit., pp. 41-3). Many Western musicologists also participated in this conference. Quite a detailed summary of the final meetings and the various subjects treated was published in 1934 as *Recueil des Travaux du Congrés de Musique Arabe* (Cairo).

[24] See the report of the conference in Cairo, pp. 593-603, 653-5.

[25] The different organizations of the *maqamat*, and their collection into *Diwans*, at various periods past and present, are described by Idelsohn (op. cit., pp. 52-6). Actually, the organization of the *maqamat* suggested by most scholars is mainly according to types of scales. Thus, for instance, d'Erlanger divides them into four types:

Present-day theoreticians, though continuing the tradition of the Middle Ages to a certain extent, are adopting and adapting Western concepts and systems. The influence of Western thinking is particularly felt in the younger generation of musicians and theoreticians.[26] In their writings, however, no exact statement has been found of the theoretical frameworks and the relationships among them. The word *maqam* can mean 'system of intonation', 'mode', or 'tetrachord'.

In the textbooks on the theory of Arabic music customarily used,[27] this music is described after a discussion of Western

---

1) *Diatonic*, including:
   a) the diatonic scales according to Western conceptions;
   b) the modes obtained from the system in which E and B are flatted by a quarter-tone;
2) *Chromatic*, which contain the augmented second in the framework of the fourth;
3) *Special*. A different organization of the *maqamat* according to the pitch of basic note of the scales: scales whose 'feet stand' on G (Yaka), then those beginning on A, afterwards on B flat (ʿAgam), on B (Iraq), on C (Rast), etc. (See the report of the Conference in Cairo, pp. 522-92; d'Erlanger, op. cit., pp. 111-15; Idelsohn, op. cit., pp. 55-6.) In this manner, emphasis is given to the distinction between the intonation of the scales. An interesting organization of the scales of the *maqamat* was suggested by the Israeli composer, Abel Ehrlich, who divided them into six groups according to the sizes of the seconds contained:

   a. Scales containing seconds of 1 and $\frac{3}{4}$ tones.
   b.   „   „   „   1, $\frac{3}{4}$ and $\frac{1}{2}$ tones.
   c.   „   „   „   1$\frac{1}{2}$, 1, $\frac{3}{4}$, and $\frac{1}{2}$ tones.
   d.   „   „   „   1 and $\frac{1}{2}$ tones.
   e.   „   „   „   1$\frac{1}{2}$, 1, and $\frac{1}{2}$ tones.
   f.   „   „   also $\frac{5}{4}$ tones.

   Each group was also divided into sub-groups in accordance with the order of the seconds in the scale, with each sub-group containing all the modes obtained by shifting within a specific system.

[26] See d'Erlanger, op. cit., pp. xii-xiii. A typical example of this is the beginning of the widely distributed text on theory, *Miftah al-alhan al-arbii* (in Arabic) (The Key to Arab Melodies), by Muhamad Salah al-din (Cairo, 1947). This text opens with a description of the 'cycle of fifths' and the identification of the Western major and minor scales.

[27] There are quite a few books on the theory of Arabic music available nowadays, for example Tufik al-Sabar, *Al-dalil al-musiqi al-ʿam* (The General Guide to Music) (Syria, 1956), and Mahmud Hufni, *Al-musiqi al-nazariyah* (The Musical Theory) (Egypt, 1958). This book includes: (a) the theory of Western music; (b) the theory of Arabic music (the *maqamat*, the different rhythmic metres); (c) musical instruments in general, and Arabic instruments in particular; (d) musical forms in Western and in Arabic music. Other books are by Salim Hilu, *Al musiqi al-nazariyah* (Beirut, 1961), and Sami al-Shawa, *Al-qawaʿid al-faniyah fiʿusul al-musiqatayin al-arabiya wa-al-garbiya* (The Artistic Principles of

music. The oriental musical forms are explained after the Western forms. The *maqamat* scales are introduced after the major and minor scales. The octave is divided into twenty-four equal parts, and methods of transposition are listed for each of the twenty-four quarter-tones. The concept of *maqam* is not dealt with in any book; but from what is written, it seems that the *maqam* is defined only by scale, which itself is a result of various combinations of tetrachords.

d'Erlanger tried to define the 'true' framework of the *maqam*. Like Idelsohn, he defines it by the following elements:[28]

1) the ambitus and the tessitura;
2) the scale, or the specific combination of tetrachords (not necessarily identical), which is at times most complicated (d'Erlanger notes that there are still debates among artists as to the manner of combination);
3) important notes:
   a) opening note;
   b) the tonic, which usually serves also as the finalis. Preceding the finalis are characteristic leading notes, not necessarily in intervals of semitones.
   c) the dominant, which may be at an interval of a third or fourth from the tonic;
   d) notes which serve as medial cadences.

There is no doubt that these definitions to a large extent correspond to practice; they are, however, still in the nature o a general sketch which could fit any modal framework.

Important points that occupied the attention of both theoreticians and executants remain as yet unclear. One of these is intonation. Intonation, very subtle at times, is one of the most important factors in characterizing and defining the music in our region. The inability to determine exact intonation by ear alone was a serious obstacle to experimental research into the music of the Middle East. As a matter of fact, until the appearance of the melograph, it was almost impossible to

---

Eastern and Western Music). The most popular book currently in print in Israel is the book mentioned previously by Muhamad Salahal-Din.
[28] See d'Erlanger, op. cit., pp. 100-8.

examine systematically the intonation of a large number of examples.[29]

Preparatory work on the significance of the *maqamat* in Arabic song was carried out by the author in 1964.[30] In this work, the *maqamat* 'Siga', 'Bayat', and 'Rast' (the most prevalent in Israel) were examined via Arab instrumentalists, some of whom knew theory to varying extents. The examination was conducted by the use of the melograph, and concentrated mainly on the problem of intonation. The conclusions of this work were:[31]

1) The significance of scale for the *maqamat* system is much deeper than for Western music. In the *maqam* scale, certain degrees are more stable, others less stable. Each *maqam* dictates the extent of stability of the degrees in its scale.

2) The 'tonal skeleton'[32] is generally different from that given in the theory. It was found, however, that the same 'type of tonal skeleton' exists for all the melodies in a particular *maqam* for all singers familiar with theory.

3) No simple relationship was found among the 'skeletons' of the *maqamat* examined. Each one had a 'world of intonation' of its own.

Similar conclusions were reached in the examination of the modal framework of the liturgical music, the *'lahan'*:[33] the

---

[29] In Jerusalem we first built a melograph in 1957. This melograph was built independently of two other known melographs that were constructed on the basis of different principles and approximately at the same time: one in California by C. Seeger and the other in Norway by O. Gurvin. On the uses and limitation of the melograph, see D. Cohen and R. Katz, 'Some Remarks Concerning the Use of the melograph', *Yuval, Studies of the Jewish Music Research Center*, i (Jerusalem, 1967), pp. 157-8.

[30] Part of that study was published in an article by this writer, 'An Investigation into the Tonal Structure of the *Maqamat*', *The Journal of the International Folk Music Council*, xvi (1964), pp. 102-6.

[31] A more detailed explanation of the conclusions will be given subsequently, in the discussion on the examination of practice.

[32] The concepts 'tonal skeleton' and 'type of skeleton' will be clarified further in on this article. Here we shall only note that 'type of skeleton' was found to be the most important framework in the organization of the complicated intonation of oriental music.

[33] The Arabs use the concept *'lahan'* instead of 'mode' or 'echos' to designate the modal framework of liturgical music. The concept *'maqam'* is applied by them to secular music.

concept of the *maqam*, at least as far as intonation is concerned, is similar to that of the *lahan*. For a certain class of singers, the concepts of *lahan* and *maqam* may sometimes be identical.

A Consideration of the Musical Practice

The detailed examination concentrated on hymn singing in the eight *alhan*.[34] A total of two hundred and thirty melodies were examined, each sung at least twice by thirty-eight individuals. The informants were of different classes: priests, cantors, members of the choir and laymen of the congregation; Orthodox and Catholic; urban and rural; young and old; people of different cultural connections, some rooted in modern Arabic music, some graduates of seminaries, and some, isolated from these influences, reared almost completely on oral tradition.

The selection of singers was made on the basis of a questionnaire.[35] Fifty-two questionnaires were filled out by the author interviewing informants from twenty-six Orthodox and Catholic communities.

Each one of them was requested to sing those hymns which he knew in the eight *alhan*. All, without exception, sang the

[34] Generally, it is possible to divide liturgical music into three classes: (a) Cantillation, a type of recitative reading in which the tone 'tuba' is predominant. Portions of the Epistles and *Evangelion*, as well as various *Declarations* are sung in this manner. (b) Hymn singing, containing melodies in different modes. The wealth of hymns so typical of Eastern liturgy are sung in these melodies. These hymns are well known and sung by almost all the participants in the Service. (c) Solo and virtuoso singing containing special hymns like the *Cherubikon*.

As a matter of fact, the distinction between these three classes is not unequivocally defined from the musical point of view. It may occur that cantillation is performed in a rather developed musical fashion, whereas hymn singing may be a kind of recitative. Hymn singing may also be performed in virtuoso fashion, with a great deal of melisma and a large ambitus, whereas solo singing may be performed like an ordinary hymn. We limited ourselves, this time, to the second class only, i.e. hymn singing.

[35] The questionnaire was made up after visiting many villages, and conversing with and interviewing various local people. Questions in different areas were included in the questionnaire: (1) activity in the church; (2) the priesthood; (3) the liturgical material actually performed, and how it is performed (choirs, soloists, etc.); (4) the study sources of the liturgy performed in a particular place; the connection with different liturgical centres; (5) the striving to preserve tradition and the degree to which this is attained; (6) the understanding of, and the attitude towards religious music; (7) musical education; the attitude towards music generally, and towards modern and folk Arab music in particular. Not everything stated by the informants turned out to be identical with what we actually found. Nevertheless, important information was obtained from the

'Resurrection Hymns' for Sundays.[36] The majority sang the well-known hymns for the important feasts, such as Easter and Christmas. Some sang hymns belonging to other days, such as those of Holy Week, the 'Transfiguration', the 'Exaltation of the Cross', the 'Nativity of the Virgin', and hymns of local festivals. Each hymn was sung by the same informant a number of times. Thus it was possible to compare:

1) different melodies in the same *lahan*;
2) melodies in different *alhan* for different occasions;
3) the same melodies sung by different informants;
4) different melodies sung by the same informant;
5) the same melody sung a number of times by the same informant.

As previously mentioned, the folk-musical material in the well-known *maqamat* was also examined: one hundred and thirty-five vocal melodies in three *maqamat* ('Siga', 'Bayat', 'Rast'), performed by fifteen informants in six places. Five of the informants knew theory and played the *Ud* (the most popular Arabic instrument in Israel).

All the musical material was recorded both in conventional notation (in great detail) and in graphs obtained from the melograph (for information on intonation). From these records the musical characteristics were summarized. This summary of characteristics was cross-related. On the one hand, each characteristic was summarized individually, and its significance for the different *alhan*, occasions, and informants was investigated. The extent of relationships among the musical components was also examined. All the characteristics were also summarized from the standpoint of factors determining performance: the informants, the occasions of performance, and the *alhan*. The summary of how different features depended on the *lahan* helped to clarify the character and meaning of the *lahan* in this music. The summary of how characteristics varied

---

questionnaires, and the very lack of identity in answers helped to show the informant's grasp of certain matters.

[36] These hymns, sung after the 'Little Entrance', and varying cyclically according to the Octoëchos, are well known to the public as a whole. For most of the Christian Arabs, the 'Resurrection Hymns' are used as a guide for orientation in the *alhan*, a kind of criterion of the melody from the viewpoint of *lahan*.

between one performance and another helped us to understand the influence and effects of specific factors on performance.

A. *Musical Aspects*

1) *Degree of Melisma*. It was found that the degree of melisma depends to a certain extent on the *lahan*, on the occasion of performance, on the position of the phrase in the song, and on the class of informant.[37] In order to facilitate the comparison of this quality in different songs, melisma was defined quantitatively: the degree of melisma is the ratio between the number by which notes exceed syllables and the number of syllables itself. For convenience, this ratio was expressed as a percentage. For example, if a certain text contains ten syllables, and the accompanying musical phrase consists of fifteen notes, then the degree of melisma is 50%. (I.e. the *surplus* of notes is 50% of the number of syllables.)

It was found that those who used melisma most frequently were informants who listened with admiration to singers of modern Arabic music on the radio, and 'isolated'[38] informants who were apparently blessed with creative powers. For 'isolated' informants, singing is generally very syllabic. The quality of the melisma was different in the performance of these two classes of informants. For the first class, the melody sometimes approached coloratura and Eastern virtuosity. An extreme example of this (see Ex. 1) is the singing of Mr. Elias Fawsi, who adds melismatic and virtuosic portions to a hymn generally sung syllabically.

Those using the least melisma were mainly children and 'isolated, non-creative' informants. A fine example of how the

---

[37] Thus, for example, there is a regularity in the position of melismatic notes within the song, even though there are informants who sing almost entirely syllabically, and others who add many melismatic notes. In all the performances, the minimum melisma was found in the second-last phrase, and then in the first opening phrase. In all the performances, an increase of melisma occurred in the second phrase in comparison to the first phrase; and for many informants, the degree of melisma of the last phrase took second place. As to the dependence of melisma on *lahan*: for most of the informants, the greatest degree of melisma was found for melodies in the second *lahan*; and the least in the seventh *lahan*. The dependence of melisma on *lahan* was summarized in a diagram. A detailed discussion of the dependence of melisma on various factors may be found in the author's doctoral dissertation, pp. 63-6.

[38] For a definition of this term, see ibid., p. 104.

Ex. 1

+ a quarter-tone sharp
ḍ a quarter-tone flat

melody becomes more syllabic in children's singing is given in
Ex. 2; the Easter Hymn 'The Messiah rises' as sung by the
Orthodox cantor, Mr. Wadia Huri of Nazareth, by his fifteen-
year-old daughter, and by his eleven-year-old son.

This hymn is generally sung very melismatically by the
informants; but when sung by the children, it appears almost
syllabic. In a second singing of the same hymn, the children

Ex. 2

Ma sīḥ qām mi—n. bayn 'a — l 'a — m wāt wa
wa ṭal ma ut bi — l mawt wa wa ha ba — l ḥa — jat
Li la ḍī — na fil qu bū — r

Ex. 3

Ex. 4

repeated their first performance almost identically (only increasing the tempo slightly), whereas the father, in a repeat performance in Greek, Ex. 3, actually increased the degree of melisma.

Generally, Arabs singing in Greek use more melisma than the Greeks do, as in Ex. 4 in which the Easter Hymn in Greek is presented as sung by the Arabic cantor, Wadia

Huri of Nazareth, and by the Greek Deacon Vikentius of Jerusalem.

2) *Tempo.*
   a) *Changes in Tempo*—Changes in tempo were found to be dependent on the structure of the melody and the class of informant, but independent of the *lahan* or the occasion.
   b) *Absolute Value of Tempo*—In consideration of the important place which changes of tempo occupy, the value of tempo in a specific song was defined as the average unit of beat in the whole song. It was found that the value of tempo was dependent to a considerable extent on the particular *lahan,* and on the melisma; and to a lesser extent, on the class of the informant.[39]

3) *Range of Singing.*
   a) *Ambitus and Tessitura*—To a certain extent, both the ambitus and the tessitura (i.e. the range of the ambitus relative to the central notes) are dependent on the different *lahans,* and also the class of informant.[40]
   b) *Absolute Pitch of the Singing*[41]—In order to compare the absolute pitch of various melodies, the absolute pitch of relative D in each melody was examined. Two kinds of comparisons of pitch were made:
      1. between different melodies sung by the same informant in order to discover whether any relationship in scale is preserved between the melodies in the different *alhan;*
      2. between different melodies in the same *lahan,* to find out whether absolute pitch plays any role

---

[39] The dependence of tempo on *lahan* was summarized in diagram form. For details see Dalia Cohen, 'The meaning of the model framework in the singing of religious hymns by Christian Arabs in Israel', *Yuval: Studies of the Jewish Music Centre,* vol. II (Jeruselem, 1971,) pp. 38-39.

[40] Generally, when the same melody, or different melodies in the same *lahan,* were sung in a different ambitus, it was due to the 'isolated' informants who sang in a smaller ambitus. The dependence of ambitus on *lahan* was summarized in a diagram. For details, see ibid., pp. 39-41.

[41] The role of absolute pitch in contributing to the definition of a modal framework has occupied the attention of many investigators. Up until the present, however, no systematic work has been done on this subject.

whatsoever in defining the *lahan*. Interesting but complicated results were obtained.[42]

4) *Central Notes.* After much testing of the different components which characterize a collection of liturgical melodies, it became apparent that the central notes are the most stable and important determining factor in defining a *lahan*. They were found to be invariable for all informants.[43] It is worth emphasizing that while the intervals between the central notes are almost invariable (e.g. in all performances the interval between the central notes is a fourth in the first *lahan* and a third in the second *lahan*), the size of the interval, i.e. its exact intonation, varies considerably in the different performances, and is characteristic of the singing of local informants.

5) *Characteristic Intervals.* Sometimes, a single appearance of an interval in different melodies can be used as a means of identification of the *lahan*; and at times the degree of frequency of an interval determines the *lahan*. In any case, they are doubtlessly very influential in defining the *lahan*.[44]

6) *Recitation Notes.* The amount and type of recitation were found to depend on the informants. The notes on which the recitation appears are usually typical of the different *alhan*.[45]

7) *Structure of the Melodies and Musical Motifs.* A collection of musical motifs defines a *lahan* to quite a considerable extent.

Ex. 5

---

[42] It appears that in order to reach decisive conclusions about the role of absolute pitch, it is necessary to carry out more tests. It seems to us that the investigations already made by the author point to a certain meaning of absolute pitch in relation to *lahan*, in which the meaning varies for the different groups of informants. For details see ibid., pp. 41-43.

[43] This sentence concerns only main central tones. For a number of informants, not including any 'isolated' informants, additional central tones were sometimes found which were used as medial cadences, a sort of mediant. The summary of the main ambiti of the *alhan*, and of the main tones in the motifs surrounding the central tones, is given in ibid, p. 45.

[44] A summary of the characteristic intervals in the different *alhan* is given in ibid., p. 47.

[45] A summary of the recitation notes for the different classes of informants and for the different *alhan* is given in ibid., pp. 47-48.

Sometimes, specific motifs can appear in several *alhan*, but in each *lahan* the context is different, as in Ex. 5.

The melodic formula marked *x* appears in the performances of several informants, both in the fifth and in the third *lahan*, in the same intonation; but in each *lahan* the context is different.

To a certain extent, the sequence of the motifs is also a determining factor. There are motifs whose place in the different melodies of the *lahan* is fixed and well defined. These motifs determine their environment: what precedes and what follows them. On the other hand, there are mobile motifs, exchangeable by another motif. As an example of the change in the sequence of motifs resulting from the performance of different informants, we shall use the 'Resurrection Hymn' in the third *lahan* in various performances. The main motifs used as internal cadences in the hymn are marked by different letters (see Ex. 6). Of course these motifs appear in several different variations. Pronounced variations are marked by the sign ~.

Ex. 6

A summary of the motifs for cadences within the hymn as performed by nineteen singers is given in a table, Ex. 7.

A strong correlation was found between the class of informants and the properties of the melody, namely the structure, the degree of flexibility in the use of the motifs and the manner of combining them into one melody, the number of motifs, the type of connection between them, the extent to which they are fixed in place, the extent to which they are used in common among the *alhan*, and the relationship between the motif and its intonation.[46]

---

[46] A detailed discussion of the influence of performance will follow immediately.

Ex. 7

A	a	h	b	a	d	f				
B	c	h	b	h	j	c	f			
C	c	h	f̃	c	ã	h	c	a	b	d̃	f
D	b	h	b	d	h	j	a	f		
E	c	h	b	d	h	j	f			
F	f	c	h	c	d̃	b	h	f̃	f	
G	b̃	h	c	b	h	j	a	f		
H	c	h	b	h	j	c	a	f		
I	b	h	b	d̃	f	c	b			
J	b	h	b	b	h	f				
K	b	ĥ	b	d	b	h	c	b		
L	c	h	a	d̃	h	j	f			
M	b	h	b	b	d	h	c	a	c	
N	b	h	b	d̃	h	j	a	f		
O	ç	h	b	d̃	h	j	b	f		
P	c	h	b	e	h	j	c	f		
Q	c	h	b	d̃	h	j	c	a	f	
R	b	h	b	b	j	b	f̃			
S	b	h	j	a	b	h	j	f		

8) *Intonation.* Intonation, i.e. the pitch of the notes contained in a melody, was determined by the use of the melograph. Details of the method used will not be treated here (the subject is dealt with in a separate article).[47] Only the important findings and conclusions will be presented here.

In Arabic song, great importance is to be placed on notes stable and unstable in pitch. The intonation of a group of songs is often determined by the position and 'degree of scatter in pitch' of the notes ('degree of scatter in pitch' is the range of change in pitch occurring in the appearances of a specific tone). The intervals between adjacent notes, especially seconds, were found to be important in contrast to large intervals such as fourths and fifths. (A method was found which enabled us to summarize the intonation of a song in diagram form, by marking each second individually. All sizes in which each second appears, of type C – D, type D – E, etc., are measured and registered in a diagram near the axis of the size of the seconds.

[47] This article has appeared in the *Journal of Music Theory*, Vol. xiii (1969), pp. 66-92.

Thus a graphic summary characteristic of a song is obtained for each type of second and its degree of scatter of pitch.)

The 'tonal skeleton' was obtained by averaging the size of each scattered second, and the term can be defined as: a sequence of averages of successive intervals of seconds surrounded by the scattered seconds used in performance. (The summary of the explanation of 'scatter' is: in every vocal performance, especially in the performance of oriental music transmitted orally, there exists a scatter or spread in the pitch of the different tones making up the melody, and in the size of the intervals. This implies that the intervals are not fixed as in the theoretical scale, but are variable within a specific range.) It is very convenient to make comparisons between different tonal skeletons. As a matter of fact, in theory we are never given more than a skeleton.

Usually, two identical skeletons were not obtained, not even for the same song in a different performance. However, sometimes there does exist a certain similarity between the skeletons. This similarity is expressed in a specific relationship that exists between the seconds in the skeleton. This relationship is not defined quantitatively, but by 'larger' or 'smaller', i.e. by which seconds in the skeleton are equal to one another, which are larger, and which are smaller. The term 'type of skeleton' was given to denote a group of similar skeletons. It became clear that two or three types of skeletons are found in each *lahan*, and sometimes the same type is found in different *alhan*. The quantitative intonation (the exact size of the intervals) was found, to a large extent, to be dependent upon the singer.[48] Thus it became apparent that this whole 'chaos' of intonation, which upon first hearing seemed altogether arbitrary, is in reality founded on a framework which can be formalized. This framework (the type of skeleton) is one of the determining factors in defining the *lahan* (the modal framework in actual

---

[48] For 'isolated' informants, relatively few 'types of skeleton' were found, especially in comparison with the number found for informants rooted in modern Arabic music. Thus we found that the isolated informants sang melodies of different *alhan* in one system of intonation. This single system of intonation (or type of skeleton) varied for different informants. For different isolated informants, different systems of intonation predominated. This implies that to a certain extent intonation was found to be a local element, a kind of dialect in the musical language.

practice) and corresponds to the 'scale' in theory. It was found that different modes, distinguished by types of skeletons, are not related to a single scale system (as is also the case in the *maqamat*),[49] in contrast to Western modes which are related to one scale system only. (The scale of each Western mode is obtained by shifting stepwise within the same, single system.)

It is worth while emphasizing that we found similarity between some of the types of skeletons of the different *alhan* and types of skeletons of folk-songs in the popular *maqamat*. For example, one of the two types of skeletons found in the first *lahan* is similar to the type of skeleton found in the *maqam* 'Bayat'. In the practice of folk singing in this *maqam*, we found an ascending series of seconds: $D - E < E - F < F - G < G - A$. (The sign $<$ indicates that the interval to the left is smaller than that on the right of the sign.) The scatter of the second $E - F$ was found to be especially large, almost half a tone. Let us recall that the skeleton of this *maqam* in present-day theory is completely different:

$$D - E - F - G - A - B - C' - D'$$
$$\tfrac{3}{4} \quad \tfrac{3}{4} \quad 1 \quad 1 \quad \tfrac{1}{2} \quad 1 \quad 1$$

The unit of interval here is a whole well-tempered tone.

In the practice of liturgical singing in the first *lahan*, we found two types of skeletons: The average sizes of the seconds in the different skeletons found in these two types are (in units of one-tenth tones, i.e. each unit is twenty cents):

	D	E	F	G	A	B
Type I:	$7\tfrac{1}{2}$–10	$5\tfrac{1}{2}$–$8\tfrac{1}{2}$	$8\tfrac{1}{2}$–$10\tfrac{1}{2}$	10–12	5–8	
Type II:	6–8	$7\tfrac{1}{2}$–$8\tfrac{1}{2}$	$8\tfrac{1}{2}$–$9\tfrac{1}{2}$	$9\tfrac{1}{2}$–$10\tfrac{1}{2}$	$4\tfrac{1}{2}$–$5\tfrac{1}{2}$	

Type II is similar to the type of *maqam* 'Bayat'.

One of the four types of skeletons found in the second *lahan* is similar to the type of skeleton found in the *maqam* 'Siga', and is similar to one of the theoretical scales of this *maqam*. The average sizes of the seconds in the skeletons found in this *maqam* (in units of tenth-tones) are:

[49] In practice, we found that the scales of the *maqamat* are not related to one another; in theory, however, related scales also exist. Thus, for example, within the intonation system of the scale *maqam* 'Rast', different scales are derived by shifting within the system; and from another independent system of *maqam* 'Bayat', other scales are derived.

E	F	G	A	B
5–8	8–12	3–7	8–16	

In theory, at least three variants are given for the scale of *maqam* 'Siga':

	E	F	G	A	B	C
1) In units of whole tones:	$\frac{3}{4}$	I	I	$\frac{3}{4}$	$\frac{3}{4}$	
In units of tenth-tones:	$(7\frac{1}{2})$	(10)	(10)	$(7\frac{1}{2})$	$(7\frac{1}{2})$	
2) Called 'Huzam'	$\frac{3}{4}$	I	$\frac{1}{2}$	$1\frac{1}{2}$	$\frac{1}{2}$	
	$(7\frac{1}{2})$	(10)	(5)	(15)	(5)	
3) Called 'Mustar'	$\frac{4}{5}$	$\frac{3}{4}$	I	$\frac{1}{2}$	I	
	$(12\frac{1}{2})$	$(7\frac{1}{2})$	(10)	(5)	(10)	

That is to say, there is a similarity between the skeleton of live music in the *maqam* 'Siga' and the theoretical skeleton of the second variant called 'Huzam'.

In the practice of liturgical singing in the second *lahan*, we usually found three types of skeletons:

$$\text{Type I:} \quad E-F = F-G = G-A < A-B$$
$$B-C > E-F$$

The sizes of the average seconds (in units of tenth-tones) were:

E	–	F	–	G	–	A	–	B
	8–9		8–9		8–9		$10\frac{1}{2}$–$12\frac{1}{2}$	
	6–$8\frac{1}{2}$		6–$7\frac{1}{2}$		6–$7\frac{1}{2}$			

$$\text{Type II:} \quad E-F < F-G$$

The seconds A – B are larger than the rest of the seconds, and their degree of scatter is particularly large.

E	–	F	–	G	–	A	–	B
	9–10		6–8		7–10		10–13	

It is interesting that the first type of skeleton in the first *lahan* is almost identical with the second type of skeleton in the second *lahan*. This similarity of intonation was found mainly in the melodies of the isolated informants, who received the tradition almost only by ear. Most of the tonal skeletons in the second *lahan* were of the first type.

The type of skeleton in the eighth *lahan* is similar to that found in the *maqam* 'Rast'. In practice, the type of skeleton found may be defined by the following system of relationships:

$$C - D < D - E < E - F$$
$$F - G < G - A$$

The sizes of the seconds in all the skeletons in this *maqam* (in units of tenth-tones) are:

$$C \quad - \quad D \quad - \quad G \quad - \quad F \quad - \quad G \quad - \quad A$$
$$10\text{--}12 \quad\quad 7\text{--}10 \quad\quad 5\text{--}8 \quad\quad 9\text{--}12$$

According to the theory, the sizes of the seconds in *maqam* 'Rast' are different from that found in practice. They are:

	C – D – E – F – G – A – B – C						
In units of whole well-tempered tones:	1	$\frac{3}{4}$	$\frac{3}{4}$	1	1	$\frac{3}{4}$	$\frac{3}{4}$
In units of tenth-tones:	10	$7\frac{1}{2}$	$7\frac{1}{2}$	10	10	$7\frac{1}{2}$	$7\frac{1}{2}$

In the practice of liturgical singing in the eighth *lahan*, one type of skeleton was found. The sizes of the seconds in the different skeletons in this one type were (in units of tenth-tones):

$$C \quad - \quad D \quad - \quad E \quad - \quad F \quad - \quad G \quad - \quad A \quad - \quad B$$
$$10\text{--}15 \quad 7\text{--}9.5 \quad 5.5\text{--}8.5 \quad 9.5\text{--}13 \quad 8\text{--}11.5 \quad 4.5\text{--}11$$

It is interesting that the size of the seconds C – D is very large, sometimes exceeding the value of an augmented second; one does not hear this second as augmented, however, because of its special context (series of descending seconds).

It is important to mention that for some of the informants the concepts *lahan* and *maqam* are identical in the following way:

first *lahan* = *maqam* 'Bayat'
fourth *lahan* = *maqam* 'Siga'
sixth *lahan* = *maqam* 'Hedjaz'
eighth *lahan* = *maqam* 'Rast'

Thus it was found that the musical components contributing to the determination of style are usually dependent upon the occasion of the performance, on the *lahan*, on the class of performer, or on all of them together; sometimes they are interdependent and interrelated.

9) *The Modal Framework*.[50] The modal framework was found to be extremely significant in the material examined. The modal frameworks reflect quite reliably the types of melodies and each mode has a different value and importance. The number of different modes used actually varies between four and ten among the different informants, and also depends on some other factors. It is likely that from the standpoint of a particular factor, such as scale (or more exactly, type of skeleton), certain modes are identical, whereas from the standpoint of other factors, these same modes may be different. The kind of inter-dependence between the different determining factors in the modal framework also depends on the informant and his capability for abstraction. Many factors contribute to the definition of the modal framework, but each in a different manner and to a different extent. There exists a kind of spread in the definition of each factor. The fact that there is a degree of indeterminacy in the laws governing the framework is, apparently, one of the identification marks of live music as actually performed, and is contrary to the 'sterile' laws of music decreed by most theoreticians who cannot tolerate disorder and deviation from strict rules. The modal framework was found to be defined not only by groups of motifs, central notes and characteristic intervals, but also by tempo, melisma, tonal skeleton, and even to a certain extent by the relative and absolute ambitus.[51]

The degree of formalization of the *alhan* according to the factors mentioned above, is not equal for the different *alhan*.

[50] By the term 'modal framework' we mean the conventional frameworks in which a particular musical repertoire is organized: for example, the *maqamat* framework in which Arabic music is organized; or the raga framework for Indian music, etc. These frameworks are usually thought of as 'melody types', according to Apel's definitions. An exact definition of the essence of each melodic type does not, however, exist. Even in the various theories, no exact determination of the modal framework was found; all the more so for various practices where the essence of the frameworks in which they are organized has not been defined. Up to the present, no systematic comprehensive study has been undertaken which would exactly clarify what are the determining factors, and how they influence the modal framework. A detailed discussion on the meaning of the modal framework in the liturgical music of the Christian Arabs in Israel is given in an article by the author, to be published in *Yuval*, No. 2, *Studies of the Jewish Music Research Center* (Jerusalem, 1971) pp. 23-57.

[51] It is worth mentioning that in *maqamat* theory there are a number of scales which receive a different name when they are given in another pitch.

B. *Influences Affecting Performance*

It is possible to describe the performance of the group as a whole by general features common to all the performances. It has already been mentioned, however, that both the isolated informants and other sub-groups of informants play an important part, sometimes even a decisive role, in the final shaping of the music.

The different sub-groups in which a certain similarity was observed, may be described as follows:

1) The class of 'isolated informants' characterized by:

   a) Receiving oral tradition only, through participation in church services, or through instruction (by rote) within the family, without any specific connection with the study centres of liturgical music.
   b) The desire to guard this tradition without introducing changes.
   c) Lack of activity in folk music.
   d) Lack of interest in music in general, and in modern, artistic oriental music in particular.

In this sub-group of isolated informants, it is also possible to distinguish between those who preserve the tradition without any personal intervention, and those who allow themselves more freedom in performance and who may be considered as creative artists, although they do not look upon themselves as such. None of the isolated informants are conscious of the 'concert aspect' of singing.

2) The sub-group of those having a more or less close connection with the liturgical centres: There are some who studied in one of the centres, know theory and can read Byzantine notation; some who study for a limited period (though more than a year) in one of the centres; and some who did not study at all in any of the centres but studied for a long time with a person who was trained in one of the centres.

3) The sub-group of those involved and rooted in modern Arabic music: Some of them know Eastern musical theory (including the *maqamat* system), play oriental instruments, and take an active part in the cultural events of their locality; some are satisfied with listening to the radio, especially the 'Voice of

Cairo', greatly admire Arabic singers (Um-Khulthum, Abdu-(a)l-Wahab, Firuz, Wadi'a Asaf), sometimes even try to imitate them, and see similarity between religious song and secular Arabic song.

The distinction among the various performances was generally expressed in the quantitative measure of the features defining the performance, in the relation between the features, and the consistency of flexibility with which they were used.

For the isolated informants, restriction dominates most of the features. Thus, in the singing of isolated informants in comparison to that of others, restricted use was found in the ambitus of the melody, in the number of central notes, in the number of musical motifs with recitation notes being dominant (see Ex. 8) in the number of tonal skeletons, and in the number of *alhan* actually used. For the very isolated singers, the number of *alhan* became restricted to only three: the first, second, and third, the second *lahan* having 'swallowed' the other five.[52]

Ex. 8

In the singing of isolated informants, there is a close interdependence between features. A musical motif is never found in two different intonation systems. They have a special freedom in improvisation, which is expressed in the remarkable phenomenon of 'mosaic' change: that is, exchange of the position of

---

[52] A number of 'isolated' informants sang all the melodies from the fourth to the eighth *lahan* as though they were in the second *lahan* (with central notes and motifs typical of the second *lahan*), without realizing it.

Ex. 9

the motifs in a repeated performance by the same informant.[53]

[53] Thus, for example, the structure of the melody in accordance with the cadential motifs in the singing of an 'isolated' informant was, in the first performance: A B C B A B C̃ (the symbol ≈ designates a considerable variation). The structure of the same melody in the repeated performance was: A B A B C B C̃. That is to say, an exchange of position took place between motifs A and C in the repeat performance of the same melody. This phenomenon is quite rare.

This phenomenon was found in the singing of isolated informants only. For creative isolated informants, the amount of melisma was greater, and the use of motifs and the way of combining them was freer. The melodic line in the performance of creative isolated informants was no longer a simple combination of closed fixed units, 'frozen' motifs, but rather a continuous line in which the motifs blend so well one into the other that it is almost impossible to tell where one motif ends and the other begins, as demonstrated in Ex. 9.

Variation in the appearance of the motifs is much more frequent and developed in their singing. Another typical phenomenon common in their singing is the frequent change in unit of beat, to such an extent that it is even difficult to sense the beat.

Some similarities were found between creative isolated informants and the enthusiasts for Arabic music. The latter show a large amount of melisma and flexibility in the use of motifs. But these changes are much less limited than for the isolated informants, and sometimes even deviate from the ambitus and intonation of the song.[54] The outstanding discovery

---

It was found only in thirteen out of two hundred and thirty melodies. Not more than one exchange of this type was generally found within a melody.

[54] As an example, let us consider the third *lahan* as it appears in theory and in practice. According to neo-Byzantine theory, the scale of mode III consists of two conjunct tetrachords. According to the theory of Chrysanthos, there are two possibilities of intonation for this scale:

	C	D	E	F	G	A	B	C
1.		12	9	7	12	9	7	12
2.		12	13	3	12	12	5	11

(Here the sizes of the seconds are given according to the system of Chrysanthos, in which each unit is equal to one-sixty-eighth of an octave.) The second possibility approaches the major scale, with E raised a quarter-tone. According to the later, revised theory, there exists only one scale with the following ratios:

	C	D	E	F	G	A	B
		12	10	8	12	10	8

(The sizes of the seconds in the revised system is one-seventy-second of an octave.) In the practice of the third *lahan*, we found one 'type of skeleton', defined by the following relationships:

$$F - G > G - A > A - B$$
$$C - D > D - E > E - F$$

These relationships are also valid for the first possibility of Chrysanthos and for the revised theory, i.e. they both have the same 'type of skeleton' as that found in

in this sub-group is the multiplicity of intonation systems, and the phenomenon of similarity between the *lahan* and the *maqam*.

In the sub-group of those closely connected with the centres of liturgical study, it was found that the ambitus of the melodies was relatively large. The number of motifs used is the largest, and their combinations within the melody were sung without change in tempo. The musical motif is not always related to its intonation, and to a specific *lahan*. At times, a single motif appeared in different *alhan* and in different intonations as in Ex. 10. This last phenomenon is evidence of awareness of scale.

Ex. 10

To summarize: theoretical knowledge tends to result in a separation and independence of the musical characteristics, a quantitative increase in the musical components (ambitus, number of central notes, number of motifs, etc.), and a decrease in the role of performance.

Knowledge of and familiarity with modern Arabic music tends to produce an increase in the number of sets of intonation; continuous blending of the motifs; and increase in the amount of melisma.

In the singing of informants in which local tradition was best preserved and the external influences were minimal, a tendency was found towards curtailing most of the elements and musical frameworks, e.g. the number of modes, number of motifs, systems of intonation, and ambitus. The additive prin-

---

practice. The sizes of the seconds found in the different 'skeletons' in practice were:

$$C \; - \; D \; - \; E - F \; - \; G \; - \; A \; - \; B$$
$$10\text{--}12\tfrac{1}{2} \quad 8\text{--}10\tfrac{1}{2} \quad 5\text{--}7 \quad 10\text{--}12 \quad 9\text{--}10 \quad 5\text{--}7$$

(The units here are in tenth-tones: a whole tempered tone equals ten units.)

ciple in composition was most outstanding, and was expressed in the 'mosaic change' of motifs. Recitation was prominent in their singing.

Comparison of Theory and Practice

Many musical components which were found to be characteristic of practice are totally absent from theory. To examine this 'filtering' of theory (i.e., the subjects which it treats or neglects) can be instructive as to the character of theory and its relation to practice. Naturally, the comparison can be made only for those subjects with which theory deals.

We will examine the appearances in theory and practice of the following concepts:

1) The meaning of scale from the standpoint of intonation.
2) The internal organization of the scale into tetrachords, trichords, and pentachords.
3) The relation between melisma and other characteristics.
4) The relation between the musical motif and its intonation.
5) The relationships among the intervals.
6) The equality or lack of equality between *alhan*.

1) *The Meaning of Scale from the Standpoint of Intonation.* In all theories of music a scale is conceived to be a stepwise progression of notes according to pitch, with fixed intervals between the steps. In practice, however, we found that the intervals are *not* fixed. Even the average of all the sizes in which a particular interval of a second appears varies among the informants. There is a regularity, however, governing the relations between successive seconds. We found that in practice, the best definition of 'scale' was 'type of tonal skeleton'. This concept was derived by the author from many experiments in intonation. The concept 'type of skeleton' discussed earlier was found to be most important in determining the essence of intonation in practice. However, it is not readily apparent; it is rather a kind of hidden organization 'acting behind the scenes', not an easy matter to discover.

According to the neo-Byzantine theory, the basic scale contains three types of seconds, similar to the three main sizes of seconds in the *maqamat*: half, three-quarters, and whole tempered tones. In practice we found an abundance of seconds ranging in size from four to eighteen-tenths of a tone. The majority of the seconds, however, ranged from six to twelve-tenths of a tone.

According to the neo-Byzantine theory and the *maqamat* theory, an integral connection exists between the modal framework and the scale: the scale is one of the important components in defining the mode. Different modes and also different *maqamat* are typified by their relevant scales, which are not necessarily related to one tonal system (in contrast to Western modes which are all related to a single tonal system).

We also found a similar relationship, in the practice of liturgical music, between *lahan* and type of skeleton; and in the practice of secular music between the *maqam* framework and type of skeleton.

In addition to the agreement between practice and theory shown by the existence of the above relationship, there is also actual similarity between the types of skeleton found in the practice of specific *alhan*, and the theoretical scales of the relevant modes; and also similarity to the types of skeleton of certain *maqamat*.

Similarity to Theoretical Scales. Such a similarity can really only refer to the relationships of seconds in the scale, not to the absolute size of seconds. A similarity of this kind was found between the theoretical scales of modes III, V, VI, and VII, and the types of skeleton found in the relevant *alhan*.[54] In the sixth *lahan*, other types of skeleton were found which are not similar to the theoretical scale of the relevant mode.

Similarity to the Well-tempered Scale. Only one type of skeleton was found to be similar to the well-tempered scale, and that only partially. This was one of the two types of skeleton found in the fifth *lahan*, and was similar to the natural minor scale.[55]

[55] For mode V, Chrysanthos suggests four different types of melodies with different central notes. According to the revised version, only two types are suggested. In practice, we also found only two types, with central notes like those in theory. One of the two scales given in the theory of Chrysanthos, for mode V is:

D	E	F	G	A	B	C	D
9	7	12	12	3	12	11	

This scale is very similar to *maqam* 'Bayat', as previously explained, and is not very different from the natural minor scale.

In practice we found in one of the two types a scale similar to the natural, tempered minor scale, including the absolute size of the seconds. Only in one

Similarity to the Maqamat. It is interesting that despite the profusion of scales given in *maqamat* theory, very few were found to be similar to those observed in practice, both in liturgical and in folk singing. Only three *maqamat* scales were found to be similar (in the sense defined above) to types of skeleton found in practice:

1) The type of skeleton found in the practice of folk music in *maqam* 'Siga', and one of the four types of skeletons of the second *lahan* in liturgical music, was similar to one of the theoretical scales suggested for *maqam* 'Siga' (as was shown in the discussion on the *maqamat*).

2) One type of skeleton found in the second *lahan*, was similar to one of the theoretical scales attributed to *maqam* 'Saba'.[56] (It is interesting that this system of intonation, which sounds very strange to the Western listener, was also suggested in the theory.)

3) The type of skeleton of the sixth *lahan* was similar to the *maqam* 'Hedjaz'.[57]

---

second (A – B) was there considerable deviation from the tempered size. The average sizes (in tenths of a tempered tone) of the seconds found in the practice of the fifth *lahan* are:

D	E	F	G	A	B
10–12	5–6	$9\frac{1}{2}$–11	9–$10\frac{1}{2}$	6–7	

[56] In theory, at least four variants of *maqam* 'Saba' are found (the unit being a whole tempered tone):

	D	E	F	G	A
1.		$\frac{3}{4}$	$\frac{3}{4}$	$\frac{1}{2}$	$1\frac{1}{2}$
2.		1	$\frac{1}{2}$	$\frac{1}{2}$	$1\frac{1}{2}$
3.		$\frac{1}{2}$	1	$\frac{1}{2}$	$1\frac{1}{2}$
4.		$\frac{3}{4}$	$\frac{3}{4}$	$\frac{3}{4}$	$\frac{5}{4}$

The fourth variant called 'Rakb' forms an unusual system of intonation for the Western listener. This system was found in the second *lahan* and was defined by the fact that the first three seconds are equal, while the fourth second is larger than all the other seconds.

[57] According to theory, the scale of *maqam* 'Hedjaz' is given by the following ratios:

D	E	F	G	A	B	C	D
$\frac{1}{2}$	$1\frac{1}{2}$	$\frac{1}{2}$	1	$\frac{1}{2}$	1	1	

For the first tetrachord, there also exists the following possibility:

D	E	F	G
$\frac{3}{4}$	$\frac{5}{4}$	$\frac{1}{2}$	

4) One type of skeleton found in the fifth *lahan* was similar to the scale of *maqam* 'Nahawand', which is identical to the natural minor scale.

It is here worth while recalling Thibaut's experiments in

A variant of the scale of this *maqam* occurs when the second tetrachord is identical to and disjunct from the first:

$$\overbrace{D - G} \qquad \overbrace{A - D}$$

In this case, it is called *maqam* 'Hedjaz Kar'.

The influence of *maqam* 'Hedjaz', on both practice and theory of Byzantine music, is outstanding. This influence is expressed in mode VI, whose scale is almost identical, even theoretically, with the scale of *maqam* 'Hedjaz'. According to Chrysanthos, two possibilities exist for mode IV:

	D	E	F	G	A	B	C	D
1.		7	18	3	12	9	7	12
2.		7	18	3	12	7	18	3

(each unit is one-sixty-eighth of an octave).

The second possibility, in which the scale consists of two identical disjunct tetrachords, is similar to the scale of *maqam* 'Hedjaz Kar'.

According to the revised theory, the tetrachord typical of mode VI, which is similar to the tetrachord of 'Hedjaz', is given by the following ratios:

$$\begin{array}{cccc} D & E & F & G \\ & 4 & 20 & 6 \end{array}$$

(Each unit here is equal to one-seventy-second of an octave, i.e. one-half a tempered tone equals six units.) In performance of the sixth *lahan*, several 'types of skeleton' were found. (As already mentioned, this *lahan* is rarely found, and mainly in villages in which the influence of modern Arabic music is strong.) One of them is similar to *maqam* 'Hedjaz', and is made up of conjunct non-identical tetrachords. From the numerical point of view, the following sizes of seconds were found in the different skeletons of the sixth *lahan*:

$$\begin{array}{ccccccc} D & E & F & G & A & B & C \\ 4\frac{1}{2}\text{–}8\frac{1}{2} & 12\text{–}18 & 4\text{–}6\frac{1}{2} & 8\frac{1}{2}\text{–}12 & 3\frac{1}{2}\text{–}6\frac{1}{2} & 7\text{–}11 \end{array}$$

(The units are in tenths of a tone.)

It is worth mentioning that the 'Hedjaz' tetrachord also appears in the text-books in mode II. This scale of mode II is given in the following intonation:

$$\begin{array}{ccccccc} E & - & F & - & G - A & - & B & - & C \\ \frac{1}{2} & & 1 & & \frac{1}{2} & & 1\frac{1}{2} & & \frac{1}{2} \end{array}$$

In practice, we found, in one of the types of skeleton of the second *lahan*, that the size of the second A – B ranged from eleven to thirteen-tenths of a tempered tone. Here it is important to recall Idelsohn's hypothesis that the augmented second is a 'foreign import' into our region (see Idelsohn, *The History of Hebrew Music* (Devir, Tel-Aviv–Berlin, 1924), p. 6), and also the remark of Gerson-Kiwi (see E. Gerson-Kiwi, *The Persian Doctrine of Dastga-Composition* (Tel-Aviv, 1963), p. 28) that the characteristic interval was five-fourths of a tone, whereas the interval of one and one-half tones was a 'correction' which is found in Greece and other Balkan countries, and in the tradition of Eastern Europe.

finding the intonation of neo-Byzantine scales.[58] Comparison
with his results show that his results are similar to the present
one in the discovery of the importance of classifying notes
according to their stability or variability. Our experiments did
not, however, uncover Thibaut's 'gravitational power' towards
the 'natural scale', which in his opinion is the hidden guide of
performance. A quantitative similarity was found only between
the type of skeleton of the sixth *lahan* and the scale Thibaut
found in the mode IV.

In view of the discussion above, we should not be surprised
at the results of measurements of Alfred Berner, published
by Curt Sachs in 1937, which show the great frequency of
deviations in singing, even for excellent singers familiar with
the theory.[59]

2) *The Internal Organization of the Scale into Tetrachords*

[58] The problem of exact intervals found in neo-Byzantine singing has occupied the
attention of clergy and musicians. In 1881 they began to deal with this problem
experimentally with the assistance of the monochord. The first group of experiments, the report on which is far from being clear, was described by J. B.
Thibaut. Thibaut himself conducted the measurements of the singing of the
Arch-mandarin, who, in the opinion of Thibaut, was an accomplished musician.
The measurements were made, with the help of physicists, on a sonometer (on
which the intervals of certain scales are marked under the strings). He summarized these experiments in his article 'L'harmonique chez les Grecs
Modernes', *Échos d'Orient*, 3 (1900), pp. 211-20. His experiments provided a
reference point for the discussions of subsequent scholars (J. Jeanin and J.
Puyade, op. cit., i, pp. 137-40; J. Parisot, op. cit., pp. 52-5; Rebours, and
others). There are several limitations to Thibaut's experiments: 1) the use of
the monochord as a measuring instrument; 2) the examination of the singing
of one person only; 3) the representation of each interval of the singing in a
particular mode, by one measurement only. An additional limitation stems from
the fact that Thibaut was convinced that the 'natural' scale has a 'natural
gravitational power' (as he expressed it), and there is no doubt that this con-
viction 'guided' him in his measurements. In spite of this, if we consider the
results of his measurements as approximate representations of a tonal skeleton,
it is interesting to study them.

[59] Without going into the problem of the system of measurement (only one result
is given there), it seems to the author, in contrast to the opinion of Curt Sachs,
that the results are quite reasonable. The sizes of the seconds in the pentachord
of *maqam* 'Nahawand' (natural minor scale) were measured as performed by
two singers.

> Singer A: in cents—179, 108, 193, 222; in tenth-tones—9, 5½, 9½, 11
> Singer B: in cents—180, 144, 209, 169; in tenth-tones—9, 7, 10½, 8½

In accordance with the conclusions on intonation, it seems that for the two
tetrachords there is complete similarity to *maqam* 'Nahawand' (the quantitative
deviations being exceedingly small). Only the top second deviates slightly from
the framework.

D

Trichords and Pentachords. In theory, there are several distinct internal organizations within the scale. The scale is divided into groups of pentachords, tetrachords, and trichords, even though the definition of 'groups' is not altogether clear. In theory, a 'group' of notes is not specifically defined; in practice a group of notes is defined by its internal division according to a particular fixed intonation, and is related to central notes and musical motifs. Even in theory, however, there are many exceptions to this rule, and there are even contradictions in the descriptions in theory.

It is interesting that most of the musical theories dealing with scales rely only on the tetrachord unit. In classical Greece, the scales were classified according to combinations of tetrachords with fixed intonation; in practice, however, the few surviving examples suggest that non-identical tetrachords were combined.[60] Strunk has suggested a scale system for Byzantine music consisting of combinations of tetrachords having the same intonation. Thodberg suggested another system with a similar basis.[61] Thodberg related the concept of the tetrachord both to scale and to musical motifs in which the fourth was dominant. Strunk, on the other hand, apparently limited this concept only

[60] See Curt Sachs, *The Rise of Music in the Ancient World* (New York, 1943), pp. 214-15.

[61] Strunk assumed that one scale system exists in which one tetrachord is predominant for all the modes (see his article: 'The Tonal System of Byzantine Music', *The Musical Quarterly*, xxviii (1942), pp. 190-204). The assumption seems rather arbitrary to us. It was challenged by C. Thodberg in his studies (see his article 'The Tonal System of the Kontakarium', *Historish-filosofiske Meddelelser*, Bind. 37, 7 (Copenhagen, 1960). Out of considerations which seem most justified, and which are similar to those of Strunk in his analysis of the collection of Kontakia melodies in the *Psalticon* (which appeared in the fourth volume of *Monumenta Musica Byzantinae*), Thodberg arrived at the conclusion that the tonal system suggested by Strunk:

is suitable to the Hirmologium and the Sticherarium, whereas for the 'Kontakarium' the following system is suitable:

to the scale aspect: from the aspect of musical motif, organization into tetrachords is suitable to a few modes only, especially mode I, but is entirely unsuitable to mode II. We have no information on intonation from the Byzantine period, either in practice or in theory, so that, despite several logical considerations, the suggested organization remains doubtful. In the theory of the *maqamat* scales, also, tetrachords predominate. Here, however, in contrast to the previous case, almost no combinations of identical tetrachords were found even in theory. At times it seems that the division of the scale into tetrachords is quite artificial and the tetrachord organization loses its meaning for both intonation and musical motifs.

In actual practice, it seems to us that for the musical material in this work there is significance in the division of the scale into small groups of notes, as suggested in theory. These groups are not defined only by specific, fixed, internal divisions (though this possibility also exists), but by central notes, musical motifs, and characteristic intervals. According to this definition, it was found that the majority of melodies were organized in tetrachords only (identical or not), in trichords (identical or not), in pentachords plus tetrachords, in pentachords plus trichords, and in tetrachords plus trichords.

3) *The Relationship between the Melismatic Quality of a Melody and other characteristics*. In this matter, we did not find agreement between theory and practice.

According to theory, a relationship exists between melisma and other musical characteristics like scale, intervals between notes in the scale, organization of the notes into trichords or tetrachords or pentachords, ambitus, and central notes of the melody. Thus syllabic hymns in a particular mode will be different from very melismatic hymns (called 'papadikes') in the same mode. The difference will occur both in the scale and in central notes. That means that in each mode there are several types of melodies in accordance with their melismatic quality.

In practice, almost no such relationship between melisma and type of melody was found. We did find, however, a relationship to other characteristics and factors. The degree of melismatic quality in practice was determined quantitatively (as described previously), and was found to be dependent, to a certain extent, on the *lahan*, the occasion of performance, the position of the phrase in the song, the rhythm, and especially on the class of performer. It is true that we sometimes found in practice (as well as in theory) several types of melodies in a particular *lahan*, but to a lesser degree than suggested by theory, and without any relationship to the amount of melisma. (One exception to this rule was the fifth *lahan* in which a relationship between the amount of melisma and two types of melodies existed. These two types were determined by scales and central notes, as well as the amount of melisma.) Apparently, the discrepancy between practice and theory occurs for two reasons:

a) the collection of melodies in the group examined was relatively small. Theory deals with a much larger collection of melodies. Most of the melismatic melodies dealt with in theory are 'out of bounds' in practice;

b) the degree of melisma was found to be closely related to performance itself; obviously, therefore, practice seriously blurs the relation between melismatic quality and other characteristics.

4) *The Relationship between the Musical Motif and its Intonation.* Theoretically, no such relationship exists, and in the literature we find (though infrequently) the same musical motifs may appear in different scales, in different *alhan*, and in different intonations.[62] In practice, an intrinsic connection was found between the motif and its intonation, for the two are inseparable. Usually a particular motif was not likely to appear in a different intonation from the same informant. Only three informants sang the same motif in eight *alhan*, in a different intonation for each *lahan*. This relationship certainly must have been dominant in the Byzantine music of the Middle Ages, supplying Strunk and Thodberg with one of the important bases in their reconstruction of the tonal system of Byzantine music. It was also found in the collection of melodies recorded by Jeanin: the same motif, and even a whole melodic formula, appearing at

[62] In Rebours' book, we found the musical motif, presented in Ex. 3 in mode IV on G (p. 103), and in mode VII on F (p. 208). In the frequently used books (with Western notation), this phenomenon is quite rare. It was found to a very small extent in the Lebanese book in mode I (p. 27), in mode III (p. 31), and in mode VIII (p. 35). In the *Syllitourgikon*, it was found in mode II (p. 57), and in mode III (p. 76). In the *Melodecte*, no such example was found.

different times in different modes but always in the same intonation.[63]

The separation of musical motif and intonation is evidence of highly developed scale-awareness. The absence of such a separation, as found in the practice of our group, reveals that the scale concept has not yet developed, and that this music is still in the stage in which melodic formulas predominate.

5) *Relationships among the Intervals.* In theory, there is no preference for a particular large interval. The very existence of different organizations within the scale divides the 'power' of large intervals equally among the third, fourth, and fifth. Most theoretical thought on the subject of intonation has been focused on determining the sizes of the various seconds, and their different combinations. To the author it seems that this subject is related to the additivity of Byzantine musical notation: a note is defined by its interval from the preceding note, and not by reference to a specific central note.[64] In this way, emphasis is placed on the relationships between successive intervals, and not on their sum. A certain use of relationships of this kind was found in practice. We observed that the intonation framework is determined by the relations of successive seconds (almost without consideration of their sum). In other words, in Western music the stable interval is the large interval (with preference for the octave, fifth and fourth), whereas in the music examined here, it is the relations between successive seconds which are stable.[65]

An echo of this approach is already found in essays by Arab authors of the Middle Ages on Greek music. They considered a

---

[63] See Jeanin, op. cit., vol. II for the comparison of the musical examples in mode I p. 279, mode II p. 3, mode III p. 148, mode IV p. 13, mode VI p. 272, mode VII p. 192.

[64] In this way, the broken triad will be designated as a third plus a third (3, 3), in contrast to the system of the figured bass, founded on the bass note according to which the chord will be designated as a third plus a fifth (3, 5). It is understood, of course, that the second system mainly concerns the designation of chords, while the first system is suited for monophonic music only.

[65] In his discussions on the problem of stability of intervals, Kunst shows that 'skeleton notes', which are more or less fixed, exist also in the music of primitive tribes. But as to the internal division into seconds in this music, it seems to him that the division is far from being fixed, so that it is possible to define only the direction of the progress of the melody but not the exact size of the intervals. Size does not seem to him to be an important and determining factor (see J. Kunst, *Ethnomusicology* (The Hague, M. Nijhoff, 1959), p. 42).

tetrachord 'weak' when its minor seconds were equal in size (without the exact size being designated). A tetrachord was considered 'energetic' when one of the minor seconds was twice as large as the neighbouring interval. According to this definition, the two chromatic tetrachords of 'Ptolemy' presented here are 'energetic':

The sizes of seconds in tenth-tones:

a) 3   6   16
b) 4   7½   13½

Whereas the three chromatic tetrachords of Aristoxenos are 'weak': (This is according to Kuttner,[66] whose figures are slightly different from those of Curt Sachs.)

a) 3¾   3¾   17½
b) 5   5   15
c) 3   3   19

(In the last example, our attention is drawn, of course, to the ratio between the two small seconds. The *sum* of the three seconds in the tetrachord is always fixed, its value being a perfect, 'holy' fourth.)

6) *Equality or Lack of Equality among the Alhan.* In the neo-Byzantine theory, all the modes are equal in value, and emphasis on this fact is shown by the organization and consolidation of the collection of chants in the Octoëchos. This equality between the modes was certainly enforced artificially (a by-product of every theoretical arrangement).[67] In performance, this equality was not found; a preference was found for particular *alhan*. This preference shows itself in the attitude to the *lahan*, and in the frequency of occurrences. The attitude to the *alhan* is not neutral. *Alhan* may be (in the words of the informants) 'beloved', 'cheerful', 'respected', 'beautiful', 'difficult', and other similar adjectives. *Alhan* may be frequent, sung at every opportunity, or neglected. All the singers expressed a strong personal preference for one *lahan* or another. To a large extent, the attitude to the *lahan* is determined by festivals, and to a certain extent also by the similarity to folk-song. Thus, for

[66] See F. A. Kuttner, 'The Theory of Classical Greek Music', Introductory Notes to Musurgia Records, 1955.
[67] See the remarks of E. Werner, *The Sacred Bridge* (New York, 1960), pp. 398-402.

example, the *alhan* most liked and popular were the first, used for baptism feast days and similar to *maqam* 'Bayat', and the fifth, used for Easter. Following these, the eighth and the fourth *lahan* were preferred. The sixth *lahan* (similar to *maqam* 'Hedjaz') was the rarest, and was included among the most popular *alhan* only in villages where the influence of modern Arabic music is strong. It is interesting that none of the informants pointed out the great frequency of the second *lahan*, similar to *maqam* 'Siga', whereas from our data we observed that it was the most widespread of all (especially in isolated places). Most of the responses of the congregation are in this *lahan*, and sometimes it even replaces another *lahan*, without attention being paid to the fact. Perhaps it is so natural for them that they do not notice its distinctiveness. This is the *lahan* without a 'label'. It is interesting that in this *lahan*, several types of skeleton were found.[68]

Summary of the Comparison between Practice and Theory

The comparison of practice and theory was undertaken in the realization that we are dealing with two quite different activities and must therefore 'translate' appropriately from the language of theory to practice and, if possible, vice versa. Thus, for example, it was found that in practice, the concept which corresponded best to the theoretical scale was 'tonal skeleton' or even 'type of tonal skeleton'.

In contradiction to the conclusions of Villoteau, who examined practice and theory of Arabic music in Egypt,[69] we found that the number of rules on which practice is based is larger than the number of rules used in theory; but also that each practical rule (rules not necessarily consciously known by the performers) is defined differently from the corresponding theoretical rule.

In our comparison we found many parallels between practice

[68] On the importance of this *lahan* in the liturgical music, before the consolidation of the Octoëchos, we can read in Werner's book, ibid., p. 442; and Kenneth Levy's article 'The Byzantine Sanctus', *Annales Musicologiques*, vi (Paris, 1963). The mode described by them agrees with the second *lahan* customarily used by the Arabic group, excepting intonation about which we have no information from the early periods.

[69] See G. H. Villoteau, 'De l'état de l'art de musique en Égypte', *Description de l'Égypte*, iv (Paris, 1799).

and theory concerning their roles in the musical frameworks; generally, however, we did not find a quantitative identity of the frameworks. Agreement between practice and theory can be summarized in the following findings:

1) Both in theory and in practice, the mode, or *lahan*, or *maqam* is defined by an intonation system, i.e. the scale in theory and the type of skeleton in practice. Real similarity between the scale and the relevant type of skeleton is rare. Similarity was found between several *alhan* and *maqamat*.

2) In both theory and practice much more importance is placed on the internal organization of the scale into trichords, tetrachords, and pentachords (not necessarily identical ones). Usually little actual similarity was found between small groups of notes in practice and theory.

3) In both theory and practice, the relationships of seconds is quite important, but not necessarily their total sum. The actual similarity of these relationships was limited.

Apparently this lack of quantitative agreement among the frameworks is evidence of local tradition, and also confirms the hypothesis that intonation is a locally rooted factor, not easily transferred.

No similarity between practice and theory was found:

a) for characteristics largely dependent on performance, like melisma;

b) for the relative importance of *alhan*. In practice, the *alhan* are not equal, whether from the point of view of distribution, or of formalization (i.e. to what an extent the *lahan* is defined), or of the attitude of the performers to the *lahan*;

c) for the mutual relation between the characteristics. In contrast to theory, in practice, a close relation was found between motifs, and their intonation and tempo.

Concluding Remarks

We have found, therefore, that there is a certain regularity underlying a musical practice, which was and still is functional in character. This practice is one in which performance is predominant, and is one in which Rebours said there existed a total lack of regularity. The regularity that was discovered changed in accordance with the class of performers. Part of this regularity went completely unnoticed by the performers, and most important of all, we found that it was frequently defined within certain boundaries of change.

We found, furthermore, that neo-Byzantine theory and the *maqamat* system were fairly reliable determinants for a considerable part of the rules of this practice, if only the correct interpretation for the theory were found. This means that we must not expect absolute agreement between the laws of practice and those of theory, the latter being presented in a precise numerical form.

The musical material transcribed in books was found to be of value especially for the general design of the melody, and the determination of its central notes.

In order to deepen our understanding of the nature of the relations between practice and theory, we found it worth while to examine in detail practices of different local traditions, all related to the same neo-Byzantine theory, as well as practices with a similar cultural background related to the *maqamat*, but belonging to a different musical ritual. The groups, for example, whose practice is related to the neo-Byzantine theory are as follows: one belonging to the Arab countries, Cyprus, Turkey, and Greece, all connected to a certain extent with the same theological centres, although of course, each has its own local tradition; another group belonging to the Balkan countries: Albania, Yugoslavia, Rumania, and such areas as Georgia and Hungary, a group with separate local centres. It would be interesting to examine the practice of Christian Arabs not belonging to the Byzantine group, yet within the sphere of influence of the *maqamat* system, such as the Maronites, Latin Arabs, and Syrians.

Comparisons, even partial, between different groups will contribute most certainly to a better understanding of the processes of change in religious music as well as an understanding of the creative power of Arabic musical cultures. From these we may secure a better understanding of Byzantine music in the Middle Ages, and the changes in the course of its development.

We might venture to ask, at this point, whether it is really necessary to assume the existence of a single scale system for all the collections of hymns, in such a way that all the modes are related to this single system (as has been assumed by Western scholars of Byzantine music). One may also doubt whether a particular scale system must consist of identical tetrachords,[70] since it appears that a rigid application of the concepts of Western scales to vocal music which is built as a chain of motifs acting as organic units, is quite artificial, and perhaps far removed from reality.

[70] It is interesting that although Thodberg was bold enough to assume a different scale system for a particular group of hymns, he did not give up the idea of 'holy' tetrachords.

2

Helen Breslich-Erickson

NEW HAVEN, CONNECTICUT

The Communion Hymn
of the Byzantine Liturgy of the
Presanctified Gifts

THE communion hymn Γεύσασθε καὶ ἴδετε, together with Psalm 33 from which its text is taken, reflects the oldest communion usage of the Christian Church.[1] However, by the eighth or ninth century this once-popular hymn is found only in the Liturgy of the Presanctified Gifts,[2] which is served[3] during Great Lent.[4] In the course of its development the Presanctified,

---

[1] See H. Leclerq, 'Communion (rite et antienne de la)', *Dictionnaire d'archéologie chrétienne et de liturgie*, iii, cols. 2427-36, and J. A. Jungmann, *The Mass of the Roman Rite* (New York, 1959), pp. 514-16.

[2] The Codex Barberinus LXXVII (eighth or ninth century) is the earliest known textual manuscript of the liturgies of St. Basil the Great, of St. John Chrysostom, and of the Presanctified Gifts. Parts of the service assigned to the choir are indicated only by incipit, as the manuscript specifically contains only the part of the celebrant. The text of the Presanctified as it appears in this manuscript is published in C. A. Swainson, *The Greek Liturgies* (Cambridge, 1884), pp. 95-9. A discussion of the manuscript and its dating is found on p. xv.

[3] The Presanctified is said to be 'served' rather than celebrated, as the term 'celebrated' refers to the consecration of the bread and wine distributed in communion. The communion elements distributed in the Presanctified have been previously consecrated and therefore no consecration occurs during this liturgy.

[4] Apparently the Presanctified originally was served on other days as well. See H. W. Codrington, 'The Syrian Liturgies of the Presanctified', *The Journal of Theological Studies*, v (1904), p. 374; and I. Ziadé, 'Messe des présanctifiés', *Dictionnaire de théologie catholique*, xiii, col. 102. During the period of the musical manuscripts to be discussed in this article, it was apparently served only during Great Lent. See V. Janeras, 'La partie vésperale de la Liturgie byzantine des Présanctifiés', *Orientalia Christiana Periodica*, xxx (1964), p. 212. In current Byzantine practice the Presanctified is served on every Wednesday and Friday of Great Lent and on Monday, Tuesday, and Wednesday of Holy Week (the week immediately preceding Easter Sunday).

originally a simple communion service without attendant consecration,[5] acquired this communion hymn along with many
other features of the Divine Liturgy;[6] but when the modern
cycle of communion hymns was introduced into the Divine
Liturgy, the ancient communion text was retained in the
Presanctified.

Thus the Presanctified apparently ceased to be an object of
liturgical development considerably before the period in which
our earliest musical manuscripts were written;[7] and Simeon of
Thessaloniki tells us that by the beginning of the fifteenth century it was not used as often as in previous times.[8] Yet in spite
of this, the Akolouthiai manuscripts of the fourteenth and
fifteenth centuries almost invariably contain music for this
service, and the number of settings for a particular text is often
considerable. It is most interesting that almost all of these
musical settings were composed between 1300 and 1450 and
that they are ascribed by rubric—with remarkable accuracy—
to composers more or less contemporary with the manuscripts
themselves.

For this study six manuscripts have been chosen, all of which

[5] The origin of the Presanctified has been much discussed, but the traditional
ascription of it by Gregory Bar Hebraeus (d. 1286) to Patriarch Severus of
Antioch (patriarch 511-18, d. 538) appears to be by far the most reasonable
hypothesis. According to Bar Hebraeus, Severus instituted this service as a
replacement for the weekday Eucharistic services (i.e. on Wednesdays and
Fridays) which had been forbidden during Great Lent by the canons of the
Church (Canon 49 of the mid-fourth-century Council of Laodicea). See
Codrington, op. cit., pp. 369-77, which includes (p. 371) a translation from the
Syriac of Bar Hebraeus' comments on the origin of the Presanctified; and D. N.
Moraïtis, 'Ἡ Λειτουργία τῶν Προηγιασμένων (Thessaloniki, 1955). For a
different theory concerning its origins, see Jean-Baptiste Thibaut, 'Origine de
la Messe des Présanctifiés', Échos d'Orient, xix (1920), pp. 36-48.
[6] Among the features adopted from the Divine Liturgy (the Byzantine 'Mass')
was the Hymn of the Great Entrance (or offertory) which is clearly foreign to a
service in which there is no consecration. The Chronicon Paschale for the year 617
(Migne, Patrologia Graeca xcii, col.. 989. records the introduction of this hymn into
the Liturgy of the Presanctified in Constantinople in that year. By the time of
the Barberini Codex, the assimilation of elements from the Eucharistic Liturgies
of St. Basil the Great and of St. John Chrysostom has been so complete that the
services are grouped together as the 'Three Liturgies'.
[7] See P. N. Trempelas, Αἱ τρεῖς Λειτουργίαι (Athens, 1933), pp. 195-221. This
edition of the Presanctified is compiled from 84 manuscripts in Athens libraries
dating from the eleventh to the seventeenth centuries, with all variants
indicated.
[8] See Janeras, loc. cit.

are currently in the National Library in Athens: MSS 2458, 2622, 2456, 899, 2406, and 2837.[9]

MS 2458 is the earliest dated Akolouthiai (1336)[10] and comes from the area around Thessaloniki, where it may have been written under the supervision of Koukouzeles.[11] MS 2622 also originated in northern Greece[12] and is dated within the period 1341–c. 1360 (the period of the regency of Anne of Savoy) on the basis of acclamations contained in it.[13] MS 2456 is dated to the late fourteenth or early fifteenth century and also comes from northern Greece.[14] MS 899, according to its watermark and repertory, was copied in the first half of the fifteenth century and is also, in all probability, from northern Greece.[15] MS 2406 was written in the Monastery of St. John the Forerunner near Serres (north-east of Thessaloniki in northern Greece) and is dated 1453, as the fall of Constantinople is recorded in it.[16] MS 2837 is dated 1457 by colophon.[17]

No less than sixteen different settings of Γεύσασθε καὶ ἴδετε are found in these manuscripts. The composers are indicated by rubric in almost every case, and in the thirty-nine appearances of this text (some hymns are found in up to six copies) there is no instance of a setting being attributed to more than one composer. In only one instance do we find an unidentified setting. The setting labelled 'palaion' ('old') in three of our manuscripts is not identified by rubric in the other two manuscripts in which it appears.

The following tentative chronology of the composers indicated by rubric is possible:

[9] A complete table of the locations of settings and concordances is to be found in the Appendix. Consequently references to specific settings and examples will be identified by manuscript number only. I would like to thank the staff of the Music Library of Yale University for making the microfilms of these manuscripts available to me.

[10] For more information on this manuscript and for general information on this type of manuscript see O. Strunk, 'The Antiphons of the Octoechos', *Journal of the American Musicological Society*, xiii (1960), p. 53.

[11] E. V. Williams, 'John Koukouzeles' Reform of Byzantine Chanting for Great Vespers in the Fourteenth Century' (unpublished doctoral dissertation, Yale, 1968), p. 78.

[12] Idem.   [13] Strunk, op. cit., pp. 53-4.   [14] Williams, loc. cit.   [15] Idem.

[16] M. Velimirović, 'Byzantine Composers in MS Athens 2406', *Essays Presented to Egon Wellesz* (Oxford, 1966), p. 7. I would like to express my appreciation to Professor Velimirović for his suggestion that I work on the Presanctified and for his invaluable assistance throughout the preparation of this article.

[17] Williams, op. cit., p. 75.

a) Early to mid-fourteenth century:
   John Koukouzeles (*c.* 1280 to *c.* 1375)[18]
   Xenos Koronis (mid-fourteenth century)
   Gerontios Moschianos (mid-fourteenth century).
b) Late fourteenth century to early fifteenth century:
   John Glykes (*c.* 1400)[19]
   John Lampadarios of Klada (*c.* 1400).
c) Early to mid-fifteenth century:[20]
   Redestinos (by 1453)
   Gavalas (by 1453)
   Gerasimos the Hieromonk (by 1453)
   Manuel Chrysaphes (by 1453)
   Markos the Hieromonk (by 1453)
   Archon of the Monastery (by 1457).[21]

The setting labelled 'palaion' was in existence by 1336 and that labelled 'asmatikon' by the mid-fourteenth century, although there is good reason to believe that these compositions are of an earlier date than the Akolouthiai manuscripts in which they are found.

The manuscripts reflect the above dating in their ordering to an astonishing degree—see Table I opposite. As can be seen from the table, there is often confusion in the ordering of composers more or less contemporary with each other, as in the case of Koukouzeles and Koronis. Yet, on the whole, the order in which the settings of Γεύσασθε are found in these manuscripts reflects to a high degree the chronological ordering of their composers.

Concerning the lives of most of these composers not much is known, except in the case of Koukouzeles, whose life has been extensively studied.[22] It is believed that John Lampadarios, Manuel Chrysaphes, John Glykes, and possibly Xenos Koronis

[18] Ibid., p. 387.
[19] There is some indication that Glykes may be an older contemporary of Koukouzeles. See K. Levy, 'A Hymn for Thursday in Holy Week', *Journal of the American Musicological Society*, xvi (1963), p. 156, n. 47.
[20] The dates of these composers have been tentatively ascribed on the basis of the appearances of their works in these manuscripts.
[21] This setting occurs only in Athens MS 2837, which suggests that he was connected with the (unknown) monastery in which this manuscript may have been written.
[22] Williams, op. cit., pp. 303-77.

Table I. Ordering of Settings of Γεύσασθε in the Manuscripts

	2458	2622	2456	899	2406	2837
'asmatikon'		#1			#1	
'palaion'	#1	#2	#1	#1		#1
Koukouzeles	#2	#3	#2	#3	#3	#3
Koronis		#4	#3	#2	#4	#2
Moschianos		#5			#6	
John Lampadarios						
a) 'tetraphonos'				#5	#2	#4
b) Nenano			#4	#4	#5	#5
c) Barys			#5			#6
Glykes			#6			
Redestinos					#7	#7
Gavalas					#8	
Gerasimos					#9	
Manuel Chrysaphes						
a) Nenano					#10	
b) Barys					#11	
Markos the Hieromonk					#12	#8
Archon of the Monastery						#9

were associated with the 'imperial' choir or clergy in Constantinople.[23] It is possible that Moschianos may be either a family name or the name of a monastery. The place of origin of Demetrios Redestinos is most likely Raidestos, on the shores of the Sea of Marmara, not far from Constantinople.[24] Nothing is known of the other composers, aside from appearances of their works in musical manuscripts.

The structure of the text Γεύσασθε καὶ ἴδετε appears to be the single most important factor in the musical organization of these settings. The text is divided into musical phrases in this manner: Γεύσασθε/καὶ ἴδετε/ὅτι χρηστός/ὁ Κύριος//. The structure of the refrain, although basically determined by the varying number of repetitions of the word 'Alleluia', differs from setting to setting. Full cadences almost always occur on the final syllable of 'ἴδετε' and 'Κύριος' and conclude major sections of the refrain. It is common practice throughout the repertory to increase the rhythmic value of a note either at the end of a textual division or at the beginning of the subsequent division to indicate a clear break between the sections.

[23] Velimirović, op. cit., p. 12.   [24] Ibid., p. 159.

The introductory word 'Γεύσασθε' usually functions in a heraldic manner, defining the mode and, no doubt, also the text. A melisma may occur, most often on the second syllable of 'Γεύσασθε', but also, occasionally, on the first. These melismas are usually short compared to those found elsewhere in the setting.

As a further affirmation of the mode, the first syllable of 'ἴδετε' almost invariably falls on an important tonal centre, and this pitch is usually rhythmically extended.

The two oldest settings of the group are those marked 'palaion' and 'koinonikon asmatikon'. When these pieces

appear in a manuscript they are invariably placed at the
beginning of the collection of communion hymns for the Presanctified; and in the one instance in which both settings occur
in the same manuscript (MS 2622), the piece labelled 'asmatikon' precedes that marked 'palaion'. There seems to be little
doubt that these pieces were in existence before the introduction
of the Akolouthiai, as the musical settings usually found in this

Ex. 4

'Asmatikon' 2622

'Palaion' 2458

kind of manuscript are ascribed to their composers almost
without exception. The comparative age of these two settings
is confirmed by stylistic analysis, which notes the presence of
several early characteristics such as limited range, short and
compact phrases, and a short alleluia refrain.

Concerning the introduction of the Akolouthiai and the
musical traditions which preceded it, Levy has said:[25]

It seems that more was at stake in the general substitution of the
Akolouthiai and the Kalophonic repertory for the Psaltic and
Asmatic repertories than a simple exchange of newer for older styles.
At the root of the change there was a decline in the liturgical
tradition represented by the outmoded styles. During the 13th
century the rivalry between 'cathedral' and 'monastic' practice—
between the ceremonial Imperial rite centered at Hagia Sophia and
the more modest practice of the Palestinian Typikon ascribed to
St. Saba—reached a decisive stage. What finally transferred the
musical initiative from the clergy of the Great Church to the
monasteries of the Capital is not clear, although a ready explanation
is that it was the interruption of Imperial tradition by the Latin
conquest in 1204. In any case, the monastic usage during this
century consolidated a victory that was already won in substance
two centuries earlier. The Akolouthiai, while loyal at the outset to
relics of the cathedral tradition, are essentially monastic in outlook,
and at the root of some of their musical traditions there probably
are elements of the practice of monasteries of the Holy Land.

In the first half of the fifteenth century, Archbishop Symeon
writes of the retention of the cathedral rite in his church, Hagia
Sophia in Thessaloniki.[26] Although Thessaloniki was taken by
the Turks shortly thereafter (in 1430) and Hagia Sophia
transformed into a mosque,[27] it is apparent that the cathedral
rite, as well as the monastic rite, were well known in this area
during the period in which the majority of the manuscripts
with which we are dealing were written. Therefore it is not
unlikely that the early settings 'asmatikon' and 'palaion', which
antedate the Akolouthiai tradition of identified composers, were
retained from one or both of these earlier traditions.

Levy suggests that in the monastic tradition culminating in

[25] K. Levy, op. cit., p. 157.
[26] See O. Strunk, 'The Byzantine Office at Hagia Sophia', *Dumbarton Oaks Papers*,
ix-x (1955-6), pp. 177-202; and Janeras, op. cit., pp. 212-13.
[27] Strunk, 'The Byzantine Office . . .', p. 178.

the Akolouthiai manuscripts 'a single modal usage and a standard melodic formula for the alleluias ran through the core of the Lenten Liturgy, from the entrance of the Presanctified Gifts to the Communion'.[28] The 'single modal usage' to which he refers is the second plagal mode—the mode of the piece marked 'palaion'—and the alleluia formula[29] which he cites as common to several pieces from this section of the Presanctified is identical to the melodic formula which initiates the refrain of our setting of '*Γεύσασθε*' labelled 'palaion'. Thus it seems probable that this setting is of monastic origin and dates from a period prior to the introduction of the Akolouthiai.

The setting labelled 'asmatikon' is in the first mode and does not share the melodic tradition of the setting labelled 'palaion'. Perhaps the most immediately noticeable difference is the presence in this setting of many non-textual syllables—*χ*-, *γγ*-, and *ου*—which appear throughout the text and refrain. These syllables occur in no copy of 'palaion'. It has been suggested that these syllables or letters, which in the earliest Greek sources occur only in the Asmatikon, represent the practice of the small choir or psaltists of Hagia Sophia in Constantinople.[30] A possible source for this style, Hagia Sophia in Thessaloniki, was not distant from the assumed place of origin of these manuscripts, and it seems probable that the piece 'asmatikon' is a remnant of the music sung at that cathedral. The preservation of this setting in an essentially monastic manuscript is not at all surprising. One has only to consider the close connection between the vespers of the Presanctified—an older form of vespers which during this period generally appears only as a preface to this Liturgy—and the cathedral tradition.[31] The conservatism of the Lenten season, which no doubt was responsible for this retention of part of the cathedral rite, could just as easily contribute to the preservation of some part of its music.

Other differences besides the obvious ones of mode and of presence or absence of non-textual syllables are apparent in these two settings. In 'palaion' textual declamation is not dis-

---

[28] Levy, op. cit., p. 162.   [29] Ibid., p. 159.

[30] K. Levy, 'The Slavic Kontakia and their Byzantine Originals', *Queens College Department of Music Twenty-Fifth Anniversary Festschrift* (New York, 1964), p. 83.

[31] Janeras, op. cit., p. 222.

turbed by the brief melismas which interrupt the text; in 'asmatikon' the more extensive melismas occasionally obscure the word rhythm and distort the basic shape of the text. The structures of the refrains are also somewhat different. In 'palaion' the word 'Alleluia' is stated twice, the only deviation from straight declamation of the text being the repetition of the first two syllables of 'Alleluia' after a melisma on the second syllable ('Alle-, Alleluia').[32] In 'Asmatikon' the refrain begins with a short melisma on 'A-' which employs the non-textual syllables 'χ-' and 'ov'.[33] This melisma is concluded by a '$\lambda \acute{\varepsilon} \gamma \varepsilon$' formula, separating it from the rest of the refrain, which consists of extensive melismas employing fragments of the word 'Alleluia' as text. The refrain is, however, concluded by a clear and concise statement of the word itself. Stylistic features of both settings are found in the later repertory contained in our manuscripts.

Throughout the repertory, a close correlation exists between chronology and the choice of mode:

Table II. Chronological Table of Modes

	I	II pl.	Nenano	Barys	Nana
asmatikon'	x				
'palaion'		x			
Koukouzeles		x			
Koronis		x			
Moschianos		x			
John Lampadarios					
a) 'tetraphonos'	x				
b) Nenano			x		
c) Barys				x	
Glykes					x
Redestinos			x		
Gavalas			x		
Gerasimos			x		
Manuel Chrysaphes					
a) Nenano			x		
b) Barys				x	
Markos the Hieromonk					x
Archon of the Monastery					x

[32] This type of repetition of syllables after a melisma is found in all settings except 'asmatikon'. In the later pieces it is used more extensively, particularly in the text.

[33] It may be that this introductory melisma developed into the first statement of the word 'Alleluia', which is notable for its concision and which is often separated from the rest of the refrain by a $\lambda \acute{\varepsilon} \gamma \varepsilon$ formula.

The most popular mode for the setting of Γεύσασθε in the mid-fourteenth century appears to be plagal second, while that of the later fourteenth and fifteenth centuries is Nenano. The setting in plagal second owes a great deal to 'palaion', not only in the choice of mode and in general compositional style, but in more specific features such as the use of a melodic leap (replacing a fifth with a sixth) to reinitiate the word 'Alleluia' after the characteristic melisma on the second syllable of that word. This melodic feature borrowed by Koukouzeles recurs in a large number of settings in the repertory, becoming as large as an octave in several of the later pieces.

Ex. 5

'Palaion' 2458

λη-'   'Αλ- λη-

Koukouzeles 2458

λη-   'Αλ- λη-

Moschianos 2406

λη-   'Αλ-

The choice of second plagal mode by Koukouzeles and the choice of Nenano by John Lampadarios was influential in determining the popularity of these modes. The piece by Koukouzeles was the prototype for compositions by Koronis and Moschianos, and, in a similar manner, the setting by John Lampadarios was incorporated into the work of Redestinos and Chrysaphes. The settings in Nana, the other most popular mode for the setting of Γεύσασθε in this period, are apparently unrelated.[34]

The way in which these melodies were adapted by successive composers gives some indication both of general compositional procedures and of individual style.[35]

---

[34] A form of mode IV Plagal. See O. Strunk, 'Intonations and Signatures of the Byzantine Modes', *Musical Quarterly*, xxxi (1945), p. 349.

[35] It is well to keep in mind that these men were known for their singing and that most of this repertory bears the imprint of improvisational techniques. To think of composition in terms of pen and paper is to misunderstand the actual compositional process. Rubrics such as those found in Athens MS 2406, which indicate a composition 'as sung by', or 'as embellished by' another composer seem to confirm this opinion. See Velimirović, op. cit., pp. 15-18.

Ex. 6

* This sign is used to indicate an omission of three or more notes of the melody.

1. Only fragments are drawn from the model, rarely even a complete phrase. The musical passages taken from the original

** Variant found in MS 899 and MS 2406.

show a high degree of identity in subsequent compositions, and the rhythmic structure and phrasings are carefully preserved, although a section may be abridged, extended or transposed (scribal error?).

2. More melodic material is borrowed from the text section of the hymn than from the Alleluia refrain, perhaps because it is the refrain which shows the greatest musical development during this period. The refrains of the 'parodies' are without exception longer than those of the original settings.

3. At least in the case of the three related settings in second plagal mode, the third composer, Moschianos, seems to have been familiar with both earlier versions (by Koukouzeles and Koronis) and to have drawn his material from both sources. This impression may of course be due in part to later scribal interference. MS 899, for example, attributes to the settings of both Koukouzeles and Koronis a short melodic addition found in none of the earlier copies of these pieces.[36]

---

[36] In a similar manner the setting labelled 'palaion' is furnished with additional melismas in all manuscripts of the late fourteenth and fifteenth centuries.

4. This practice of adaptation was not a substitute for originality. Chrysaphes, the second composer to recast Lampadarios' setting of Γεύσασθε in Nenano, shows himself capable of composing a completely original setting for the same text in Barys, even though Lampadarios had previously composed a setting in Barys from which the younger composer no doubt could have drawn his material had he chosen to do so. Furthermore, the musical development found in the refrains of his 'parody' settings offers ample proof that he was capable of composing in a style very much his own. The same can be said of the refrains composed by Redestinos, Koronis and Moschianos. Religious music, like religious painting, occasionally utilized a prototype, adapting it to the style of the period and of the individual composer while maintaining ties with the past.

Two other settings in this repertory show evidence of melodic borrowing: the setting by Glykes and the 'tetraphonos' setting of Lampadarios. The setting by Glykes appears in only one of our six manuscripts—MS 2456—where it is accompanied by the rubric 'προς Σῶμα Χριστοῦ' ('to the melody of "The Body of Christ" '), which indicates a melodic relationship to the communion hymn for Easter Sunday.[37] Among the numerous settings of this hymn found in the Akolouthiai manuscripts, there is one version essentially identical to our setting of Γεύσασθε, also attributed to Glykes. The copy found in MS 2456 lacks a modal signature, and a comparison with other manuscripts reveals a confusion both of the mode and of the melodic structure of the first line of the text.[38]

As the majority of manuscripts indicate the mode as Nana, it seems likely that both copies of Γεύσασθε are correct in their modal signatures. However, two melodic traditions exist for the first line of the setting of Σῶμα Χριστοῦ—that of Sinai 1293 and that of Athens 2406, Sinai 1462, and Athens 899. Both melodic variants make possible an internal cadence on c′ at the end of the first line, although one version records most of this line a

---

[37] By application of the principle that every Sunday is a 'small' Easter (the day of the Resurrection), this communion hymn came to be used throughout the year. The full text is: Σῶμα Χριστοῦ μεταλάβετε πιγῆς ἀθανάτου γεύσασθε. Ἀλληλούϊα.

[38] Folio numbers appear in the Appendix.

step lower than does the other.[39] Each version has, of necessity, a slightly different closing formula to maintain the internal cadence on *c′*. Therefore it seems reasonable to assume that our setting of Γεύσασθε, despite the melodic variants of its incipit, is an adaptation of the Σῶμα Χριστοῦ melody contained in Sinai 1293, in which appears the same internal cadence formula found in both of our copies of Γεύσασθε.

Table III. Modal Signatures and First Line of Glykes' Setting

a) Modal signatures

	Nana	II pl.	None
Γεύσασθε καὶ ἴδετε	Athens 2456 Sinai 1293		
Σῶμα Χριστοῦ	Sinai 1462* Sinai 1293* Athens 2406	Athens 899	Athens 2456

b) Notation of first line of text

Γεύσασθε
- Athens 2456 — *(Byzantine neume notation)*
- Sinai 1293 — *(Byzantine neume notation)*

σῶμα Χριστοῦ
- Athens 2456 — *(Byzantine neume notation)*
- Sinai 1293 — *(Byzantine neume notation)*
- Athens 2406 / Sinai 1462 / Athens 899 — *(Byzantine neume notation)*

* The microfilms with which I am working are not sufficiently clear to make the reading of this modal signature completely certain.

The adaptation of the new text shows several interesting features, for its placement was carried out with great care. Word changes occur and accented syllables fall in identical places, and the non-textual syllable 'χ-', which appears on the second syllable of 'γεύσασθε' in Σῶμα Χριστοῦ and on the first syllable of

[39] The lower version is found in Athens MS 2406, Sinai MS 1462, and Athens MS 899.

the final 'Alleluia' in Γεύσασθε καὶ ἴδετε is found in the same melodic position in both settings. The melisma on the final syllable of 'γεύσασθε' in Σῶμα Χριστοῦ is duplicated in the contrafactum by a melisma on the last syllable of the final 'Alleluia'. A melisma in this position occurs in no other setting of Γεύσασθε, the refrain being concluded in all cases by an almost syllabic statement of the word 'Alleluia'.

Another setting of Γεύσασθε, attributed to Lampadarios, is accompanied by the rubric 'tetraphonos'. An examination of one of the most extensive of the manuscripts under discussion, MS 2406, reveals that this rubric is attached to perhaps a dozen other musical examples by almost every major composer whose works are found in the Akolouthiai. All the settings, while differing in text and liturgical function, agree in one respect: they are without exception composed in the first mode, and within almost every composition both the version of mode I beginning on D and the version beginning on A are employed. The majority of settings begin on D, indicated either by the signature 𝄞>-< with a descending fifth as the first pitch of the melody, or by the signature 𝄞 . In the case of the latter signature, the starting pitch of D is invariably confirmed by a medial martyria of 𝄞>-< on A.

Among these settings labelled 'tetraphonos', one finds a large group of communion hymns,[40] including our setting of Γεύσασθε by Lampadarios and three other communion hymns with different texts by the same composer. The liturgical use of these other texts (Αἰνεῖτε τὸν Κύριον, Ποτήριον σωτηρίου, and Ἐξηγέρθε)[41] suggest that Lampadarios' setting of Γεύσασθε belongs to a set of communions composed specifically for Great Lent. This hypothesis of their interrelationship is confirmed by

[40] The hymns composed by Lampadarios represent perhaps a third of the total number of communion hymns to be found in the manuscripts under discussion. Some of these hymns (e.g., those of Chrysaphes) are parodies of earlier settings of the same texts.

[41] All three texts are used during Great Lent (see Table IV); however, Αἰνεῖτε and Ποτήριον are also commonly used throughout the Church year. The former is the first of two communion hymns sung every Sunday; the latter is the ordinary chant for Wednesdays or for lesser feasts of the Theotokos. Ἐξηγέρθε is sung only on Holy Saturday. I am grateful to Professor David Drillock of St. Vladimir's Orthodox Theological Seminary in Crestwood, New York, for pointing out the special Lenten usage of Αἰνεῖτε and Ποτήριον.

the existence of a probably later 'tetraphonos' setting of
Εἰς μνημόσυνον by John the Deacon of Sgouropoulos, which
expands this cycle of Lenten communions.[42]

Table IV. Communion Texts Proper to Great Lent

Incipit of Text	Liturgical position
Γεύσασθε καὶ ἴδετε	Every Wednesday and Friday of Great Lent, and Monday, Tuesday, and Wednesday of Holy Week. Liturgy of the Presanctified.
Αἰνεῖτε τὸν Κύριον	1st, 2nd, 4th, and 5th Sundays of Great Lent. One of two communions. Liturgy of St. Basil.
Ποτήριον σωτηρίον	5th Saturday in Great Lent. Liturgy of St. Basil.
Ἐξηγέρθε ὁ ὑπνῶν	Holy Saturday. Liturgy of St. Basil.
Εἰς μνημόσυνον	1st Saturday and 2nd, 4th, and 5th Sundays in Great Lent. Liturgy of St. Basil. (Not set by Lampadarios.)

The four Lenten communion hymns by Lampadarios do not
appear to be derived from a prototypical melody, although they
occasionally share melodic fragments; for example, an initial
ascending fifth and a closing descending fifth[43]—features also
found in many of the other 'tetraphonos' settings. As in all of
Lampadarios' settings of *Γεύσασθε*, this group of hymns shows
greater length than the hymns of his immediate predecessors.
It may be for this reason that the hymns are composed of
carefully articulated sections which make use of the apparently
characteristic juxtaposition of first mode centred on D and first
mode centred on A. Certainly the use of both versions of first
mode is to some degree responsible for the increased range of
intervals found in these four settings—particularly in our
setting of *Γεύσασθε*, which has a range of a twelfth.

In general, the range of the settings increases as they move
into the fifteenth century, and with the increase in range of the
entire piece, a large range appears specifically in the refrain.
Neither 'palaion' nor 'asmatikon' places much emphasis on the
refrain, but from the time of Koukouzeles onward the refrain
develops in size, finally dwarfing the text. Unlike the earlier

---

[42] This text is also an ordinary communion hymn for Tuesdays and for feasts of
prophets, martyrs, or saints other than the Theotokos.

[43] These melodic features are found in Lampadarios' settings of *Γεύσασθε, Αἰνεῖτε*.
and *Ποτήριον*.

settings, in which the range of the text and the refrain are essentially identical, the range of the refrain is often greater in these later pieces, and in the cases in which it is not, the refrain is higher in pitch and tessitura than is the text.

Table V. Ranges of Settings

	Total range in intervals	Text	Refrain
'asmatikon'	7th	7th	7th
'palaion'	6th*	5th	5th
Koukouzeles	8th	7th	8th
Koronis	8th	7th	7th
Moschianos	10th	6th	8th
John Lampadarios			
a) 'tetraphonos'	11th	6th	11th
b) Nenano	11th	8th	8th†
c) Barys	8th	7th	8th
Glykes	7th	6th	7th
Redestinos	9th	7th	9th
Gavalas	10th	9th	9th
Gerasimos	8th	8th	7th
Manuel Chrysaphes			
a) Nenano	8th	8th	7th
b) Barys	9th	8th	8th
Markos the Hieromonk	9th	7th	9th
Archon of the Monastery	9th	7th	6th

* The range is increased to a 7th by the additional melismas found in late fourteenth and fifteenth-century copies of this setting.

† The range is increased to a 9th by the variant version found only in Athens MS 2456.

As the range becomes larger, the melodic style changes somewhat. Instead of the predominantly conjunct intervals of the earlier settings we find an increasing number of thirds, fourths and fifths, and, occasionally, larger intervals, such as an octave. At the same time, the melodic style becomes more improvisatory and less moulded in character, making greater use of sequential passages and expansive phrases. Although there is a tendency in all the settings to dwell on a certain restricted melodic area before moving to another, this development of greater range makes possible a rhapsodic melody that occasionally sweeps from one end of the melodic ambitus to the other.

As the refrains become longer, more careful formal organiza-

Ex. 8
Gerasimos 2406

Γεο-   . σασθε

tion is necessary. Regular internal cadences, melodic repetition and 'entrance motives' to introduce the recurring word 'Alleluia' are among the most common devices used for this purpose. The refrains become sectionalized, and the formulae 'λέγε' (to say or sing) and 'πάλιν' (repeat, again)[44] are often used to articulate the sections.

Table VI. Appearances of λέγε and πάλιν Formulae

	λέγε	πάλιν
'asmatikon'	after 1st 'A——'	
'palaion'		
Koukouzeles*		
Koronis*		
Moschianos*		
John Lampadarios		
a) 'tetraphonos'	after 1st 'Alleluia'	
b) Nenano†	after 1st 'Alleluia'	
c) Barys	before refrain	after 1st 'Alleluia'
Glykes		
Redestinos†		after 1st 'Alleluia'
Gavalas		
Gerasimos	before refrain	
Manuel Chrysaphes		
a) Nenano†	after 1st 'Alleluia'	after 2nd 'Alleluia'
b) Barys	after 1st 'Alleluia'	after 2nd 'Alleluia'
Markos the Hieromonk	after 1st 'Alleluia'	after 2nd 'Alleluia'
Archon of the Monastery	after 1st 'Alleluia'	after 2nd 'Alleluia'

    * Settings related to Koukouzeles' piece in plagal second mode.
    † Settings related to Lampadarios' piece in Nenano.

As can be seen from the table, the λέγε formula is not present in the refrains of most of the earlier pieces related to the monastic tradition through 'palaion' and through Koukouzeles

[44] For a thorough discussion and description of λέγε and πάλιν formulae, see Williams, op. cit., pp. 183-4 and 230-1, and J. Raasted, *Intonation Formulas and Modal Signatures in Byzantine Musical Manuscripts, MMB, Subsidia,* vii (Copenhagen, 1966), pp. 66-7.

and his followers. Moschianos, the only composer in this group
to employ the formula, uses it between the text and the refrain—
thus causing a greater division between the two major sections
of the hymn, but not creating any significant structural division
within the refrain itself.

The use of the *λέγε* formula found in 'asmatikon' is unique,
falling after the first melisma (on 'A-') of the refrain. However,
it may well be that the use of *λέγε* in many of the later settings
is based on this precedent. Lampadarios, who is the first
composer to employ the *λέγε* formula within the refrain itself,
places it in more or less the same position—after the first
statement of the word 'Alleluia'. This usage becomes relatively
standard in the later repertory, appearing in the settings by
Chrysaphes, Markos the Hieromonk, and the Archon of the
Monastery.

The presence of the formula *πάλιν* always indicates a musical
repetition of an entire section of music, sometimes with subtle
melodic variations.

Ex. 9
Lampadarios 2456

Barys   *λέ-*   *γε*   *͜͜*   'Αλ-   *λη-*   *, πά-*

λιν   *͜͜*   'Αλ-   *λη-*

It is in the Barys setting by Lampadarios that we first
encounter the use of the *πάλιν* formula, and, as we have already
noted, his refrains are consistently longer than those of his
predecessors. His placement of the formula after the first
statement of the word 'Alleluia' is copied by only one subsequent composer, Redestinos. In both settings by Manuel
Chrysaphes the formula appears after the second statement of
the word 'Alleluia', and it is this usage which is characteristic
of our four latest settings.

One of these four late settings—that of Markos the Hieromonk—affords an interesting example of highly developed
form. The refrain is divided into three major sections, the first
set apart from the second by a *λέγε* formula, and the second

from the third by a πάλιν formula. The first section consists of
one statement of the word 'Alleluia', the second of two state-
ments of the word (with new music). The third section consists
of a repetition of the entire second section, concluded by an
elaborate final statement of the word 'Alleluia'. This refrain is
the most highly developed and, needless to say, the longest in
the repertory.

Another interesting development in the later settings is the
return of the non-textual syllables. As mentioned above, they
do not occur in the 'palaion' setting. In Koukouzeles' setting
there are several occurrences of the syllable 'χε-' both in the
text and in the refrain; however, the use differs from that found
in 'asmatikon', for here the syllable is used only once in any
given position and is not repeated. Syllabic repetitions after
melismas occur in his setting, of course, as they do throughout
the repertory with the single exception of 'asmatikon'.

It is in the setting by Moschianos that the syllables 'ουα-γγα'
first appear on the final syllable of the last 'Alleluia' of the
refrain. This feature subsequently is found in the setting in
Barys by Lampadarios, in the settings in Nenano by Redestinos
and Gavalas, and in the setting in Barys by Chrysaphes.

Ex. 10
Lampadarios 2456

Barys -α-   ουα-   γγα

Finally, in the work of Chrysaphes and the Archon of the
Monastery, totally extraneous syllables—such as 'κη-κη-κη' and
'τι-τι-τι'—are introduced into the refrain. The syllables

Ex. 11·
Chrysaphes 2406

Nenano -λη-   κη-   κη- κη-   κη-

Chrysaphes 2406

Barys -λη   κη- κη-   κη.   κη-

The Archon of the Monastery 2837

Nana -λη-   τι- τι- τι- τι-   τι- τι- τι- 'Αλ-   λη-

invariably appear on the second syllable of 'Alleluia', and are followed by a repetition of the first two syllables of that word.

This rather brief repertory of communion hymns reflects the stylistic practices of over a century of music development. Remnants of earlier monastic and cathedral traditions are preserved in the settings labelled 'palaion' and 'asmatikon'. The 'palaion' setting no doubt influenced Koukouzeles in his choice of the second plagal mode for a new and larger piece on the same text, a piece which was parodied slightly later in the fourteenth century by the composers Koronis and Moschianos. At the end of the century John Lampadarios composed several completely new settings of this text, among them a piece in mode Nenano, which was also parodied by two composers— Redestinos and Chrysaphes. In this manner Nenano was also firmly established as an appropriate mode for the setting of this communion hymn, and during the fifteenth century two more original settings appeared in that mode. The settings of Lampadarios show a great development in size, particularly in the refrains, and also achieve a greater ambitus, a higher tessitura and a more rhapsodic line than the pieces of the early and mid-fourteenth century. The fifteenth-century settings continue this trend towards expansion and employ sequences, repetition, and carefully planned points of articulation to organize the longer 'Alleluia' refrains.

APPENDIX

a) Settings of Γεύσασθε καὶ ἴδετε:

	Athens MSS					
	2458	2622	2456	899	2406	2837
	1336	1341–c. 1360	14th–15th c.	early 15th c.	1453	1457
'asmatikon'		376r			284r	
'palaion'	175v	376r	216v	144r		197r
Koukouzeles	175v	376v	216v	144v	284v	197v
Koronis		376v	217r	144v	284v	197v
Moschianos		376v (inc.)			285r	
Lampadarios						
a) 'tetraphonos'				145v	284r	198r
b) Nenano			217r	145r	284v	198v
c) Barys			217v			198v
Glykes			218r			
Redestinos					285v	199r
Gavalas					285v	
Gerasimos					286r	
Chrysaphes					286r	
a) Nenano					286r	
b) Barys					286v	
Markos the Hieromonk					287v	199v
The Archon of the Monastery						200r

b) Settings of Γεύσασθε and Σῶμα Χριστοῦ by Glykes:

	Athens MSS			Sinai MSS	
	2456	899	2406	1462	1293
	14th–15th c.	early 15th c.	1453	14th–15th c.	early 15th c.
Γεύσασθε	218r				282r
Σῶμα Χριστοῦ	219v	148v	289v	149r	284r

c) 'Tetraphonos' settings of communion hymns by Lampadarios:

	Athens MSS					Sinai MS
	2456	899	2401	2406	2837	1293
	14th–15th c.	early 15th c.	mid 15th c.	1453	1457	early 15th c.
Γεύσασθε		145v	284r	198r		
Αἰνεῖτε	201r	123v	210v	251v	162v	261r
Ποτήριον	201r	124r	210v	251r	163r	
Ἐξηγέρθε		148r	185v	286v	202v	

F

3

Jerzy Gołos

WARSAW, POLAND

Manuscript Sources of Eastern Chant before 1700 in Polish Libraries

POLAND never came under the long-lasting influence of the
Eastern Orthodox rite and, consequently, has not accumulated
as many historical documents about Eastern chant as have
countries with long-standing associations with Eastern Christen-
dom. Students of the subject generally agree that the Greek rite
made moderate advances in the early years of Polish history,[1]
but these missions were short-lived and limited to the southern
provinces of medieval Poland. Traces of any versions of the
Eastern rite in Poland are very scanty. This is due to a deliberate
attempt on the part of the Roman Catholic clergy to destroy
such traces after the Great Schism,[2] an attempt almost

---

[1] Hieronim Feicht, 'Die heiligen Cyrill und Methode in polnischen Choral-und
Liederbüchern', paper read at the congress in Salzburg, 1963. J. Golos, 'Traces
of Byzantino-Slavonic Influence in Polish Medieval Hymnody', *The Polish Review*
vol. ix (New York, 1964); J. Gołos, 'Z problematyki obrządku słowiańskiego w
Polsce', *Muzyka*, iii (1968); S. Kętrzyński, 'O zaginionej metropolii czasów
Bolesława Chrobrego', *Prace Instytutu Historii Uniwersytetu Warszawskiego*, i
(Warsaw, 1947); T. Lehr-Spławiński, 'Dookoła obrządku słowiańskiego w
Polsce', *Księga pamiątkowa ku czci Stanisława Pigonia* (Kraków, 1961); T. Lehr-
Spławiński, 'Pierwszy chrzest Polski', *Slavia Occidentalis*, 19 (1960); T. Lehr-
Spławiński, 'Czy są ślady istnienia liturgii cyrylo-metodejskiej w dawnej Polsce',
Od piętnastu wieków (Warsaw, 1961); K. Lanckorońska, 'Studies on the Roman-
Slavonic Rite in Poland', *Orientalia Christiana Analecta* 161 (Rome, 1961); A.
Steffen, 'Greckie ślady w regeście Dagome Iudex', *Antemurale*, iii (1956); M.
Tobiasz, 'Kraków benedyktyński w XI w.', *Nasza Przeszłość*, 14 (1961); J.
Widajewicz, 'Prohor i Prokulf', *Nasza Przeszłość*, 4 (1948); J. Umiński, *Obrządek
słowiański w starodawnej Polsce i zagadnienie drugiej metropolii polskiej w czasach
Bolesława Chrobrego* (Wrocław, 1953).

[2] *Monumenta Poloniae Historica*, ed. by A. Bielowski, i (Lwów, 1864), pp. 90 and 92;
see also M. Tobiasz, op. cit., pp. 7 and 13; K. Lanckorońska, op. cit., p. 6.

entirely successful, at least in the realm of written documents.

There are no known extant musical sources that can be dated prior to the fifteenth century, at which time a second wave of Eastern influence was felt in Poland.[3] From that period dates the only concrete evidence of Eastern elements in Polish Catholic liturgy, namely the Trisagion. The importance to this day of the Trisagion in local tradition is inexplicable in terms of its limited use in the Roman rite.[4] The Byzantine origin of that chant with its text has already been demonstrated.[5] A striking similarity of the Trisagion-melody to one of the oldest melodic versions in the Greek-Orthodox repertory has also been ascertained.[6] In the fourteenth and the following centuries, progressively closer ties between Poland and its neighbours to the east and south-east led to borrowings in the sphere of the fine arts, languages, and even in social customs. Church music could not have been an exception.[7]

In comparison with the more homogeneous population of the former Polish kingdom, the multi-national and multi-denominational character of the Duchy of Lithuania contributed to a different ethnic make-up when the Polish–Lithuanian Commonwealth was established in 1569.

[3] Its origins are ascribed to the founding of a Benedictine Abbey of the Slavonic rite in the Kleparz district of Cracow, in 1390, and the services in Old Church Slavonic language in the Holy Cross Church in that city. The Benedictines of the Slavonic rite were invited to Poland by King Władysław Jagiełło from the Emaus Abbey in Prague. The king's interest in the Eastern rite was not accidental. Being a Lithuanian he was familiar with it, for the Duchy of Lithuania incorporated areas inhabited by Ruthenian population. Jagiełło's fourth wife was a Ruthenian princess. Ruthenian painters were commissioned by him to decorate several churches, including Wawel Cathedral in Cracow, the Castle chapel in Lublin, Sandomierz Cathedral, and in the parochial church in Wiślica.

[4] The Trisagion is sung during the Mass, usually before the Elevation of the Host, and as a part of many other liturgical-para-liturgical services throughout the liturgical year. In the Roman rite, however, the singing of the Trisagion is limited to the Adoration of the Cross on Good Friday.

[5] Cf. J. Gołos, 'Z problematyki . . .' in *Muzyka* (1968), pp. 28-34, and 'Traces . . .' *Polish Review*, ix (1964), pp. 78-81.

[6] Similar melodic versions are found in the repertories of the Russian, Ukrainian, and Lithuanian Catholic church. Concerning the latter, Wincenty Pol pointed out in the nineteenth century that according to old chronicles the Trisagion (Święty Boże) came from that country, a point which is supported by our findings. Cf. W. Pol, *Sześć prelekcyi o muzyce kościelnej* (Lwów 1864), p. 112.

[7] It is a well-known fact that many of the Polish liturgical terms are borrowed from the Old Church Slavonic language rather than Latin.

According to the terms of the Union of Brest (1596), a part of the Greek-Orthodox clergy and population recognized the supreme authority of the Pope in the Church, thus complicating even further the religious mosaic in the country. Yet, the liturgical books of the Uniates do not differ from their other Orthodox counterparts, for apart from expressing allegiance to Rome, the Greek Catholics did not abandon the Eastern liturgy and chant. Later on, however, the quick adoption of part-singing led to far-reaching repercussions, not only in their own church music but also in the Orthodox churches of the Eastern Ukraine and Muscovy. This led to a decline and abandonment of the centuries-old chant traditions in much of North-Eastern Europe.

The Uniate Church not only favoured adoption of part-singing, but also broke the strict Orthodox ban on the use of instruments in church services. Although it is generally believed that the Greek Catholics observed their traditions, the data from various sources indicates that from about 1650 a number of Uniate communities in the Polish–Lithuanian State introduced instruments into their religious services. [8] While such a development was a sign of acceptance of West-European musical currents, it was a disaster for the traditional forms of liturgical music.

This is, in brief, the history of Eastern chant and liturgy in Poland and Lithuania before A.D. 1700. Such a long and colourful history was bound to leave traces of chant or part-

[8] Cf. MS 10002 [olim 127/56] of the Jagiellonian Library in Cracow. The use of instruments was favoured by the Uniates' Archbishop Cyprian Żochowski (d. 1693). In 1679 he organized an 'ecumenical' service in the Jesuit Church in Połock with instrumentally accompanied church music of the Slavonic rite. J. Bartoszewicz's entry 'Żochowski Cyprian', *Encyklopedia Powszechna*, 28 (Warsaw, 1863), pp. 1005, 1010. Organs must have also been used occasionally from about that time until recently. There is, for instance, a positive organ from the eighteenth century in Opole (district Lublin, Włodawa county) in a parochial church which originally belonged to the local Uniate church (the old building was in use from 1643 to 1805, and then was rebuilt between 1805 and 1811). This church building was later forcibly taken over by the Russian-Orthodox clergy. Very illuminating is the report of Alojzy Karwacki, a Franciscan at Kalwaria Pacławska monastery, a place of pilgrimages for both Roman and Greek Catholics. Karwacki wrote in 1915: 'the local organ is played by various self-taught organists, among them Ruthenian organists, for at times their deacons come with pilgrims from such parishes as have had organs preserved from old times' (cf. *Archiwum O. O. Franciszkanów w Kalwarii Pacławskiej, Inwentarz O. Alojzego Karwackiego z 1915 r.*).

music, as the manuscript sources listed at the end of this article demonstrate.[9]

From the first and undoubtedly the most interesting period of Polish history, between the tenth and the fourteenth centuries, there are no musical sources comparable to those found in Bulgaria, Serbia, Macedonia, or Russia.[10] The earliest sources containing musical notation date from the sixteenth century. With rare exceptions these belong to the so-called Kievan staff notation group which is typical of the overwhelming majority of sources from the next two centuries. No attempt has been made to distinguish between Uniate and Orthodox chant books in the appended list nor was it possible, at this stage, to identify all the species of the chant.[11] Finally, we encounter liturgical part-music recorded in either Kievan or Western mensural notation, at times even with *basso continuo*.[12]

Among the most interesting manuscripts in Poland are the Heirmologion of 1591 with the Russian *kriuki* notation and a copy of *Azbuka iz staroznamyennago pyenia* with cinnabar signs (*kinovarnya pomyety*). Based on the Mezenets treatise the copy of this 'alphabet' dates from the late eighteenth century. In the early nineteenth century it belonged to a Saint Petersburg merchant. In spite of its late date this manuscript is worth mentioning here for there are not many manuals of that kind still in existence.

[9] This list does not pretend to be complete. More manuscripts may still be recovered in private possession or in church holdings which have been only partially examined. Those interested in later developments will find many eighteenth-century manuscripts omitted from this list. In several libraries, especially in the National Library in Warsaw, there is also a sizable collection of non-musical items (*Oktoich, Akaphistnik, Časoslov*) from the fifteenth, sixteenth, and seventeenth centuries. Deliberately omitted are also the well-known manuscripts from the former Staats und Universitätsbibliothek in Breslau/Wrocław. Cf. E. Koschmieder, 'Über einige Kyrillische Neumenhandschriften der Universitätsbibliothek zu Breslau,' *Festschrift für Hans Jessen*, (Würzburg, 1967).

[10] The important Old Church Slavonic source, the famous *Codex Suprasliensis*, was recently returned to Poland from the United States.

[11] Except for instances where the source expressly calls a chant 'Kievan', 'Greek', or 'Bulgarian'.

[12] Cf. J. Gołos, 'Nowoznaleziony rękopis Biblioteki Jagiellońskiej jako źródło do historii kontaktów polsko-ruskich', *Polsko-rosyjskie miscellanea muzyczne* (Warszawa, 1967), pp. 49-52.

Biblioteka Narodowa—Zbiory Specjalne. Warszawa

Type of Manuscript[13]	Date	Call number	Microfilm no.	Former owner	Notation	Remarks
Irmologion	1672	2472	13044	BCRGC-Przemyśl[14]	Kievan	
Irmoloi	17th c.	2526	13461	"	"	Contains inscriptions: Kievan, Bulgarian chant.
Irmoloh	17th c.	2529	13568	"	"	Contains *Irmosy stolpowye*
Irmoloh	17th c.	2552	13590	"	"	Contains inscriptions: Greek, Kievan, Bulgarian chant.
Irmoloh	17th c.	2556	13594	"	"	
Irmoloh	17th c.	2593	14346	"	"	
Irmoloh	17th c.	2598	14283	"	"	
Irmoloh	17th c.	2601	14286	"	"	On folio 143r fragment of a polyphonic composition.
Irmoloh	17th c.	2602	14287	"	"	
Irmoloh	17th c.	2603	14288	"	"	
Irmoloi	1668	2604	14289	"	"	
Irmoloi	1639	2606	14292	"	"	Contains inscriptions: Greek, Kievan chant.
Irmoloh	17th c.	2608	14294	"	"	Contains inscriptions: Kievan liturgy, Greek, Bulgarian chant.
Irmolohion	17th c.	2609	14295	"	"	
Irmoloh	1667	2610	14296	"	"	
Irmoloh	16th c. (?)	2611	14297	"	"	
Irmoloh	17th c.	2613	14301	"	"	Contains inscription: Kievan chant.
Irmoloh	17th c.	2614	14302	"	"	
Irmoloh	17th c.	2616	14304	"	"	
Irmoloi	17th c.	2617	14316	"	"	
Irmoloh	c. 1680	2618	14317	"	"	

Irmoloh	1675	2619	14318	BCRGC-Przemyśl[14]	Kievan	
Irmolohion	17th c.	2687	15119	„	„	Contains *kanony bolgarskie*
Irmolohion	17th c.	2689	15121	„	„	
Irmolohion	17th c.	2690	15122	„	„	
Irmoloh	17th c.	2691	15123	„	„	
Ustav	16th–17th c.	2774	15384	„	„	Notation only on f. 289r–v.
Irmologion	17th c.	2788	15396	„	„	
Irmolohion	17th c.	2911	15553	„	„	
Irmolohion	17th c.	2916	15558	„	„	
Irmolohion	17th c.	2917	15559	„	„	
Irmoloi	17th c.	2932	15629	„	„	Contains among other things a Bulgarian *tropar*.
Irmolohion	17th c.	2935	15632	„	„	
Irmolohion	17th c.	2947	15645	„	„	
Irmoloh	1591	2954	15685	„	Kriuki	Table of neumes with their names on ff. 258v–259r.
Irmolohion	1670	2961	16048	„	Kievan	
Irmolohion	17th c.	2962	16053	„	„	
Irmolohion	17th c.	2963	16054	„	„	Among other things Kievan, Greek, Bulgarian *Stikhiri*.
Słożenie himnov	17th c.	2973	16067	„	„	
Azbuka	18th c.	8982	—	private	Kriuki	*Azbuka iz staroznamyennago pyenia.*
Irmologion	c.1700	10019	—	private	Kriuki	

[13] According to the library catalogue.

[14] Bibliotheca Capituli Ritus graeco-catholici Premisliensis. Biblioteka gr. kat. kapituli v Peremishli. Library of the Greek-Catholic Chapter in Przemyśl. The older seals are in Latin, the later in Ukrainian.

[15] At the time when this article was being prepared, the library catalogue did not record the presence of musical notation. This has been added later at my suggestion and on the basis of my observations.

Biblioteka Jagiellońska. Kraków

Type of Manuscript	Date	Call number	Microfilm no.	Former owner	Notation	Remarks
Antifony na osm hlasov	16th–17th c.	5118	—	—	Kievan	Latin title: *Antifonae cum notis musicis.*
without title[16]	before 1680	10002	—	Ostromeczew church	Western	b.c. and Church-Slavonic text.

Biblioteka Czartoryskich. Kraków

Type of Manuscript	Date	Call number	Microfilm no.	Former owner	Notation	Remarks
Osmohlasnik	1660	2358	BN 12918[17]	—	Kievan	Library catalog calls it *Śpiewnik ruski z nutami.*
Irmologion	16th–17th c.	2413	BN 9131[17]	private	Kriuki	Library catalog calls it *Śpiewnik ruski Pieśni religijne z nutami.*
Irmologion	17th c.	13783	BN 12942[17]	—	„	Library catalog calls it *Śpiewnik ruski.*
Irmologion	17th c.	2055	BN 9112[17]	—	Kievan	Library catalog calls it Śpiewnik kościelny cerkiewno-słowiański.

Jasna Góra Archive, Częstochowa

Type of Manuscript	Date	Call number	Microfilm no.	Former owner	Notation	Remarks
Irmologion	17th c.	I-216	—	—	Kievan	—

[16] Source edition prepared by J. Gołos, J. and Z. Steszewski entitled *Staropolskie Silva Rerum muzyczne z XVII w.* has appeared as vol. xvi of the *Źródła do historii dawnej muzyki polskiej* series (Sources for the History of Old Polish Music) (Kraków, 1969).

[17] Microfilms in the National Library in Warsaw—Biblioteka Narodowa, Stacja Mikrofilmowa, Warsaw 1, Plac Krasiński ch 5.

4

Michel Huglo

PARIS, FRANCE

L'Introduction en Occident des formules Byzantines d'intonation

LES plus anciens monuments qui nous transmettent le 'chant grégorien', aux huitième et neuvième siècles, se divisent en deux catégories: les livres liturgiques qui contiennent le texte intégral des pièces de chant, sans notation musicale, suivant l'ordre liturgique d'exécution à l'Office (Antiphonaire et Responsorial) ou à la Messe (Graduel, Cantatorium); les livres de théorie musicale qui classent les pièces de chant suivant l'ordre des huit tons psalmodiques grégoriens (tonaires) ou qui analysent ces huit tons en citant quelques exemples tirés du répertoire liturgique (traités).

Le classement des chants du répertoire grégorien suivant les huit tons est attesté par le traité d'Aurélien de Réomé, *De musica Disciplina*,[1] vers 850, mais encore par un tonaire de la fin du huitième siècle:[2] ce tonaire, écrit dans le nord de la France à l'usage de l'abbaye de *Centula* (St. Riquier, près d'Abbeville) où Charlemagne fut solennellement reçu le jour de Pâques de l'année 800, contient précisément cette division en huit tons et donne le classement par tons d'une centaine de pièces du Graduel: antiennes d'introït et de communion, mais encore graduels, alleluia et offertoires, qui se chantent sans psalmodie.

---

[1] Gerbert, *Scriptores* I 28-63. Transl. J. Ponte (Colorado Springs, 1968). Critical Ed., L. Gushee, *Diss. Yale Univ. 1962*, Vol II.

[2] E. A. Lowe, *Codices latini antiquiores*, V, n° 652. — M. Huglo, *Un tonaire du Graduel de la fin du VIIIᵉ siècle (Paris, B.N. lat. 13159): Revue grégorienne*, 31 (1952), pp. 176-86; 224-33. — *Les tonaires* (Paris, 1971), pp. 25-9.

C'est dans ce tonaire que, pour la première fois, se rencontre l'attestation de l' 'octoëchos occidental': AVTENTVS PROTVS, PLAI PROTVS, AVTENTVS DEVTERVS, PLAI DEVTERVS, AVTENTVS TRITVS, / / / / / / / (la fin manque, par suite d'une lacune matérielle).

Le mot *plai* est une variante de *plagi* (*plagalis*), qui vient naturellement du grec πλάγιος:[3] cette variante *plai* pour *plagi* est d'origine gallicane.[4] La numérotation des modes est évidemment adaptée de la numérotation usuelle byzantine: *protus* πρῶτος, *deuterus* δεύτερος, *tritus* τρίτος, *tetrardus* τέταρτος. Mais d'où sort le mot '*authentus*'? Il est inconnu de l'ancienne terminologie musicale byzantine qui emploie, dès le septième siècle au moins, le terme ἦχος là où les Occidentaux usent du terme '*authentus*': en effet, si *plagi* équivaut à πλάγιος, *authentus* ne connait pas d'équivalent dans l'ancienne terminologie musicale byzantine:[5] ἦχ.α′ (*protos*) désigne le 'premier ton' (notre 'authente'), par opposition à πλ.α′, le premier plagal.

Cependant, en Occident, pour éviter de traduire ἦχος par *tonus* — ce qui aurait exclu le 'plagal', qui est, lui aussi, un *tonus* — on a adopté *authentus* ou plus exactement, suivant la leçon ancienne attestée par Aurélien de Réomé, le tonaire de Metz, du neuvième siècle, et Réginon de Prüm, *authenticus* terme qui appartient au vocabulaire canonique et liturgique de l'époque carolingienne.[6]

[3] Le terme πλάγιος apparait dans les écrits de Zosymos de Panopolis: O. Gombosi, *Studien zur Tonartenlehre des MA.*: *Acta Musicologica*, XII (1940), pp. 29-52. Cf. E. Wellesz, *A History of Byzantine Music and Hymnography*, 2nd Ed. (Oxford, 1961), p. 72 ss. Le mot πλάγιος est abrégé en πλ. dans les manuscrits grecs et dans le papyrus copte de Crum, cité par R. Ménard, *Revue de Musicologie*, 36 (1954), p. 28.

[4] Comme *aius* dans l'*Epistola I* du Pseudo-Germain sur la Messe gallicane (éd. E. C. Ratcliff, *Expositio Antiquae liturgiae gallicanae*, London, 1971, pp. 4, 7) au lieu de *agius* (ἅγιος). De même, *Noeais* pour *Noeagis* dans les formules échématiques (voir plus bas).

[5] Dans la théorie ancienne, car dans les traités plus récents, tel que celui qui est publié par L. Tardo, *L'antica melurgia bizantina* (1938), p. 167, on rencontre le terme κύριος rétroversion de *authenticus* (glosé: *authenticus sive magister*).

[6] De αὐθέντης 'qui surmonte, qui domine': étymologie donnée par J. Chailley, *Essai analytique sur la formation de l'Octoëchos latin*: *Essays presented to Egon Wellesz* (Oxford, 1966), p. 86. Cette étymologie est satisfaisante au point de vue musical, mais seulement dans la perspective de l'analyse modale médiévale. Le terme *authenticus* désigne les livres officiels romains à l'époque carolingienne: la collection canonique *Dyonysiana*, le sacramentaire d'Hadrien, etc. Voir A. Dold, '*Enthenticus-Authenticus*'... *seine Stellung in der Liturgiegeschichte*: *Münchener Theologische Zeitschr.* XI (1960), pp. 262-6.

Ainsi, la terminologie officielle adoptée pour désigner les huit tons en Occident révèle une origine byzantine, revue et adaptée à l'époque carolingienne lors de l'imposition du chant grégorien dans l'Empire. Cependant, cette question de terminologie ne touche pas à la nature même du systême des huit tons: les tonaires vont mettre en évidence des liens plus concrets entre l'Octoëchos byzantin et le systême occidental des huit tons.

Après l'énoncé du titre de chaque ton, les tonaires donnent une formule courte dont la dernière syllabe, dans les manuscrits neumés ou notés, supporte un long mélisme appelé 'neuma': il s'agit d'une adaptation occidentale des formules échématiques byzantines. Aussi, l'étude de ces formules doit être menée parallèlement d'après les sources byzantines et d'après les sources occidentales.

Dans les manuels de théorie musicale byzantine du quinzième siècle, on rencontre des listes d'echemata classées suivant l'ordre usuel en Orient: ἦχος α΄, β΄ γ΄, δ΄—πλ.α΄, πλ.β΄, πλ.γ΄, πλ.δ΄. Chaque echema est suivi d'un ou de plusieurs exemples liturgiques. Ce genre de listes, destinées à l'enseignement des tons (διδάσκειν écrit l'Hagiopolités) évoque nos tonaires abrégés occidentaux. En remontant dans le temps, Jørgen Raasted[7] a remarqué que déjà au douzième siècle des listes de formules d'intonation avaient été transcrites au début des livres de chant: 'We do not know how the tables were used. But from the coexistence of "theoretical" lists and practical books of chant within the same binding we may safely infer that the teachings of the lists were practised on the melodies contained in the manuscripts. The list obviously belonged to the classroom and the manuscripts in which they were included must have served, apart from their liturgical function, as "text-books" for teachers of Byzantine chant.'[8]

En Occident, les formules sont attestées pour la première fois par Aurélien de Réomé (vers 850) et il semble — si nous admettons que le chapitre IX du De musica Disciplina attribuant à Charlemagne l'invention des tons 'paraptères' ou 'moyens' (medii, μεσοι), contient des parcelles de véracité historique —

[7] Intonation Formulas and Modal Signatures in Byzantine Music MSS (Copenhagen, 1966), MMB. Subsidia, VII, p. 42.
[8] J. Raasted, op. cit., p. 49.

que l'adoption des formules echématiques en Occident date du
règne de Charlemagne (771–814). Les formules échématiques
figurent dans tous les manuscrits du tonaire carolingien,[9] dont
l'archétype a été daté de 830. Sans doute font-elles défaut dans
le tonaire de St. Riquier (de 799–800), mais ce tonaire est
incomplet — il ne donne en effet aucune pièce de l'Office —
et ne peut donc apporter un élément de poids dans la solution
du problème.

Aussi est-il très possible que l'origine des formules échématiques soit solidaire et contemporaine de l'adoption de la
terminologie byzantine des tons: leur introduction ne semble
pas avoir été faite après la traduction en latin des noms des
tons inscrits dans le premier tonaire carolingien. Autrement dit:
le premier tonaire qui, en Occident, a dressé une classification
des antiennes du répertoire suivant les huit tons contenait ces
deux éléments d'origine byzantine: la dénomination byzantine
des tons latinisée (*protus*, *plagis protus*...) et les huit formules
échématiques.

Cependant, la tradition littéraire et musicale des formules
échématiques se partage en deux branches. La plupart des
tonaires a condensé la variété des formules et l'a réduite à deux:
une formule longue pour les tons 'authente' (*Nonnenoeane* ou
Noeane) et une formule brève pour les plagaux (*Noeagis*). Cette
réduction à deux types est-elle ancienne? N'est-elle pas une
simplification très ancienne, faite par un théoricien dès le début
de la tradition manuscrite du tonaire?

Il est remarquable de constater qu'un groupe très cohérents
de manuscrits théoriques, qui se rattache de manière plus ou
moins étroite à la collection de textes réunis autour de la
Musica Enchiriadis, nous rapporte une liste de formules echématiques, chacune différente pour chacun des huit tons. La
tradition de ces tonaires offre un contraste d'autant plus grand
que la *Musica Enchiriadis*, transcrite dans les mêmes manuscrits
qu'eux, est le témoin de la version 'simplifiée'.

Dans l'édition de la *Musica Enchiriadis*, due à Gerbert
(*Scriptores* I, p. 158), on voit que la liste a été abrégée:
Noannoeane (pour les authentes), *Noeagis* (pour les plagaux) 'et

---

[9] Le 'tonaire carolingien' du manuscrit de Metz 351, dont l'archétype — suivant
l'éditeur, W. Lipphardt — remonte à l'année 830, nous est parvenu dans trois
autres manuscrits: voir M. Huglo, *Les tonaires* (Paris, 1971), pp. 29-43.

cetera'. Dans plusieurs manuscrits,[10] la liste est plus complète, avec ou sans neumes, et comprend les huit formules suivant l'ordre descendant (VII, V, III, I; VIII, VI, IV, II).

Il en est de même dans le plus ancien manuscrit de la *Commemoratio brevis de tonis et psalmis*,[11] alors que dans celui que Gerbert a utilisé (*Scriptores*, I 229), on est revenu à l'ordre ascendant habituel (I–VIII).

Dans plusieurs tonaires,[12] qui avoisinent des collections de traités anciens comportant habituellement la *Musica Enchiriadis*, le texte des formules échématiques est plus voisin du texte des formules tel qu'il est indiqué dans les traités byzantins:

	1	2	3	4	5	6	7	8	Variantes
PROTUS	NA			NA	NO	E	A	NE	1. NO: tous les MSS sauf Paris, lat. 4995. — 4. AN: Krakow 1965. — NE: Vercelli LXII, Clm. 14523
ἦχ.α′	α			va	v	ε	a	vες	
DEUT-ERUS	A	IA		NE	O	E	A	NE	1. AY: Paris, lat. 13252. — 2-5. NO: Paris, lat. 13252
ἦχ β′				νε			a	νες	
TRITUS				NE			AN	NES	NOYOEANE (NOEOEANE): Paris, lat. 13252, Krakow 1965, Clm. 14272
ἦχ. γ′	a			νεε			a	νεες	
TETRAR-DUS				NO I	O	E	A	NE	NO(N)ANNES: Paris, lat. 4995, Vercelli LXII, Clm. 14523. NOEOEANE: Clm. 14272. NANAANES: Cambr. CCC 473 – 8. IS: Milano H 146 inf.
ἦχ. δ′	aa			γι			a		
Protus plagal				NO	NE		A	IS	4. E: tous les MSS sauf Paris, lat. 13252. — 8. GIS: Cambridge CCC 473, Clm. 14272
πλ. α′	a				νε		a	νες	
Deuterus plagal				NO	E		A	IS	8. IA: Vercelli LXII. NE: Clm. 14523, 14272
πλ β′.				ν	εε		a	νες	
Tritus plagal							AN	NES	NONEAIS: Paris, lat. 13252
πλ. γ′							aa	νες	
Tetrardus plagal				NO	E		A	IS	8. NNES: Clm. 14523
πλ. δ′				ν	ε		a	γιε	

---

[10] Voir par exemple Paris, B.N. lat. 7202 (XIe s.), f. 56v (éd. Gerbert, *Scriptores* I, p. 158, note c); Melbourne, State Libr. 091/B.63, anc. Phillipps 3345, XIe s., f. 52 (décrit par K. V. Sinclair, dans *Archiv für Musikwiss.* XXII (1965), pp. 52-5. D'autres manuscrits seront mis en évidence par l'édition critique de la *Musica Enchiriadis* préparée par H. Schmid (München).

Ce tableau n'est pas l'édition critique des formules occidentales. Il serait vain de prétendre reconstituer le 'texte primitif'
des formules de l'archétype du plus ancien tonaire: déjà, en 850,
au temps d'Aurélien de Réomé, les variantes se constataient:
'*in plagis... est litteratura scilicet NOEANE sive secundum quosdam
NOEAGIS*'.[13]

Les tonaires cités, bien que remplis de variantes, nous font
penser qu'à l'origine de la tradition occidentale, au neuvième
siècle, les formules latines étaient beaucoup plus proches des
formules byzantines[14] que dans le cours du Moyen-Age.
Cependant, si pour plusieurs formules, le texte latin est
étonnamment proche du grec, comment se fait-il que pour
d'autres formules, on ne constate aucune correspondance?
Ainsi, en tetrardus, NOIOEANE: les variantes des manuscrits
n'offrent aucun rapport avec le texte grec ααγια. Pourtant,
cette leçon AGIA était connue en Occident: on la relève dans
le petit traité *De Modis* qui figure dans certaines collections des
écrits hucbaldiens.[15]

L'écart de temps entre l'introduction de ces formules, à la
fin du huitième siècle, et les premiers documents écrits que nous
connaissons est assez large: à cette première cause de déforma-

---

[11] Wolfenbüttel, Herzog August Bibl. 4376 (Gud. lat. 2° 72): le manuscrit de
St. Paul en Carinthie, Stiftsbibl. 29.4.2, édité par Gerbert, serait — suivant
H. Schmid — une copie du MS de Wolfenbüttel.

[12] Tonaires *italiens*: Vercelli, Bibl. Cap. LXII (2), psautier du Xes. avec tonaire
(f. 285-9); Milan, Bibl. Ambros. H.146 inf. (XIes.), f. 62; Paris, Bibl. Nat.
Nouv. acq. lat. 443 (XIIes.), f. 29ᵛ (incomplet: ne donne pas les huit formules);
Krakow, Bibl. Jagellonska, 1965 (XIes.), p. 78; Munich, Clm. 14523
(XI-XIIes.), f. 132. — Tonaires *français*: Paris, Bibl. Nat. lat. 4995
(Xes.) f. 38ᵛ; lat. 13252 (XI-XIIes.), f. 71ᵛ, tonaire de St. Magloire; Munich;
Clm. 14272 (XI-XIIes.), f. 62ᵛ (manuscrit directement copié sur un modèle
chartrain, suivant B. Bischoff): voir, sur tous ces tonaires, M. Huglo, *Les
tonaires* (Paris, 1971) p. 66, ss. — Le tonaire du tropaire de Winchester (Cam-
bridge, CCC 473), issu d'un modèle français (Tours ou Fleury).

[13] *Mus. Disc.* IX: éd. Gerbert, p. 42; éd. Gushee, p. 38.

[14] Pour une étude définitive du problème, il faudrait connaître les variantes des
manuscrits byzantins sur les formules echématiques: nous avons suivi ici le
texte reçu adopté par J. Raasted, op. cit., p. 9.

[15] Gerbert, *Scriptores* I 148 A. Ce petit traité figure dans le manuscrit de Strasbourg,
aujourd'hui perdu; dans le MS de Cesena, Malatest. Plut. XXVI, 1, f. 196ᵛ et
enfin dans Oxford, Bodl. Canon. Misc. 212 (XIVes.), f. 39ᵛ. Le *De modis* donne
encore des formules echématiques pour les 'paraptères', comme l'interpolateur
du tonaire de Réginon de Prüm édité par P. Wagner dans *Festschrift G. Adler*
(Wien–Leipzig, 1930), pp. 29-30, d'après Leipzig Univ. CLXIX (actuel
Musikbibl. Rep. I 93).

tion s'ajoute l'introduction des modes paraptères ou modes 'moyens' — à l'imitation des Grecs, suivant Aurélien (GS. I 41 B) — auxquels on a également attribué des formules échématiques:[16] d'où confusion, à l'égard de laquelle la réduction des huit formules à deux seulement (*Nonenoeane*/*Noeagis*) apparaît comme une réaction. Cette réaction s'est produite à la fin du neuvième siècle et se décèle dans la *Musica Enchiriadis* ainsi que dans la majorité des tonaires.

Ces variantes textuelles ne paraissent pas avoir entrainé de variantes notables dans la tradition musicale des formules échématiques: tous les tonaires, depuis les plus anciens, notés en neumes, jusqu'aux tonaires notés sur lignes au douzième siècle, nous transmettent la même mélodie. La seule différence importante enregistrée porte sur l'absence ou la présence du *neuma* final.

La mélodie des formules échématiques est une mélodie syllabique qui rappelle les éléments architecturaux du ton: dans la tradition occidentale, les formules echématiques se terminent par un long mélisme (*neuma*), dont la restitution est donnée d'après les manuscrits notés sur tableau hors-texte.[17] Il est notable que l'intonation de ces mélodies se fait généralement sur la dominante et qu'elle retourne à la tonique par degrés conjoints: la composition de ces formules est sans analogies avec celles qui sont employées pour la centonisation des pièces grégoriennes appartenant au 'fonds primitif' du répertoire. Le *neuma* est peut-être un genre de trope ajouté en Occident à la formule echématique brève.

Les théoriciens du Nord de la France, à la fin du neuvième siècle,[18] et les tonaires aquitains[19] nous ont conservé une formule mélodique brève exactement comme les manuscrits byzantins.

Les formules échématiques ne se chantaient pas au choeur

---

[16] Aurélien, *Mus. Disc.* VIII: éd. Gerbert, 'p. 41 B-42 A; éd. Gushee, p. 36; *De modis*: Gerbert, p. 148 A; Interpolateur de Réginon: éd. P. Wagner, loc. cit. pp. 29-30.

[17] La mélodie que nous avons transcrite sur le tableau hors-texte n'est pas une version critique absolument définitive: c'est la résultante des mélodies notées en neumes par les plus anciens manuscrits et 'traduites' par les manuscrits aquitains et italiens.

[18] Aurélien de Réomé (manuscrit de Valenciennes 148 [141], f. 71, en notation paléofranque); Hucbald (éd. Gerbert, I, 118); *Musica Enchiriadis* (éd. Gerbert, I, 179). Voir le tableau comparatif.

en Occident: elles servaient à la mémorisation des tons, à l'aide du tonaire. Cependant, ces textes intriguaient la curiosité des théoriciens: Aurélien de Réomé interroge un grec sur le sens de ces formules (GS. I 42); l'auteur de l'*Enchiriadis* (GS. I 158 B), Réginon (GS. I 247 B) et Bernon (GS. II 77 A) font observer qu'il ne faut pas leur chercher un sens. Elles sont simplement des *syllabas modulationi attributas* (GS. I 158 B), *syllabae ad investigandam melodiam apte* (GS. I 216), c'est à dire aptes à la vocalisation. Ce n'est qu'au début du XIe siècle qu'on tente de trouver, malgré l'avis des maîtres cités, une interprétation des textes mystérieux: *Noe dicitur a greco quod est nus* (νοός—νοῦς). Ce texte a connu quelque diffusion,[20] mais il n'a cependant pu assurer la survie des formules échématiques qui, dès le dixième siècle, se trouvèrent en concurrence avec des antiennes latines: *Primum querite regnum Dei, Secundum autem simile est huic... Octo sunt beatitudines.*[21]

Ces antiennes latines ne sont pas des antiennes liturgiques, mais des pièces composées pour le tonaire et destinées à la mémorisation des intervalles caractéristiques de chaque ton: leur mélodie a repris le mélismes final ou *neuma* des formules echématiques, mais leur formules d'intonation et la contexture de leur ligne mélodique se rapprochent des compositions grégoriennes classiques en utilisant des formules usuelles qui ne se trouvaient pas dans les anciennes formules échématiques:

Primum querite...	intonation	Dah
Secundum autem...		DA
Tertia dies est...		Gh (variante: Gc)
Quinque Prudentes...		a F a c
Septem sunt spiritus...		d–dc
Octo sunt...		F–FG

Les antiennes ont éliminé les formules échématiques byzantines de la pratique occidentale au douzième siècle: mais

---

[19] Voir J. Raasted, *Intonation Formulas*... pp. 154-6.

[20] Les références aux sources sont données par J. Smits van Waesberghe, dans CSM. 4, pp. 20, 42, 47, 56 et dans *The Theory of Music up to 1400* (RISM), I, p. 116. Le texte du manuscrit de Prague, Univ. XIX C 26 (ancien Tetschen) a été édité par E. Langer dans *Kirchenmusikalisches Jahrbuch*, XXVII, 1902, p. 79. — Cf. A. W. Ambros, *Geschichte der Musik*, I, p. 445, n. 6.

[21] Pour le développement des points exposés ici, voir *Les tonaires*, p. 386, ss.

1. Beginning of the Heirmologion of A.D. 1591, fol. 2r (see p. 77).

3. Bulgarian Academy of Sciences manuscript No. 37, recto and verso (see p. 98).

4. The Bitola Triodion (see p. 101) (a) fol. 4v, lower half; (b) fol. 7r; (c) fol. 13r, lower margin.

5. 'Persikon'. Athens MS. 2401, fol. 122v (see p. 181).

l'ancien *neuma* a subsisté dans l'usage jusqu'au dix-huitième siècle.

Ce neume, employé comme 'pierre de touche' pour reconnaître le mode d'une pièce[22] est passé dans la pratique liturgique: au douzième siècle, sinon avant, on a chanté le *neuma* à la suite de l'antienne de Magnificat à Vêpres et à Laudes.[23] Le *neuma* a encore été choisi comme ténor dans plusieurs motets du treizième et du quatorzième siècles. Plus tard, c'est l'organiste qui jouera à l'orgue la mélodie du *neuma* et qui ainsi l'enlèvera aux chanteurs. Enfin, il reste à évoquer, pour mémoire, le témoignage des liturgies néogallicanes du dix-huitième siècle qui maintinrent le *neuma* dans le nouveau répertoire, signé évident d'attachement à une tradition populaire.

L'analyse et le classement des textes a révélé la complexité de la tradition des formules échématiques en Occident. C'est à la fin du huitième siècle, en même temps que les noms grecs des huit tons, que ces formules ont été introduites dans le tonaire, dans un but didactique.

Cette influence de la théorie musicale byzantine sur l'*Ars Musica* occidentale se dénote au moment même où apparaissent en Occident les diverses pièces de la *Missa greca* en usage à St. Denys et dans plusieurs églises du Nord de la France: *Doxa en ipsistis, Pisteu(g)o is ena, Agios*, etc. Comme dans d'autres domaines — celui des Arts plastiques — le rayonnement de Byzance se révèle sur la culture occidentale et en particulier sur la Musique. Ce rayonnement n'a pas été éphémère et ses effets ont persisté durant tout le Moyen-Age, car les théories de l'*Ars Musica* ont été élaborées à partir de ces éléments contenus dans les tonaires: la terminologie spéciale désignant les huit tons de la musique ecclésiastique et la formule musicale qui les résume schématiquement ou formule échématique.

---

[22] Les tonaires italiens indiquent la méthode de comparaison: *Ad judicium primi toni haec antiphona ponitur*   etc., texte en partie parallèle à Guy d'Arezzo, *Micrologus*, cap. XIII (CSM. 4, p. 154; Gerbert, *Scriptores* II 48).

[23] Sur ce point et sur la suite, voir *Les tonaires*, p. 388.

G

TABLEAU COMPARATIF DES MÉLODIES DES FORMULES ÉCHÉMATIQUES

Mélodie byzantine[1]

Mélodie occidentale brève

Mélodie occidentale avec 'neuma'

1. D'après J. Raasted, *Intonation Formulas in Byz. Music. Mss.* (1966), p. 9.

2. Hucbald (GS. 1, 118).

3. Ms. d'Aurélien de Réomé (Valenciennes 148 [141], fol. 71, not. paléofranç.) et *Schola de la Musica Enchiriadis* (GS. 1, 179, notation dasiane).

4. A partir de cette ligne, restitution d'après les manuscrits aquitains.

5. Restitution des mélodies d'après 8 Mss. neumatiques et 10 Mss. diastématiques.

6. La restitution des deux formules du VII° ton est incertaine en raison de lacunes matérielles dans les meilleurs témoins aquitains.

5

Andrija Jakovljević

COLUMBUS, OHIO

David Raidestinos, Monk and Musician

STUDENTS of Byzantine music have been aware for some time of the great profusion of names of composers and singers listed in medieval musical manuscripts. In a recently published study[1] the number of musicians listed in a single manuscript surpasses one hundred names. It is unlikely that detailed biographical studies will be compiled for all of these musicians; in all probability many of them will only be remembered by their names and works,[2] without any additional data. Yet for a few musicians there are additional bits of information, not only in the musical manuscripts but also in the theoretical treatises.[3]

This essay will attempt to assemble data about one musician and copyist of musical manuscripts, David Raidestinos, who was active during the first half of the fifteenth century.[4] His

---

[1] Miloš Velimirović, 'Byzantine Composers in MS Athens 2406' in *Essays presented to Egon Wellesz*, edited by Jack Westrup (Oxford, 1966), pp. 7-18.

[2] E.g. the Monk Theodoulos of whom nothing else is recorded. His works may be found in a great number of manuscripts. As a point of curiosity, we have discovered in the Chilandar MS 59 a sticheron by this composer, in Greek, in honour of the Bulgarian saint John of Rila (d. 946), fols. 11r-14r. Besides the name of 'Ioasaph, the new Koukouzeles' little else is known about him, yet his works may be found in many manuscripts. This is the fate of most Byzantine musicians whose names are recorded without any other data.

[3] The best known musician appears to have been John Koukouzeles about whom some data are available in a 'vita' which has recently been studied by Edward V. Williams in his doctoral dissertation 'John Koukouzeles' Reform of Byzantine Chanting for Great Vespers in the Fourteenth Century' (Yale University, 1968). Although little is known about Manuel Chrysaphes, his treatise on the 'phthorai' was first published by A. Papadopoulos-Keramevs in *Vizantiĭskiĭ Vremennik*, viii (1901), pp. 526-45.

[4] Some material concerning him has already been published. See Marie Vogel and Victor Gardthausen, 'Die griechischen Schreiber des Mittelalters und der Renaissance' (*Zeitschrift für Bibliothekswesen, Beiheft* xxxiii) (Leipzig, 1909), p. 100;

surname 'Raidestinos' suggests that he came from the city of
Raidestos on the shores of the Sea of Marmara, not far from
Constantinople. He was one of the many singers and musicians
who gave a distinguished name to that settlement.[5]

Eustratiadis has already pointed out that in a manuscript in
the library of the Great Laura on Mount Athos (K.188) there
is an interesting inscription which reads: [τοῦ] Δανιήλ μοναχοῦ
[Ἁγιορείτου] τοῦ διά τοῦ μεγάλου σχήματος Δαυίδ. On the basis
of this Eustratiadis was inclined to suggest that in the fifteenth
century musical manuscripts references to a musician 'Daniel'
may all refer to the same person, namely David Raidestinos.[6]
Furthermore, Eustratiadis pointed out that the text of the
communion hymn Γεύσασθε καί ἴδετε appears in the Lavra
Manuscript K.188 as the work of 'Daniel Gavalas', in the Lavra
Manuscript Θ.154 as the work of David, monk from Mount
Athos (Δαυίδ μοναχοῦ Ἁγιορείτου), and in the Xeropotamou
Manuscript 317 as by David the Monk.[7] Although comparative
studies of these musical settings are lacking, Eustratiadis was
inclined to the view that all these works were a single piece and
that the various names all referred to a single person, David
Raidestinos, who may have also been known as Daniel, and
whose family name might have been Gavalas. As a logical
consequence of this reasoning, Eustratiadis further suggested
that any work attributed to Gavalas might be by David,
although he himself realized that this position could lead to
much confusion, since he knew of at least three other musicians
with the family name of Gavalas.[8] It is easy to view these
additional persons as 'relatives', yet in the absence of studies
dealing with these musical compositions one should exercise
caution, unless some tangible evidence is uncovered to sub-
stantiate the hypothesis. From a bibliographical point of view
and as a lead for further research it might be desirable to
supplement the references listed by Eustratiadis with some

---

see also Sophronios Eustratiadis, 'Θρᾶκες μουσικοί' in 'Επετηρὶς 'Εταιρείας
Βυζαντινῶν Σπουδῶν, xii (1936), pp. 54ff.
[5] See the index in G. Papadopoulos, Συμβολαί εἰς τήν ἱστορίαν τῆς παρ'
ἡμῖν ἐκκλησιαστικῆς μουσικῆς (Athens, 1890) and also Eustratiadis' study
in the Supplement to the third volume of Θρᾳκικά (1931), pp. 224-5.
[6] Eustratiadis, ΕΕΒΣ, loc. cit.   [7] Ibid.
[8] Ibid.; for an example of the surname without the first name see Velimirović,
op. cit., p. 15 in the index.

newly acquired data obtained during work in the libraries of
the monasteries on Mount Athos as well as in the National
Library in Athens. For this purpose a list of incipits and
locations is appended to this essay.

To the autographs of David Raidestinos already known may
be added the earliest dated manuscript copied by him, from
the year 1431, which we found in the library of the Monastery
Iviron on Mount Athos. This is Manuscript 544 (Lampros
5126/1006).[9] Besides being his earliest autograph this manuscript contains some additional inscriptions which suggest that
it travelled considerably before it came to be deposited in the
Iviron library. One of the inscriptions mentions the hitherto
unknown name of a John Stamiorof ('Ιωάννης Σταμιώροφ) who
may have been of Slav origin. On fols. 265r and 265v there is
a mention of another John, 'notary of the Great Church' (i.e.
of St. Sophia in Constantinople)—'Ιωάννης νοτάριος τῆς
Μεγάλης 'Εκκλησίας. It remains uncertain whether this inscription should be interpreted as indicating that the manuscript
was in use in Constantinople or not. Yet there is little doubt
that the manuscript was taken to the city of Smederevo, the
capital of Serbia in the fifteenth century, where it was pur-
chased by the Metropolitan 'Kyr Atanasije' (who died in 1456)
from a 'Turk' according to a Serbian inscription on fol. 1v
which reads:

'СΪЮ КНИГОУ КȣПИ МТРДЛИТЬ СМЕДЕРЕВСКΪЙКȣРЬ
АТАНАСΪЄ ОД ЄДНОГА ТȣРЧИНА КАГА ПРΪИ-
НМИШЄ ТРЦЫ ЦРГРАДА ТА Ю ДАДЄ МЄНЄ ГРѢЩ-
НОМЬ ПОПОУ СТЄФАНȣ И БГЬ ДА ГА ПРОСТИТЬ
АМИНЬ.'

At some undetermined time shortly afterwards it must have
been brought to Iviron, where it is now. While it was in Serbia
some additions were made there, as can be seen from the
appearance of a sticheron for the funeral rite, originally composed by John Koukouzeles, copied in its Greek form on fols.

---

[9] S. P. Lambros, *Catalogue of the Greek Manuscripts on Mount Athos*, ii (Cambridge,
1900), p. 245. Since this cataloguing the manuscripts at Iviron were renumbered
and No. 544 is the *new* number. There is, however, a good cross-index referring
to the Lambros numbering. David's subscription is to be found on fol. 252v and
reads: 'Ετελειώθη τό παρόν βιβλίον διά χειρός ἐμοῦ Δαυίδ μοναχοῦ Ραιδεσ-
τινοῦ· ἐν μηνί ἰουλλίου ἡμερα σαββάτο· ἐν ἔτει, ͵ϛϡλθ' (i.e. A.D. 1431).

131r–132v, and then translated into the Serbian version of Old Church Slavonic. Of even greater significance is the apparently unique occurrence on fols. 263r–264v of a Christmas sticheron in the Serbian language only. The inscription already mentioned is additionally important for it contains the information that the manuscript was given by the Metropolitan Atanasije to 'the confessor, Stefan the Priest'. While it cannot be stated with certainty that this is a reference to the well-known Serbian composer Stefan the Domestikos of the same city of Smederevo,[10] due to some difference in the style of Stefan's works and due to the difference in the handwritings of the musical compositions and the inscription itself, the fact remains that some of the earliest, if not the earliest, chants from Medieval Serbia have survived in this beautifully executed manuscript.[11] The data provided by this manuscript support the contention that in the fifteenth century there were increasing contacts between Constantinople and the Serbian state.[12]

David's second musical autograph is Pantocrator MS 214 dated A.D. 1433. This manuscript has been extensively used in studies of Byzantine music.[13] In its contents and the general layout it closely resembles a hitherto neglected anthology of chants in the library of the Monastery Chilandar, Manuscript 97, which contains a polychronion honouring Manuel II Palaiologos and his wife Helen Dragash (who was of Slav

[10] The first reference to this composer was made by the late Prof. Kosta P. Manojlović in his *Opšte pojanje* (Belgrade, 1935). The work of Stefan the Domestik has been studied by Dimitrije Stefanović in several of his studies, especially in his article 'Izgoreli neumski rukopis br. 93 beogradske Narodne biblioteke', *Bibliotekar*, xiii (Belgrade, 1961), pp. 373-84.

[11] On the basis of the findings in this manuscript the writer has published two studies. One of these deals with 'The Serbian Kratēma', in *Hilandarski Zbornik*, ii (Belgrade, 1972), pp. 131-41, and the other with 'Koukouzeles' Part in the Funeral Service in Medieval Serbia and Byzantium', in *Cyrillomethodianum*, i (Thessaloniki, 1972), pp. 121-30.

[12] Cf. M. Velimirović, "Ἰωακεὶμ μοναχός τοῦ Χαρσιανίτου καὶ δομέστικος Σερβίας', in *Recueil des travaux de l'Institut d'études byzantines*, viii/2 (Mélanges G. Ostrogorsky, II), (Belgrade, 1964), pp. 451-8. During his stay in the Vatopedi Monastery in July of 1969, this writer discovered in MS 1528, fol. 84, two communion hymns composed by 'John Charsianites domestikos of Serbia'—Ἰωάννου Χαρσιανίτου δομεστίκου Σερβίας. These works belong to the earliest documented proofs of Serbian contacts with Byzantium in the fifteenth century.

[13] Cf. H. J. W. Tillyard, 'The Acclamations of Emperors in Byzantine Ritual', *Annual of the British School at Athens*, xviii (1911-12), pp. 241ff. Also, Egon Wellesz, *A History of Byzantine Music and Hymnography*, 2nd ed. (Oxford, 1961), pp. 114ff.

origin). For a more precise dating of the Chilandar manuscript another polychronion may be useful which honours John Palaiologos and Gabriel, 'archbishop of Thessaloniki', whose dates are 1397–1416.[14]

David's third musical autograph is the Lavra Manuscript E.173, written in A.D. 1436. This exceedingly large anthology is one of the most beautifully executed manuscripts and one of the largest anthologies of medieval Byzantine chant. Unfortunately, this manuscript has not yet been utilized for musicological studies. On the basis of a quick perusal it is clear, however, that the number of works and composers included is greater than in either the Iviron or the Pantocrator manuscripts. The signature of Patriarch Joseph Kokkas (1465–66) at the end of the manuscript suggests that it may have been in use in Constantinople at that time, a point which only enhances its value for studies of the Byzantine chant at the time of the downfall of the Byzantine Empire.

While the number of active musicians in Byzantium during the first half of the fifteenth century cannot be estimated with any degree of certainty, there is no doubt that David Raidestinos was a first-class craftsman and probably a well-known personality. The manuscripts which he copied are extremely clear, in fact clearer to read and interpret than any other manuscripts (whether autographs or not) which may be found in the monastic libraries on Mount Athos. The total number of his compositions is relatively small, yet his works were copied from the fifteenth century until the nineteenth century. In the absence of a 'master-index' of composers and their works, the following listing, however tentative, is offered in the hope that it may stimulate additional research about this musician, one of the finest copyists of music in Byzantium.

---

[14] All references to manuscripts in the library of the Monastery Chilandar are derived from the writer's extensive catalogue *Slavic and Byzantine Musical Manuscripts at Mount Athos: I.—Catalogue of Manuscripts in Chilandar*. This catalogue was accepted for publication in the *Monumenta Musicae Slavicae* series, in Munich. For data about Archbishop Gabriel, see Θρησκευτική καί ἠθική ἐγκυκλοπαιδεία, iv (Athens, 1964), columns 112-13.

List of incipits of compositions attributed to David Raidestinos

A) With clear attributions to David Raidestinos:

1) Στέφανος ἡ καλή ἀπαρχή (sticheron for 27 December), besides Eustratiadis' reference to the Lavra MS E.155 we have located it in Athens, National Lib., MS 886, fols. 377v–378v; also in Chilandar, MS 28, fols. 222r–224r; and in Chilandar, MS 36, fols. 225v–227r.

2) Αἰνεῖτε τόν Κύριον and Γεύσασθε, two communion hymns, besides Eustratiadis' reference to the Lavra MSS E.25 and E.32, we have located the first one of these in the following MSS: Xeropotamou, MS 265, fols. 83r–84r; Vatopedi, MS 1528, fols. 86r–87v; Philotheou, MS 235 (on the 20th and 16th folios from the end; the MS is unnumbered).

The first one of these two hymns also appears in the Athens MS 893, fol. 264v with an attribution to 'David the hieromonk'.

3) Ποτήριον Σωτηρίου λήψομαι, communion hymn, not listed in Eustratiadis. Located in Philotheou MS 235, 16th page from the end.

B) With attributions to David the Monk:

1) Τῷ ἔκτῳ μηνί ἀπεστάλη ὁ ἀρχάγγελος, a sticheron for 25 March. Besides Eustratiadis' reference to Lavra MS E.155 we have located it in Athens, 886, fol. 249v.

2) Alleluias for liturgy, no additions to Eustratiades' reference to Lavra MSS I.81 and K.188.

3) The second of the communion hymns listed above has been found by Eustratiadis in Lavra MSS E.173 and Θ.154 attributed to David the Monk from Mount Athos. No new additions.

4) Νῦν αἱ δυνάμεις the substitute for the Cherubic hymn in the liturgy of the Presanctified, containing reference to Daniel as well as the name of David (cited in the article, just prior to footnote 6). No new documentation of this inscription has yet been found.

C) Works attributed to Daniel the Monk (or Daniel the Monk from Mount Athos):

1) Οὐρανοί ἔφριξαν (sticheron for 6 August), to the references in Lavra MSS K.168 and K.173 add Athens, 893, fols. 394r–394v.

2) Ἡ παγκόσμιος χαρά (sticheron for 8 September), no new additions to the reference in Lavra MS E.46.

3) Ἰδοῦ δή εὐλογῆτε τόν Κύριον

4) Κύριος εἰσακούσεταί μου

5) Τό ἐλεός σου Κύριε

6) Θεός ἐν τῷ ὀνόματ'σου σῶσόν με

7) Ἡ βοήθιά μου παρά Κυρίου

8) Ὁ Θεός ἀντιλήπτωρ μου

9) Ὁ Κύριος ἐβασίλευσεν

Incipits numbered 3 to 9, unknown to Eustratiadis, have been located with an attribution to Daniel the Monk in the Chilandar MS 50, starting from fol. 62r.

10) *Τί σέ καλέσωμεν Προφήτα*

11) *Χορός τετραδέκα πύρσευτος*

  Incipits 10) and 11), unknown to Eustratiadis, were located in Chilandar MS 100. The first of these is to be found on fols. 645v–646v; the second on fols. 257r–258v. The latter is also found in Athens 893, fols. 384v–385v.

N.B. References to Daniel Gavala as well as other possible mentions of the Gavala surname were disregarded when compiling this temporary listing.

6

Stefan Lazarov

SOFIA, BULGARIA

A Few Pages from the History of Bulgarian Music

I.—An Eleventh-century Palimpsest Triodion

IN the library of the Bulgarian Academy of Sciences in Sofia there is a unique document under the call-number No. 37. It consists of a single parchment folio, measuring 24 cm. by 17 cm. To judge by the orthography and some of the peculiarities of the text, it dates probably from the end of the eleventh century, or at the latest from the twelfth century. It represents the only surviving folio from a Triodion containing a fragment of a text which is sung at the Morning Office of Thursday of the fourth week of Lent. The manuscript apparently originated in the small town of Resan, in Macedonia, and was discovered in 1963 in the Bulgarian town of Gabrovo by Christo Kodov, an expert on Bulgarian literature and linguistics, who studied and published it. Kodov called to the attention of scholars the fact that 'between the lines there are, in red ink, ekphonetic signs of the earliest type, such as oxeia, bareia, double bareia, apostrophos, kathiste, apeso-exo, teleia. These ought to be studied separately.'[1] Unfortunately, these signs are not visible in the facsimiles published in Kodov's study.[2] The author nowhere mentioned that this is a palimpsest and that the signs belonged to the erased text.[3]

[1] Chr. Kodov, 'Fragment ot starobŭlgarski rŭkopis s glagolicheska pripiska', in *Kliment Ohridski-sbornik ot statiĭ po sluchaĭ 1050 godini ot smŭrtta mu* (Sofia, 1966), pp. 121-31.

[2] Ibid., p. 122.

[3] The information is completed in Chr. Kodov's 'Opis na slavyanskite rŭkopisi v Bibliotekata na Bŭlgarskata akademiya na naukite' (Sofia, 1969), p. 61.

In the accompanying photographs of this folio the ekphonetic signs are recognizable since they were not erased to the same extent as the original text. These signs were profusely yet not haphazardly used, obviously with some purpose in mind. There are eleven ekphonetic signs, some of which appear in more than one form. In the order of their appearance they are: bareia, apostrophos (two forms, one of which leans quite horizontally), kathiste, oxeia, teleia, a sign akin to the 'tzakisma' (?) (line 17 on the recto page), kentemata, double bareia, double oxeia (akin to diple of the later musical notation) and parakletike. Most frequently used is the oxeia followed by the kathiste. It would be significant if one could determine what the original text utilizing these signs was.

The superimposed text, of only a page and a half with a total of thirty-five lines (twenty-four on the recto and eleven on the verso), has peculiarities of its own. In its orthography it reveals archaic traits, e.g. only the soft sign (ь) is used and the hard sign (ъ) is missing; there are no iotacisms (ѥ , ѭ , etc.), there are no accentual marks and only the abbreviations appear. The text originated in the Southwest Bulgarian linguistic domain suggesting that this may be an early and quite authentic version of the Slavic translation of the Triodion, different from that in use after the fourteenth century. Of exceptional interest in addition to this text is an inscription in Glagolitic characters written in the empty space on the verso page. Transcribed into Cyrillic characters it would read: ПОПЕ ДРАГОСЛАВЕ ЗЛѢ СТВОРНШЬ ('Oh, priest Dragoslav, you are doing badly' (or 'you are wronging'[?]). This sentence is quite interesting and important not only from the standpoint of paleography and as evidence that the Glagolitic characters were used not only for the official liturgical writings, but in another sense as well, to be discussed below. Beneath this inscription at the bottom of the page a much later hand added the incipit of the dogmatic hymn of Mode I beginning with ВЬСЕМИРЬНОУЮ СЛАВОУ ѿ . ЧЛОВЕКЬ... (i.e. τὴν παγκόσμιον δόξαν). Above the Glagolitic inscription there is an ornament. In all the empty spaces on that page and beneath the inscriptions and ornament, one can notice faint traces of letters, altogether some thirteen lines, which, unfortunately, are much more visible on the film than on the print of this page.

By utilizing special photographic filters it is possible to discern that some groups of letters make words and that the letters are those of the Cyrillic alphabet. The erased text remains, however, illegible. An attempt to reconstruct the now lost text surpasses the limits of this study. A reconstruction would be helpful in learning which Cyrillic text had already been notated at such an early date.

The superimposed text of the palimpsest appears to have been written fairly soon after the original, probably only a few decades later. It is interesting that in the process of erasing the older text, the notational signs were preserved, not only between the lines but also within the lines, as if the scribe had done that on purpose. What the actual purpose of this action was remains conjectural, whether to utilize these signs as decorations, or to re-use them for another copying of the erased text. It is doubtful that the intent was to utilize the notation for decorative purposes. The re-use of the notation appears also to be out of the question since the newly copied text does not correspond in its structure in any way with the notational stresses. In this quest it may be useful to come back to the Glagolitic inscription and by means of it seek a hypothetical solution to this palimpsest. It seems that this inscription was written down by the same hand which copied the Cyrillic text of the Triodion, yet in the writing of the Glagolitic characters it reveals some lack of skill, not only because of the radical differences between these two alphabets, but perhaps also because the scribe was not ex-perienced in the use of Glagolitic letters. The appearance of the Glagolitic inscription here may be another instance of a crypto-gram which medieval scribes often used. Such inscriptions frequently contained data about the scribe and the date of the writing. It seems, nevertheless, that this is a different case. The name of the scribe is not connected with the work but with a moral or ethical question. What is it that the scribe is reproaching himself for? For having damaged an older manu-script? For having erased its script in order to copy a part of the text of the Triodion? It appears that he needed a single sheet for a purely practical purpose. In the process of erasing the old script he noticed the notational signs which (we should assume) he both knew and understood. If he had been ignorant of the meaning of these signs he would have behaved differently.

The priest Dragoslav then conveyed his spiritual pain confining it in a Glagolitic inscription. This story, which may seem quite romantic, is told by the document itself. It would have been delightful to have additional support for the plausibility of this interpretation. An indirect confirmation appears to be available in line 8 on the verso page. Still another hand began writing there the words ЛЮТѢ МНѢ ГРЕШ[НАГО] ('oh what a bitterness') as if a philosophical thought was about to be spelled out, as if someone had recognized the content of the palimpsest, became acquainted with the Glagolitic inscription of priest Dragoslav and probably connected it with the fate of the manuscript.

It is quite likely that this single folio may have been a part of a large manuscript which disappeared without any further trace. This folio may have fallen into the hands of the scribe when it had already been detached as a single leaf. The scribe, paradoxical as it may seem, must have recognized the signs which are nowadays so precious for a music historian. Their origin is undoubtedly Byzantine, yet some of the features of their writing reveal a somewhat different manner of writing. It would be tempting to pursue the hypothesis further. Yet, such as it is, this palimpsest represents one of the earliest Bulgarian musical documents found to date and it may have had an interesting fate of its own. It is a pity that so much of it remains illegible.

II.—*The Twelfth-century Bitola Triodion*

In the archives of the Bulgarian Academy of Sciences there is an important manuscript from the end of the twelfth century (call-number No. 38) known as the *Bitola Triodion*. It was discovered in 1907 in the town of Bitola by the well-known Bulgarian scholar Iordan Ivanov who was the first one to study and describe it. This manuscript is important in more than one way. The linguistic features of the text reveal that it is not a direct translation from the Greek, but that it represents a copy from an earlier Bulgarian original. Its paleographic, orthographic, and phonetic characteristics place this manuscript on the borderline between the Old Bulgarian and the Middle Bulgarian literary documents. Nearly every page contains lines in the Glagolitic characters (of a peculiar angular and rounded shape) written by a skilled and sure hand. The text reveals traces of the vocabulary in use in Western Macedonia where this Triodion was written. Last but not least, the document contains some personal remarks of the scribe. In these, a priest George recorded how he worked on this manuscript during winter, experiencing the bitter cold, having a toothache, expressing gratitude to those who were bringing him hareskins (for use as parchment) and food. In every sense of the word he appears to have been a literate and erudite man. Yet his circumstances eloquently demonstrate the fate of the Bulgarian clergy under Byzantine domination toward the end of the twelfth century.[4] The manuscript lacks beginning and end. It now consists of one hundred and one parchment folios, measuring 27 cm. by 19 cm. with twenty-eight lines per page.

It appears that priest George had some inkling of music, for in the lower part of folio 4v, in the kanon for St. Theodor the Martyr (celebrated on 17 February) there are a few neumes above the text, specifically above the words in line 3 and above one word in line 6 (see Plate IIa). In the margin of folio 7r there is the letter *omega*, standing alone surrounded by some signs suggesting the possibility of musical meaning (see Plate IIb). On folio 13r in the margin at the bottom of the page there are several signs, among which one is quite similar to ४ . This, however, does not appear to be the ligature consisting of letters *omikron* and *ypsilon* ($o+v$) as known in the contemporary manuscripts, but reminds this writer of a neume known in Russian musical manuscripts where it carries the designation 'pauk' (i.e. 'spider') (see Plate IIc).

We assume that priest George did have some knowledge of musical notation. He did not, however, use it systematically as these signs appear rather haphazardly. Much more interesting than these instances, however, is folio 91r containing indications for the vespers for the feast of the Annunciation. This folio seems to have been used more frequently due to its dog-eared appearance. The striking point is that the text is not copied in a continuous script but in segments which are separated one from another by red double bars. Also conspicuous is the frequent appearance of the sign (Θ) thematismos (or 'fita' in

4 I. Ivanov, *Bŭlgarski starini iz Makedoniya*, 2nd ed. (Sofia, 1931), pp. 452-67.

Russian terminology) (we find it also on the folio 10^r, 10^v, 26^r, 65^r). There is no apparent continuity between the text which precedes or follows this page. After listing these instances, the question arises whether these neumes constitute a peculiar system of notation. On folio 4v, the sequence of neumes seems to suggest the use of a melodic formula which does not reappear either on that or the following pages. The letter *omega* on folio 7r reminds this writer of some signs in the Russian Kondakarian notation.[5]

There are, on the other hand, some external resemblances to signs in the important Middle-Bulgarian document from the thirteenth century, the Zograf Trifologion.[6]

This relationship to the Zograf Trifologion is even more pronounced in the case of signs on folio 91r of the Bitola Triodion. It is curious to observe that in the Zograf Trifologion, two of the three signs which represent a Bulgarian variant of the thematismos appear above the word РАДȣИСА ('rejoice') while in the Bitola Triodion there is a simple thematismos at that point. In the later manuscripts the thematismos is to be found above other words on the same page. In two instances this neume appears above abbreviated words demonstrating the fact that musical signs could be placed even above words which are not spelled out in full.

In the beginning of line 10 of that page in the Bitola manuscript there is a bareia. The ison can also be found and, curiously enough, most frequently above the diphthong *ia*. It thus appears that the ison may have served here for prosodic purposes. Most curious, however, are the double bars in red ink separating one phrase from another. A careful reading of the text seems to imply that their function is to maintain a steady and logical rhythm of the thought. In other words, it may be assumed that they serve for the scansion of the text. The scansion is not a simple declamation but akin to a recitative with line 10 seems to become more dynamic and complex: text one does occasionally encounter the thematismos as a sign for a melodic formula. The rhythm of these 'phrases' starting

[5] Mme R. Palikarova-Verdeil, *La musique byzantine chez les Bulgares et les Russes*, MMB, *Subsidia*, iii (Copenhagen, 1953), p. 114.

[6] Ivanov, op. cit., 1st ed. (1908), p. 38; cf. *Zografskiĭ trifologiĭ* with studies by A. I. Sobolevskiĭ, M. Lisitzyn, V. Metallov, and A. V. Preobrazhenskiĭ (Petersburg, 1913), plate v.

with line 10 seems to become more dynamic and complex:
the number of syllables between the double bars diminishes
from fifteen to thirteen, to five, to eight, to seven, etc. This
manner of indicating the rhythmic dynamism of the text is
quite original.

The appearance of the notational signs in the Bitola Triodion
and especially of the signs on folio 91^r may lead to interesting
thoughts. It appears that the scribe priest George was an
educated man familiar with some musical signs, but the manner
in which he used them does not reveal any relation to the
contemporary uses of the musical notation either in Byzantine
or in Russian manuscripts of the period. The manner in which
he interspersed them suggests an almost indigenous approach
to the idea of notation. As I. Ivanov had indicated, the Bitola
Triodion was based on an even earlier Bulgarian model in
which the system of signs was quite primitive, not an elaborate
one. In all likelihood, whatever these signs may designate, it
would seem plausible to assume that they may designate a
recitative-like rendition rather than a melodic musical style. It
remains something of a mystery as to why these signs were used
at all and so haphazardly, rather than systematically when in
contemporary Russian musical documents similar pages were
fully notated. The Bitola Triodion raises some intriguing
questions and thus it continues to remain an enigma for
scholarship.

III.—Musical Notation in a Thirteenth-century Triodion

The thirteenth-century Triodion, manuscript No. 933, in the
Cyril and Methodius National Library in Sofia, consists of
fifty-eight parchment folios in eight incomplete quires; the
measurements are 24·5 × 19·5 cm. The text recension is
Bulgarian; some of the letters have an archaic appearance and
two words are even written in Glagolitic characters. Some
orthographic peculiarities suggest the possibility that it may
have been copied from a Glagolitic model.[7] In the description
of the manuscript it is stated: 'On the upper part of folio 31v
the full text of the oikos for the vespers of Maundy Thursday

[7] M. Stoyanov and Chr. Kodov, *Opis na slavyanskite rŭkopisi v Sofiĭskata narodna biblioteka*, iii (Sofia, 1964), pp. 93-4.

contains musical notation (neumes) in red ink.'[8] These signs do
not seem to have been a later addition since space for these
signs was provided in the process of the copying of this manuscript. We suggest that they may have been written in by the
copyist of this manuscript himself. Only eight lines of a complete text contain notation. Either a single neume or a group of
signs accompanies each syllable, although there are omissions
as well. On the whole they seem to be logically organized in a
system of signs. A listing of these neumes according to their
order of appearance gives the following picture: see p. 106.

The sum total of these signs is quite interesting as it seems to
suggest that some of the signs may be of Slavic origin (as
traditionally interpreted) and that others were in use by both
Greeks and Slavs.

It thus appears that in neither the graphic aspects nor the
use of notation in this very interesting document agree completely with the notation in either Russian or Byzantine
sources. It is obvious, however, that there are clear Byzantine
elements as well as those encountered in the earliest samples of
notation in Russian sources, even some signs known from the
ekphonetic notation. Yet in spite of the presence of these
elements in a single source, it would be difficult to state that
this document reflects influences from either Byzantine or
Russian sources, especially since linguistically the manuscript
is a typically Bulgarian document. The question which this
document raises deals more with the nature of its origin rather
than with the chronology or territory from which it may have
originated. It appears that the notation in this document
follows an established procedure and not an innovation. The
question may be raised as to whether this is the missing link
between the Byzantine and Russian practices representing a
point of departure for the evolution of the neumatic notation
in Russian musical manuscripts, or whether this is something
different that evolved concurrently? There is no doubt that the
ultimate origin of this notation harks back to Byzantium and
that this notation in this particular form originated in the
Balkan Peninsula. This document is contemporary to those
already published in the two volumes of *Fragmenta Chiliandarica
Paleoslavica* as well as to a number of Byzantine manuscripts

[8] Ibid.

H

Signs	Combinations			
1		‿	Petastē Крюкъ	Gr./Slav.
	1	⌃		
2		⁄	Oxeia	Gr.
3		⸲	Klasma-mikron	Gr.
	2	⸲⁄	Ison + ...	Gr.
4		⸜	Bareia	Gr.
5		⸗	Diplē Статья	Gr./Slav.
	3	⸿	Ison + ison	Gr.
6		ⸯ	Apostrophos	Gr.
	4	⸲⸴·	Стрела	Slav.
7		⸗‿	Xēron-Klasma Подкоулизма	Gr./Slav.
8		⸌⸌	Seisma, Piasma	Gr.
9		ⸯ	Kouphisma? Kathistē	Gr.
	5	⌣ ⌢	Чашка + Облачко	Slav.
10		⸲ⸯ	Палка	Slav.
11		⌣	Ison	Gr.
	6	⟨⟩ ‿	Челюстка + ...	Slav.
	7	⸌⫽	Стрела	Slav.
	8	⸲⸲		
	9	ⸯ⌣		
12		∴·	Kentēmata	Gr.
13		⟨⟩	Челюстка	Slav.
	10	⁄⌣		
	11	⸲⁻		
14		ⸯ	Petaste (?)	Gr.
15		⸮	Облачко	Slav.
16		2	Paraklētikē	Gr.
	12	⸜ⸯ	Крюкъ + Палка	Slav.
17		⸮·	Голубчикъ?	Slav.
18		⌣	Стопица	Slav.

19	⌣/		
20	⌣	Параклитъ	Slav.
21	⌐		
22	/⟍		
	13	//∪//	
	14	/\	
	15	⌐\	
23		⌐	
24		⌣	Чашка	Slav.
	16	//⌐7	
	17	2ᴬ	Стопица...+Ison...	Gr./Slav.
	18	⌐⟍	Paraklētikē+paraklētikē	Gr.
	19	⌐⟍⌐	Kathistē+kathistē	Gr.
	20	⌐⟍	Ison+Hyporrhoē	Gr.

containing Middle Byzantine notation. This document, however, differs from these by some archaic features. Whether the
scribe of this manuscript knew the notation as found in Russian
manuscripts or not, is irrelevant; if he was familiar with that
notation he was not influenced by its graphical appearance.
The same may be said about his attitude toward the contemporary Byzantine notation.

The use of the notation on a single folio of this manuscript
does represent something of a mystery. At any rate, the unique
use of the notation seems to suggest the idea of an actual
composition rather than the copying from a model. In spite of
a visual impression of a rounded entity, an analysis reveals that
there were some stumbling blocks in the writing. The absence
of neumes above some syllables appears to suggest a groping
for a new rendition in a way similar to a compositional sketch
rather than a completed work which is being copied from the
beginning to the end.

IV.—Bulgarian Musical Education in the Fourteenth Century

The concept of education, whether in our own days or in the past, is a rather broad one, implying some knowledge of a foreign language and literature, of foreign arts and practices. A high level of education and lack of bias made it possible for Arabs to preserve in Arabic translations the works of authors from Antiquity. The role of education played an exceptionally important role in the translations of the Bible and creation of new literature, as can be observed in the course of the fourth century among the Armenians and Georgians, and in the ninth century with the Slavs. The fact that an important person, statesman, or monk, leader or thinker, was literate and educated, was recorded in their biographies, in historical chronicles, and other writings of medieval authors. There are also different records to be encountered in manuscripts which testify to the educational level of the period. These often appear in the form of comments, brief explanations, or marginal notes of a purely practical nature. Such records may prove to be quite significant.

Similar records may be found in musical documents as well. Some time ago, the late Mme Palikarova-Verdeil published a page from a Greek manuscript from the fifteenth century which originated in the Bachkovo Monastery. That manuscript was at one time known as No. 14 in the Library of the Ecclesiastical Historical Museum of the Holy Synod in Sofia, and at present is preserved in the Cyril and Methodius National Library in Sofia. The page in question is to be found on folio 112^r where below the text with Neo-Byzantine notation there is a marginal comment in Bulgarian referring to the Cherubic hymn. Mme Verdeil's note reads simply: 'Manuscrit grec avec titres de chants en slavon.'[9]

In the library of the same museum there is another similar manuscript, No. 816, consisting of two hundred and thirty folios on paper, measuring 23 × 18 cm., having also originated from the Bachkovo Monastery. It is a carefully executed and initials are of a faded reddish-pink hue which contrasts strongly with the dark brown ink of the main body of the text. The many Bulgarian words and expressions to be found in this manuscript were written in a now faded reddish ink. Although

[9] Palikarova-Verdeil, op. cit., plate xviib.

the manuscript had endured considerable use it is still relatively well preserved.

The Bulgarian textual comments are to be found on thirty-one pages; a full list of these inscriptions is:

108ᵛ	херувн на пр꙯ежес꙯щеннаа	159ᵛ	с꙯томоу 'аплоу пе꙯тр꙯ѕ
112ʳ	херувн вс꙯ꙗ ве꙯	164ʳ	с꙯томоу аплоу па꙯вл꙯ѕ
117ʳ	с꙯томоу архнгг꙯лѕ мнханлѕ	168ᵛ	на пр꙯ѣкѡ꙯ѣражен꙯іе гн꙯е
119ᵛ	на в꙯ъвеніе пр꙯тыꙗ б꙯цꙗ	174ᵛ	въ т꙯ъж празннкъ
122ᵛ	с꙯томоу са꙯вы	177ᵛ	сты тре ст꙯іе
125ʳ	с꙯томоу ннкѡлѕ	181ʳ	на оус꙯ѣкнивеніе
127ᵛ	на рож꙯ъство хв꙯о	185ᵛ	на цвѣтонѡ꙯сіе
129ᵛ	въ т꙯ъ пр꙯а	189ʳ	на въскр꙯сеніе гн꙯е
133ʳ	въ т꙯ъже празннкъ	192ʳ	въ т꙯ъ пр꙯а
135ᵛ	на вг꙯о꙯являніе	195ʳ	въ т꙯ъжде празннкъ
137ᵛ	въ т꙯ъ пр꙯азннкъ	198ᵛ	на в꙯ъзн꙯еніе гн꙯е
141ʳ	на ср꙯ѣтеніе	201ʳ	въ т꙯ъ пр꙯а
144ʳ	на бл꙯гов꙯ѣщеніи	205ʳ	на съшествіе ст꙯го д꙯ха
148ᵛ	въ т꙯ъже пр꙯а	227ᵛ	προφίτα
153ʳ	с꙯томоу геѡргіѕ	234ᵛ	на оуспеніе пр꙯тыꙗ б꙯цꙗ
156ʳ	на рож꙯ъство꙯ іѡаннѕ		

This listing includes one Greek entry (folio 227ᵛ) omitting one Slavic inscription which is to be discussed separately. Although thirty-one inscriptions in a manuscript of some two hundred and thirty folios suggest an average frequency of one inscription manuscript with Neo-Byzantine musical notation. The heading on every seventh folio, this is a deceptive reckoning since al

Slavic inscriptions are to be found between folios 108 and 234. Such a disposition of these inscriptions may be interpreted only by presuming that that particular part of the manuscript had certain significance in the mind of the scribe and the compiler of this manuscript.

The long list cited above consists of remarks and explanations of a purely practical character. As a rule such inscriptions are to be found in margins and seem to appear as later additions. Yet there is no doubt that they were all written by the same hand which copied the main text of the manuscript. After the decorative ornament in the upper part of page 232^r, there is a title in a rich uncial lettering which reads: НАЧАЛО ЛТ8РГЇИ ('The beginning of the liturgy'), a designation identical to those utilized in Slavic manuscripts.

On the basis of this description the significance of this manuscript begins to emerge. It was compiled as an anthology with a practical purpose, namely, to be utilized by Bulgarians in the process of studying the Byzantine religious poetry and music. The scribe who wrote the remarks obviously knew the Bulgarian language as well as the Byzantine manner of calligraphy of the epoch. From the paleographic standpoint there are also similarities in the shape of several letters common to both alphabets. The question of the nationality of the scribe is therefore of secondary importance in the light of circumstances which led to the compilation of this document in the first place.

This manuscript was found in the Bachkovo Monastery and it is therefore possible that it may have originated there. This monastery in Southern Bulgaria in the midst of the mountain-chain of the Rodopes, some twenty-eight kilometres from Plovdiv, was founded c. 1083 by two brothers from Georgia (Gruzia) who were high Byzantine dignitaries, Gregory and Abasius Pakurianos. With its unique architecture and frescoes, it was a focal point at which influences from Georgia and Byzantium as well as Bulgaria converged. To this day there are relics preserved in the monastery among which there is a twelfth-century 'miracle working' icon representing the Virgin, a work of Georgian origin. In the following centuries the monastery was connected with events of Bulgarian history, e.g. it was the last residence of St. Euthimius, the Patriarch of Trnovo in the Second Bulgarian Empire, who was deposed by the Turkish conquest of Bulgaria in 1396. The literary school founded by him flourished in the monastery long after his death. The monastery played an important role in the Bulgarian national awakening. Also, the well-known Bulgarian artist Zacharias Zografos was active in this monastery during the nineteenth century. In the large library, there were at one time large collections of Bulgarian, Greek, Georgian, and Armenian manuscripts, many of which were dispersed or lost in the stormy events of the past centuries.

It was in that part of Bulgaria that cultural contacts with foreign countries were the most active, both in the past as well as in recent events connected with the liberation of Bulgaria from Turkish domination, as recently as 1879. It should therefore come as no surprise that in the normal course of events in the life of that monastery it may have been necessary to study the Byzantine hymnography and music and to prepare comments in Bulgarian in manuscripts dealing with these subjects. We suggest that the manuscript in question may represent a hitherto neglected silent witness of such events.

7

Maureen M. Morgan

ARDSLEY, NEW YORK

The Musical Setting of Psalm 134
—the Polyeleos

IN comparing manuscripts of a particular psalm one is eager to find concordances between the sources and at the same time the unique features within each manuscript. The musical settings of the Polyeleos, as set forth in manuscripts Athens MS 2406 and Sinai MSS 1276 and 1293, yield many examples of both types. For the purposes of this study only the *first stasis* in these three manuscripts was used for comparison, that is, Psalm 134 according to the numbering and verse division found in the Septuagint.[1] Although a few words of the text of the Polyeleos as found in the musical manuscripts are found only in the Psalterion, it is none the less apparent that the Septuagint version served as the basis for the textual pattern in the Polyeleos.[2]

The Typikon specifies that the Polyeleos, a selection of verses from Psalm 134 and 135, be sung during the Orthros for the Feasts of the Lord and on several other occasions. Since the manuscripts examined date from a relatively short span of time in the fifteenth century, the comparisons in this study will not show an evolution but rather present the manner of the chanting of the Polyeleos at a given point in time. The Sinai MSS 1293

---

[1] The psalms in the Septuagint and King James version agree in the numbering of Psalms 1-8 and 148-50. The Septuagint version of Psalm 9 is broken at verse 22 to make two Psalms in King James. Agreement in numbering is restored when in the Septuagint Psalms 146 and 147 are combined to make the King James version of Psalm 147.

[2] Verses 5, 10, and 14 of the Septuagint version have been slightly altered in the printed Psalterion.

and 1276 (which are available in the microfilm collection at the Library of Congress) date from the first half of the fifteenth century. The Athens MS 2406 is dated A.D. 1453. A microfilm of this manuscript was obtained from the National Library of Athens by the Music Library of Yale University in New Haven, and copies of the pertinent folios (90v–99v) were used for the transcription.

Athens MS 2406 is a comprehensive anthology of the type referred to as 'akolouthiai'. Kenneth Levy has described the akolouthiai as 'loyal at the outset to relics of the cathedral tradition, they are essentially monastic in outlook and at the root of some of their musical traditions there probably are elements of the practice of monasteries of the Holy Land'.[3] The fifty-four pieces in the first stasis of the Polyeleos in Athens MS 2406 are all attributed to either a composer or a particular tradition, such as 'palaion', 'latrinos', or are labelled 'other choir' indicating, presumably, the connection to the 'Great Church', or a metropolitan tradition. Since this manuscript was written in the town of Serres, at that time in the hands of the Turks, it is to the credit of the scribe that the various traditions and variants are so carefully delineated.[4]

The term 'latrinos', attached to this setting of the Polyeleos and to certain specific pieces, has never been completely explained. Velimirović suggested that it may refer to the area of Latros, the name of the monastic settlements in the vicinity of Miletos. He recognizes that this hypothetical explanation presents a problem because it implies the existence of a chant unique for an area, which then had to be transmitted to Constantinople for its place in history.[5]

A possible clue to the connection with monastic tradition presumably exhibited in this akoulouthiai may be seen in the close connection of some of the settings in Athens MS 2406 with those of Sinai MS 1293 and to a lesser degree with Sinai MS 1276. In Sinai MS 1293 every piece is attributed to either a composer or a tradition and may be said to contain the typical tradition, whereas Sinai MS 1276 is highly selective and

[3] Kenneth Levy, 'Hymn for Thursday in Holy Week', *Journal of the American Musicological Society*, 16 (1963), p. 157.

[4] Miloš Velimirović, 'Byzantine Composers in Manuscript Athens 2406', *Essays presented to Egon Wellesz* (Oxford, 1966), p. 9.

[5] Ibid., p. 13.

without any attributions. The latter manuscript is visually very attractive with wide margins while the other two are quite densely written, Athens MS 2406 extraordinarily so.[6]

Of the one hundred and twenty-seven pieces transcribed, all are in the first mode with the single exception of one which is attributed to Xenos Koronis, written in the 'nenano' or the 'ninth' mode, so called by Manuel Chrysaphes in his treatise on the phthorai.[7] In the recent *Pandektes*, a setting of the Polyeleos by Peter Lampadarios is written in the Plagios Protos mode and presumably dates back at least to the eighteenth century.[8] A possible explanation of this change of modality over three centuries is offered by Levy in his discussion of the monastic tradition of the akoulouthiai. In the kalophonic version of τοῦ δείπνου σου there is an interesting change of mode in the later manuscripts of the fifteenth and sixteenth centuries, clearly marked by the scribe: 'protos plagal, some also write this in deuteros plagal.' According to Levy, this may reflect a basic shift in the monastic conception of the tonal and modal system.[9] This change of mode may also be one of the contributing factors to the evolution of the modern tradition. However, in order to chart the course of the Polyeleos from the Fall of Constantinople to the present more transcriptions from the intervening centuries are required.

The arrangement of the Psalm verses in the Septuagint provides an answer to some of the patterns found in musical manuscripts. Each part of a verse is given a separate line, whereas in the printed Psalterion the verses are printed continuously, obscuring any possible pattern in the choice of text. I am indebted to Velimirović for suggesting the use of the Septuagint text for a study of the musical settings of the psalms.[10]

In order to determine a 'standard' setting of the Polyeleos,

[6] In Athens MS 2406 there are two lively illuminations. At verse 16, 'They have mouths but they speak not', a profile with an open mouth is used to form the initial letter of 'Stoma'. Likewise, for verse 17, 'They have ears but they hear not', a very large ear forms the first letter of the verse.

[7] A. Papadopoulos-Kerameus, 'Μανουηλ Χρυσάφης λαμπαδάριος τοῦ βασιλικοῦ κλήρου', in *Vizantiiskii Vremennik*, vii (1901), pp. 526-45.

[8] Μουσικὸς Πανδέκτης, vol. ii (Athens, n.d. (vol. i 1956)).

[9] Levy, op. cit., p. 171.

[10] This verse scheme, first encountered in a study of the Prooemiac psalm, is discussed by Velimirović in an article for the volume dedicated to A. T. Merritt, *Words and Music*, to be published by the Harvard University Press.

Table I

Verses always set to music (Exceptions)		Verses rarely or never set to music (Exceptions)	
Verse 1		Verse 2	(2406)
		Verse 3	
Verse 4a		Verse 4b	
Verse 5a		Verse 5b	(1276)
Verse 6a		Verse 6b	(2406)
Verse 6c		Verse 7a	
Verse 7b		Verse 7c	(2406)
Verse 8a		Verse 8b	
Verse 9a	(1276)	Verse 9b	(1276)
Verse 10a		Verse 10b	(2406)
Verse 11a		Verse 11b	(2406)
Verse 11c		Verse 12a	(2406)
Verse 12b		Verse 13a	(2406)
Verse 13b	(1276)	Verse 14a	(2406)
Verse 14b		Verse 15	
Verse 16a		Verse 16b	(1293)
Verse 17a		Verse 17b	
Verse 18a	(1276)	Verse 18b	
Verse 19a		Verse 19b	(2406)
Verse 20b	(1276)	Verse 20a	(2406)
		Verse 21	(1293)

the verses or parts of verses which are always used were separated from the verses or their parts that appear only rarely or never. In Table I the alternating pattern of verses can be seen quite clearly. There are the usual exceptions in every plan but even in the exceptions one can see patterns emerging. The most obvious consistency between all three manuscripts is the omission of verses 3 and 15. With only four exceptions in the pattern of alternating lines one can see that three of the missing pieces of a hypothetical 'standard' setting of the Polyeleos are missing from Sinai MS 1276, the more selective manuscript. On the other side of the pattern, the parts of the text which are included and only exceptionally set to music are found for the most part in Athens MS 2406, confirming the all-inclusive character of this particular anthology. Sinai MSS 1276 and 1293 offer only three exceptional pieces while Athens MS 2406 contributes ten pieces. The alternating pattern is lost after verse 19 and in both Athens MS 2406 and Sinai MS 1293 some non-scriptural material is introduced. For example, Athens

MS 2406 contains nine pieces by Koukouzeles using no part of Psalm 134. In Athens MS 2406 non-scriptural refrains had already been introduced at verse 12 in the setting by 'Kyr Andreas' entitled 'politikos, asmatikos'. Up to this point the refrain consisted of merely the word 'alleluia' in various syllabic combinations. From this point on new textual material is added to the 'alleluia' refrain. Some refrains are used more than once by different composers but normally each piece has its own refrain. At verse 17, a 'latrinon' setting, the alleluia is dropped and the new material becomes more extensive. After six more settings the psalm text also disappears and the last nine pieces, all by Koukouzeles, are non-scriptural. With this textual change comes a style shift as well, the latter being more neumatic than the earlier melismatic alleluia refrain.

In a comparison of the musical settings of the refrains in Sinai MS 1293 with those of Athens MS 2406 one would have expected or hoped to find that certain refrains were tradition-ally associated with certain verses. But this is not the case. The settings of all three manuscripts, after verse 12, may use refrains and in only one case did two settings of the same verse end with an identical refrain. This example, 'latrinon' in Athens MS 2406 and 'palaion' in Sinai MS 1293, is obviously the same piece except for two more words at the beginning of the 'latrinon' setting. In all other examples of the use of a refrain in different manuscripts, each setting of a given refrain is attached to a different verse. Another example is Agallianos' use of the refrain 'ᾄσατε τῷ Κυρί ἡμῶν ᾆσμα' for a setting of both verse 16b (in Sinai MS 1293) and verse 14a (in Athens MS 2406). The refrain 'τὸν Κύριον ὑμνεῖτε' may be found attached to three different verses: 19a (Athens MS 2406), 18a (Sinai MS 1293), and 20 (Sinai MS 1276), which illustrates the great mobility of the refrain. One must point out, however, that the *melody of a given refrain is always stable* and in these three manuscripts there was not a single exception to this rule. Thus, the same Psalm verse may be set to several different melodies but two refrains with the same text will always have the same melody.

The free non-scriptural material by Koukouzeles that appears at the end of the first stasis in Athens MS 2406 is copied as the refrain for the verse-phrase 'εὐλογήσατε τὸν Κύριον' in Sinai MS 1293. Since examples of this technique were found only in

the settings by Koukouzeles, we cannot suggest this as more than
an interesting and practical technique of migration of melodies
by this composer. There are, however, two isolated examples of
other composers' works which are also subjected to this
technique. A piece by Nicephorus Ethikos, a composer who
predates Koukouzeles, has the same refrain and incipit
'εὐλογήσατε τὸν Κύριον' as a piece by Koukouzeles, but one finds
a different melody for the verse-phrase. However, the melody
of the refrain still remains stable even when re-used by different
composers. Likewise, Klovas, in Sinai MS 1293, appears to have
taken a Koukouzelian refrain and combined it with the text
'εὐλογήσατε τὸν Κύριον'.

In cataloguing the number of different composers found in
Athens MS 2406 and Sinai MS 1293, it is clear that there was
an extraordinary amount of activity in the music of the
Eastern Church in the fifteenth century. At the same time it is
difficult to understand the remark of Manuel Chrysaphes,
concerning his six rules of the art of psalmody. The last of these
rules involves the ability to be critical of a given composition,
to be able to judge if a piece of music is well composed and
according to the rules of musical composition, and secondly, to
be able to tell, just by hearing the composition, who the
composer was.[11] Considering the great similarity of so much
melodic material in Byzantine chant, one wonders if the key to
Chrysaphes' ability to recognize any given composer may lie
in the manner of presentation rather than in the melodic
style.

Ex. 1, a setting of the second half of verse 14 by Xenos
Koronis that appears in all three manuscripts, reveals a very
definite form in textual material. By designating 'καὶ ἐπὶ τοῖς
δούλοις αὐτοῦ' as part A, and 'παρακληθήσεται' as part B, the
textual pattern of ABB AB ABB can be clearly observed in all
three pieces. The example from Sinai MS 1293 had no attribution to a composer, yet it is obviously the same piece. The close
parallel between Athens MS 2406 and Sinai MS 1293 is
notable, becoming even more pronounced after the word
'λεγε'. A curious rearrangement of words can be seen in Sinai
MS 1276 where the phrase 'ὁ κύριος' is used as a substitute for
'παλιν'. Yet later on, when Athens MS 2406 and Sinai MS 1293

[11] A. Papadopoulos-Kerameus, op. cit., p. 536.

use the words 'ὁ κύριος', Sinai MS 1276 has no comparable musical passage.

The opening melodic phrase in this example is typical of this mode but there is an example of a less typical melodic incipit that is constant in all three manuscripts. In Ex. 2 the

Ex. 1
Sinai 1276, fol. 41v   By Xenos Koronis

Example 1—*continued*

Example 1—*continued*

Example 1—*continued*

essential concordance of the three manuscripts can be seen, but the closer parallel of Athens MS 2406 and Sinai MS 1293 is still observable. This same melody for the beginning is also used consistently in the second piece of each manuscript, a setting of the complete first verse.

The last musical example is in a more kalophonic style than most of the settings in the first stasis but its rhythmic liveliness is also worth noting as well as its sequential patterns. The word 'παλιν' does not indicate a melodic repeat but rather a repeat of the word 'alleluia' which in this case does contain a repeated melodic pattern. The third statement of the word alleluia, covering the last three lines in Ex. 3, contains a syncopated figure of four notes that is repeated three times, the last twice consecutively. The contrast of a repeated melodic figure, twice in a row, is found between the syncopated figures. The compelling rhythm of this alleluia refrain is unique in the three settings of the Polyeleos used for this comparison.

The results of this study have reinforced the findings of Velimirović that alternating parts of the psalm-verses, as seen in Table I, form one of the basic patterns in a number of

I

musical settings of the Psalms. This study has also suggested that the music for a verse and for a refrain may be considered as independent entities, and that a given refrain may be used with

Ex. 3

Sinai 1293, verse 19, fol. 71r   By Christophoros

any verse at the discretion of the composer-performer.[12] Athens
MS 2406 and Sinai MSS 1293 and 1276 offer a variety of
combinations of verses and refrains, further emphasizing the
need for more research into Byzantine musical practices of the
fifteenth century.

[12] This phenomenon has also been studied at length by Edward Williams in his
study of the Psalmody for Vespers as part of his doctoral dissertation on John
Koukouzeles (Yale, 1968).

8

Grigore Panțiru

BUCHAREST, RUMANIA

Une Nouvelle Interprétation de la Notation Écphonétique d'un Manuscrit à Iași, Roumanie

On connaît les nombreuses découvertes et valorisations des monuments artistiques du passé, depuis les temps les plus reculés jusqu'à nos jours, qui se trouvent sur le territoire de notre patrie. La musique populaire et la musique byzantine sont elles aussi l'objet d'incessantes investigations, poursuivies avec le plus vif intérêt.

C'est dans le contexte de ces recherches que se situe ici notre souci de signaler et faire valoir un monument musical ancien de grande importance, non seulement au point de vue purement historique, mais aussi et surtout musical. Il s'agit de l'*Evangéliaire grec*, *MS 160* conservé à la Bibliothèque Centrale de l'Université de Jassy.[1]

Ce manuscrit a déjà fait l'objet des investigations du Prof. V. Gheorghiu. Les résultats de son étude sont consignés dans son travail intitulé *Lecţionarul evanghelic grecesc de la Iaşi* (Sur l'Evangéliaire grec de Jassy), publié en 1940 dans *Studii şi Cercetări* XLI de l'Académie Roumaine.

L'auteur nous présente le manuscrit sous ses différents aspects: description, caractère paléographique, contenu, historique de l'époque où il fut rédigé et par quelle voie il parvint à Jassy. Le même ouvrage contient aussi un rapport succint de Gh. Onciu concernant la notation musicale du manuscrit qu'il croyait, à ce moment, impossible à déchiffrer et à transcrire.[2]

Attiré par l'opinion de V. Gheorghiu — que ce monument serait le plus ancien manuscrit musical de notre pays — et à l'encontre de celle de Gh. Onciu — que ce manuscrit ne saurait être transcrit en 'notation moderne'—, j'ai attentivement étudié ce document et fort des informations recueillies dans des ouvrages de spécialité, j'ai essayé de déchiffrer l'énigme de cette notation. Les résultats de mes recherches sont consignés dans un ouvrage de proportions plus vastes sur la notation musicale byzantine, un guide nécessaire dans le déchiffrage des textes musicaux byzantins de l'époque la plus reculée à nos jours et que nous espérons voir imprimé bientôt.

En attendant jusqu'à la publication de l'étude indiquée ci-dessus et la transcription complète du manuscrit en notation actuelle, nous nous limiterons dans cet article de signaler seulement quelques aspects et problèmes ayant trait au manuscrit de Jassy.

Le MS 160 est un évangéliaire qui comprend différentes *péricopes* (fragments) des quatre évangélistes, qui se lisent solennellement dans les églises certains Dimanches et jours de

---

[1] J'exprime ici mes remerciements à MM. Grigore Botez, directeur, et Ignat Evdochim, de la Bibliothèque Centrale de l'Université de Jassy, pour l'élan avec lequel ils m'ont encouragé à l'étudier et la bienveillance avec laquelle ils l'ont mis à ma disposition.

[2] V. Gheorghiu, *Lecţionarul evanghelic grecesc de la Iaşi*, p. 33.

fête de l'année. Il existe des évangéliaires qui contiennent toutes les péricopes évangéliques de l'année, d'autres seulement pour les principaux jours de fête. Il en existe aussi qui contiennent des textes des Apôtres (Le Livre des Apôtres) ou des Prophètes (Prophétologe ou Livre des Prophètes).[3]

L'Evangéliaire de Jassy est plus réduit, ne comprenant que 18 péricopes évangéliques qui se lisent aux principaux jours de fêtes de l'année.

Dès le premier contact avec le manuscrit, on est impressionné par son aspect extérieur qui nous suggère — quand bien même il ne semble pas avoir la même ancienneté que le texte intérieur — par le genre de sa reliure et par les mots grecs et slavons qui s'y trouvent, qu'il aurait été relié à une date ne remontant pas plus haut que les quatorzième ou quinzième siècles.[4]

L'oeil y est saisi par les couvertures en cuir vert, la première portant la scène de la Résurrection de Jésus-Christ, avec les soldats gardant le Sépulcre, avec les Femmes Pieuses et, dans les coins, les quatre Evangélistes avec leurs simboles. La seconde couverture porte le Crucifiement de Jésus sur le Golgotha. La scène est représentée avec beaucoup de détails et la participation de personnages connus de l'Evangile. Les coins sont occupés par les figures des Evangélistes. Au dos, des lignes dorées.

L'aspect extérieur et le genre de la reliure nous font pressentir la grande valeur de l'intérieur. En effet, en ouvrant le manuscrit, on découvre — admirables — la calligraphie et la notation musicale, les titres des péricopes, les vignettes ornant les lettres initiales, la grandeur identique des mêmes lettres dans tout le texte.

A la page 11 se trouve une prière écrite par le Patriarche de Constantinople Génnade II Scholarios après la prise de Constantinople par les Turcs (1453). Celui-ci aurait emporté le manuscrit lors de sa retraite au monastère Serae de Macédoine (1459) où du reste il est mort. De là, le manuscrit a dû être apporté par un quelconque réfugié dans les Principautés Roumaines, où il a finalement été acquis par la

---

[3] Carsten Höeg, *La notation ecphonétique* (Copenhague, 1935), pp. 71-6 et V. Gheorghiu, op. cit., pp. 7-8.

[4] V. Gheorghiu, op. cit., pp. 10-11.

Bibliothèque de la Métropolie ou de l'Académie Princière de Jassy.[5]

Une première mention de l'existence du dit manuscrit est faite par A. D. Xenopol et Erbiceanu, dans l'ouvrage *Serbarea Scolară de la Iaşi cu ocazia împlinirii a 50 de ani de la înfiinţarea învăţămîntului superior în Moldova* (La Fête Scolaire de Jassy à l'occasion du cinquantenaire de la fondation de l'enseignement supérieur en Moldavie). En 1885, le manuscrit se trouvait à la Bibliothèque Universitaire de Jassy.

N. G. Dossios rappelle à nouveau, en 1902, son existence à Jassy et fixe son ancienneté au dixième siècle.[6]

Sur la page 2v et 3r est écrite en rouge la liste des 18 péricopes, chacune avec ses premiers mots: 1) le Dimanche de Pâques; 2) le Lundi de Pâques; 3) le Dimanche de l'Octave de Pâques (*in albis*); 4) la mi-temps des cinquante jours après Pâques; 5) l'Ascension; 6) la Pentecôte; 7) la Transfiguration; 8) la Dormition de la Sainte-Vierge (l'Assomption); 13) la Nativité; 14) vigile de l'Epiphanie; 15) l'Epiphanie du Seigneur; 16) la Purification; 17) l'Annonciation; 18) les Saints Anargyres. En plus de ces péricopes, le manuscrit contient encore une péricope de l'Evangile selon St. Mathieu (chap. XVIII, 11–20) écrite plus tard, sans notation musicale, qui se lit le Lundi après la Pentecôte (p. 66r–67r). A partir de la p. 4v commence la série des péricopes empruntées à l'Evangile de Pâques. Dans la partie gauche de chaque péricope, sauf pour celle de la Nativité, est placé le titre de la péricope, écrit en lettres d'or dans un parallélogramme, inscrit à son tour dans un rectangle contenant des figures géométriques en or, bleu, vert, ainsi que des guirlandes de fleurs dans les quatre coins. Ces ornements sont travaillés de main de maître, avec un grand sens artistique qui suscite l'admiration du chercheur.

Les péricopes sont écrites sur des feuillets de parchemin un peu jaunis, aux marges dorées; au total, 156 feuillets. Chaque page contient huit rangées de lettres onciales grecques, écrites avec un art achevé et finement ornementées. On ne saurait ne pas admirer l'exactitude de forme des mêmes lettres tout au

---

[5] V. Gheorghiu, op. cit., pp. 28-9.
[6] N. G. Dossios, *Studii greco-romane*, p. 1, fasc. II et III, p. 91, d'après V. Gheorghiu, op. cit., pp. 28-30.

long du manuscrit. Les lettres initiales des péricopes et des
commencements de phrase plus longues sont de plus grande
dimension que les autres, contournées de rouge et le corps doré.
On y trouve des ornements en forme de coeur, de feuilles de
trèfle, de pomme ou de poire, de couleur bleue ou verte. Les
lettres initiales comprises dans le texte même de la péricope
sont plus petites et déplacées vers la gauche. Les mots les plus
fréquents sont écrits en abrégé: la première et la dernière
lettre. L'écriture en est continue, c'est-à-dire que les mots ne
sont pas séparés par la ponctuation. Seuls les esprits au-dessus
des lettres grecques marquent les commencements des mots.
La fin des phrases plus longues est marquée d'une croix dorée
formée de cinq points. Celle de la péricope, d'un coeur ou
d'une feuille de trèfle.

En ce qui concerne *l'époque où ce manuscrit a été écrit*, V.
Gheorghiu est d'avis qu'il date de la fin du huitième siècle ou
du début du neuvième siècle, et cela pour les raisons suivantes:

1. Le manuscrit ne contient aucune figure d'évangéliste,
ce qui dénote qu'il a été écrit à l'époque icônoclaste (726–842)
lorsque la reproduction des Saints par la peinture était in-
terdite.[7]

2. A la page 2, en-haut, se trouve une note qui mentionne:
'Souvenez-vous Seigneur des âmes de vos serviteurs Constantin
et de son épouse Marie.' Il s'agirait ici, suivant V. Gheorghiu,
de l'Empereur Constantin VI et de son épouse Marie, qui
auraient à leurs frais fait écrire le manuscrit. On suppose que
Marie, son ancienne épouse, aurait copié ce manuscrit durant
sa détention dans un monastère.[8]

De l'existence de certains mots latins écrits au-dessus du
texte grec, aux pages 95v, 98v et 99v, on conclue que ce manuscrit aurait été employé aussi par le Patriarche latin de
Constantinople, installé en 1204 lors de l'établissement de
l'Empire Latin par les Croisés et qui aurait fait ajouter les mots
latins afin de permettre une lecture plus aisée du texte grec.[9]

La musique du manuscrit

Si l'on examine attentivement une péricope évangélique du
manuscrit, notre intérêt sera éveillé par l'existence de signes de

[7] V. Gheorghiu, op. cit., p. 18.   [8] V. Gheorghiu, op. cit., pp. 22-3.
[9] V. Gheorghiu, op. cit., p. 24.

couleur rouge, écrits au-dessus, au-dessous ou entre les mots du texte à la fin des propositions. Ils ont des formes diverses: lignes simples ou doubles, lignes droites, obliques vers la gauche ou vers la droite, lignes courbes, en zig-zag, des groupes de trois points et à la fin des phrases une croix dorée. Ils constituent ce que l'on appelle la *'notation ecphonétique'*, le premier système de notation musicale chrétienne en usage entre le sixième et le quatorzième siècle.[10] Cette notation avait pour but de 'faciliter la lecture des textes du culte, en marquant les différentes parties des morceaux d'écriture et en indiquant la manière de les moduler selon leur importance et leur place.'[11]

L'évangéliaire de Jassy emploie les signes ecphonétiques suivants:

Signes simples		Signes composés	
Oxia	⟋	Oxia doubles	⟋⟋
Varia	⟍	Varia doubles	∖∖
Syrmatiki	⤳	Chentima	
Cathisti	⌐	Apeso exo	, ... ⟋
Cremasti	⟍		
Synemba	⌣	Hypocrisis	⸵
Paraclitiki	⸜ ⸝		
Apostrophos	⸴		
Telia	+		

---

[10] I. Tzetzes, "Ἡ ἐπινόησις τῆς σημαντικῆς τῶν . . . χειρογράφων τῶν ἀνατολικῶν ἐκκλησιῶν', *Parnassos*, ix (1885), pp. 413-93; J. B. Thibaut, *Origine Byzantine de la notation neumatique de l'église latine* (Paris, 1907); E. Wellesz, 'Die byzantinischen Lektionszeichen', *Zeitschrift f. Musikwiss*, xi (1929), pp. 515-34; idem, *A History of Byzantine Music and Hymnography*[2] (Oxford, 1961), p. 249; C. Höeg, op. cit., pp. 15 et 127.

[11] Le Père I. D. Petresco, *Les idiomèles e le Canon de l'Office de Noël* (Paris, 1932), p. 39.

Suivant le R.P. I. D. Petresco, l'étymologie des signes ecphonétiques s'explique par leur forme graphique:

Oxia = accent aigu
Varia = accent grave
Apostrophos = tourné en sens contraire
Synemba = trait d'union
Telia = chose achevée
Syrmatiki = ondulation
Cathisti = accent circonflexe
Cremasti = petit crochet
Paraclitiki = inclinaison
Chentimata = points
Hypocrisis = explication, réponse[12]

En ce qui concerne la signification musicale de la notation ecphonétique, Egon Wellesz accorde aux signes l'acception suivante:

Oxia = indique l'élévation de la voix
Syrmatiki = le mouvement ondulatoire
Varia = baisse de la voix avec accent
Cremasti = élévation de la voix avec une légère accen-
          tuation
Apostrophos = baisse de la voix sans accent
Synemba = sorte de legato
Paraclitiki = exécution dans un mode de prière et
             d'imploration
Hypocrisis = signe de séparation, peut-être une pause plus
            longue ou plus courte
Telia = arrêt complet
Cathisti = style narratif sans emphase[13]

En essayant de déchiffrer le manuscrit de Jassy d'après les indications de Wellesz, je n'ai pu obtenir un résultat satisfaisant, car, les signes ecphonétiques n'indiqueraient pas, selon lui, la marche précise de la voix, mais seulement d'une manière vague l'élévation ou la baisse de la voix avec ou sans emphase.

J'ai essayé une autre interprétation des signes d'après les indications plus anciennes de Carsten Höeg qui est d'avis que

[12] Le Père I. D. Petresco, op. cit., p. 38.
[13] E. Wellesz, *History of Byzantine Music*, 1961, pp. 252-4.

chaque groupe de signes ecphonétiques (incise) indiquerait
une mélodie brève ou une formule mélodique.[14] Par exemple:

le groupe de signes

contiendrait la formule mélodique suivante: *mi, faa, fa, fa, mi,
faa, laa, faa*. Il y a en tout 14 formules mélodiques dans une
péricope. Höeg a identifié ces formules mélodiques d'après une
mélodie mnémotechnique appartenant au douzième siècle qui
portait, écrits au-dessous, en groupe pair, tous les signes
ecphonétiques. La signification que Höeg attribue aux signes
ne m'a pas, non plus, aidé à déchiffrer la notation, pour les
raisons suivantes:

1. Si les signes avaient indiqué des formules mélodiques,
leur écriture au-dessus ou au-dessous du texte évangélique
n'aurait pas été nécessaire.

2. Les signes sont écrits sous la mélodie mnémotechnique
afin d'être plus facilement mémorisés et non pas en vue d'une
signification mélodique.

3. Les formules mélodiques ne peuvent s'adapter à tous les
textes, étant donné que ceux-ci diffèrent les uns des autres, l'un
étant formé de plusieurs mots que l'autre, plus long ou plus
court, avec des propositions de longueur différente, etc.

4. Aussi bien qu'un exécutant les eût pu connaître, il
n'aurait quand même pu, pratiquement, les appliquer sans
confondre les formules mélodiques.

5. Certains signes sont inversés et dès lors on se demande:
comment pourrait-on inverser, de mémoire, la formule
mélodique à la place indiquée?

Et Höeg lui-même de reconnaître que la transcription
rencontre de 'nombreuses difficultés' et que son essai 'ne
représente qu'une adaptation possible, mais non la seule'.[15]

Egon Wellesz, se rapportant à cette transcription, dit que
Höeg 'ne nous fournit pas l'intervalle exact des cadences de la
mélodie'.[16]

Devant tant de difficultés d'interprétation et de transcription,
j'ai essayé une méthode propre, en m'appuyant d'une part sur
les observations comparatives des signes de toutes les péricopes
et des autres manuscrits, et — d'autre part — en tenant

[14] C. Höeg, op. cit., pp. 21-31.
[16] E. Wellesz, *History of Byzantine Music*, p. 257.
[15] C. Höeg, op. cit., p. 32.

compte du maintien, grâce à la tradition, jusqu'à nos jours, du mode de lecture récitative de l'Evangile et des récitatifs liturgiques en général. D'ailleurs, A. Gastoué aussi nous recommande pour le déchiffrage de ces textes d'avoir recours à la méthode du rapprochement des récitatifs traditionnels rééls et anciens.[17]

Le R.P. I. D. Petresco, l'unique chercheur de notre pays en matière de musique ancienne byzantine et défricheur de nouvelles voies dans l'oeuvre de recherche de cette précieuse musique, recommande la confrontation des textes musicaux notés, que nous donne la musique vivante, avec les textes théoriques et la tradition — même écrite —, que nous conservent les manuscrits qui datent d'après le Moyen-Age.[18] E. Wellesz, en parlant des signes musicaux du *Codex Sinaïticus 8*, affirme lui-même que ce récitatif semble être très proche de la 'cantillation' actuelle (de la manière actuelle — disons-nous — de lire l'Evangile).[19]

La manière dont les signes musicaux sont distribués et placés dans le manuscrit de Jassy nous convainct qu'il s'agit d'un récitatif simple, sans formules mélodiques, dont les signes acquièrent une signification suivant leur endroit: au-dessus, au-dessous, au milieu du texte ou à la fin, et suivant le rapport de chaque groupe avec le son de base du récitatif:

1. Au-dessus du texte on trouve les signes suivants

1. Au-dessus du texte on trouve les signes suivants

ce qui nous indiquerait l'élévation de la voix à une certaine distance par rapport au ton de base du récitatif, à l'exception de la *varia* qui baisse.

2. Au-dessous du texte nous trouvons   et   ce qui indiquerait une baisse de la voix à l'exception du dernier qui est le point de départ du récitatif (le ton de base).

3. Le groupe hypocrisis   est écrit entre les mots, probablement parce qu'il aurait occupé plus de place si on

---

[17] A. Gastoué, *Catalogue des manuscrits de musique byzantine*, p. 12.
[18] I. D. Petresco, *Aspecte si probleme ale muzicii bizantine medievale*, p. 99 seqq., dans *Studii de Muzicologie*, Vol. I.
[19] E. Wellesz, *History of Byzantine Music*, p. 257.

l'avait écrit en-dessous du texte; c'est le signe qui indique le son le plus grave du récitatif.

4. La fin de la phrase ou de la péricope est marquée par le signe ✚ , ce qui nous indique le retour de la voix au son du début.

Pour choisir le mode ou la gamme dans lesquels se développe le récitatif évangélique de Jassy, nous tiendrons compte de la dénomination même de 'ecphonétique' signifiant 'lecture à haute voix' et de la lecture traditionnelle qui utilise le mode de *do* (*Ni*) dans le registre élevé. Par conséquent, nous choisissons le mode de *do*, tel que de nos jours encore on le fait pour la lecture de l'évangile.

Dans le MS de Jassy le récitatif se développe généralement dans le cadre d'une quinte: *sol-re'*, tel que d'habitude il se présente aussi actuellement. Rarement il dépasse le son *re'*, mais seulement comme broderie; dans le registre grave, il atteint exceptionnellement jusqu'au *fa*.

Le résultat de notre examen comparatif portant sur cette notation, peut être résumé dans le tableau suivant:

Signes simples

Cathisti ▬▬▂ représente le son de base du récitatif: *do'*

Oxia ⌒ monte une seconde par rapport au ton de base et signifie *re'*

Cremasti ⟋ monte une seconde accentuée (*re'*) ou avec plus d'emphase

Syrmatiki ⟿ est un ornement qui, d'après la forme du signe, indiquerait le groupe de sons *si, do'', si, do', re'*. C'est encore une seconde ascendante ornée vers le bas.

Paraclitiki ⸙ ⸙ seconde ascendante ornée d'un mordant: *re'mi're'*. D'après la graphie du signe on voit que c'est un oxia muni d'un zig-zag.

Synemba ⌣ c'est le legato qui relie deux mots

L'apostrophe ⟩ descend une seconde légère à partir du son de base et peut représenter les sons *do', si, la* ou *sol*.

Varia ❭ descend une seconde accentuée, *si, la* ou *sol*.

Telia ✝ est le signe final de toute proposition musicale et indique le son de base *do'*.

Signes composés

Le double oxia 𝅘 monte d'une seconde accentuée et prolonge la durée (*re'*).

La double varia 𝅖 descend d'une seconde accentuée et prolonge la durée, représentant: *si, la* ou *sol*.

Les chentimas . . . représentent le son *re'* brodé de la note supérieure: *re'mi're'*.

Apeso exo ⸒ . . . 𝅗 désigne la seconde inférieure et le passage à la seconde supérieure: *si... do'... re'*.

Hypocrisis ⸴ trois apostrophes qui indiquent une quarte descendante à partir du son de base *do'*. Ce signe représente toujours le son *sol* grave.

Tous ces signes sont utilisés et n'ont de signification que par pair, identiques ou différents, tel par exemple:

■▄ . . ■▄ ⸒ . . . 𝅗

Dans notre ouvrage sur la notation, nous donnons un tableau de toutes les combinaisons de signes ecphonétiques se trouvant dans le manuscrit de Jassy. Signalons, pour l'instant, que le signe Cathisti dispose de 5 combinaisons, Telia — de 7, le groupe de signes ascendants répétés — de 5, descendants répétés — aussi de 5 et signes ascendants et descendants — 6. De l'étude comparative des 18 péricopes, il résulte:

1. 14 péricopes commencent par le groupe cathisti = *do'... do'*

2. Toutes les phrases initiales finissent par l'un des groupes:

𝅗. . . . ✝ 𝅘. . . . ✝ ⁓ . . . ✝ ⸒ . . . ✝

3. Toutes les périodes initiales ont dans leur schéma l'une des incises suivantes:

A ■▄ . . . ■▄ ■ B ⸒ . . . ⸒ C 𝅗 . . . ✝

amplifiées de la manière la plus variée.

Dans la partie médiane des péricopes, on trouve les groupes ci-dessus utilisés de manière très variée selon le texte en cause et les idées que l'exécutant doit souligner. Ainsi, par exemple, il existe des phrases typiques pour les affirmations, les interrogations, les réponses, les interrogations et réponses, les invocations etc. Nous les signalons dans notre ouvrage dans une table détaillée de chaque groupe de signes avec ses combinaisons multiples.

De la comparaison des phrases finales des péricopes, il résulte:

1. 11 péricopes se terminent avec l'incise ꝑ . . . ꝑ (do'... do') précédée du groupe des chentimas.

2. 7 péricopes ont la phrase formée d'oxia doubles et de varia doubles, ce qui dénote une intensification du récitatif et un allongement appréciable des durées.

3. 6 phrases finales reproduisent à l'aide de signes simples les phrases avec des signes doubles des autres péricopes, ce qui signifie que le final des péricopes à signes doubles devait se faire avec plus d'intensité, alors que ceux à signes simples se faisaient de manière habituelle, comme dans la partie médiane de la péricope.

4. 3 péricopes s'achèvent de manière inaccoutumée sur le *sol* ou le *fa*. Ce sont des finals qui tendaient à disparaître, pour être remplacés par des signes doublés (finals intenses) qui constituent la caractéristique des manuscrits de l'époque classique (10ᵉ–12ᵉ S.).

La détermination de la date du MS de Jassy

La notation ecphonétique apparaît et se développe à partir du sixième siècle jusque vers la fin du quatorzième siècle pour disparaître ensuite. C. Höeg considère quatre époques: 1) archaïque (6ᵉ–7ᵉ siècles); 2) époque de fixation et de consolidation de la notation (8ᵉ–9ᵉ siècles); 3) époque classique (10ᵉ–12ᵉ siècles); 4) époque de la décadence et de la disparition (13ᵉ–14ᵉ siècles).[20]

La notation du manuscrit appartient à l'époque de fixation et de consolidation de la notation ecphonétique (8ᵉ–9ᵉ siècles) parce qu'elle dénote l'existence de signes propres à cette

[20] C. Höeg, op. cit., pp. 108 et 137.

époque, et parce qu'on y trouve des finals à signes doubles à
côté d'autres à signes simples et portant sur d'autres sons que
celui de base du récitatif. Outre ces particularités, il présente
le groupe Syrmatiki utilisé rien que sous sa forme simple.

Le groupe Hypocrisis formé de deux apostrophes ne s'y
trouve nulle part, cependant que l'emploi double du groupe
de 3 apostrophes est, parfois, remplacé dans une forme abrégée,
telle que

Le groupe des Chentimas est immanquablement employé en
final et ce n'est que fort rarement qu'il est utilisé dans la partie
médiane des péricopes et jamais dans deux groupes consécutifs.
Si la notation du manuscrit peut être attribuée, pour les
motifs ci-dessus, au 8e–9e siècles, la calligraphie du texte
évangélique suggère une autre hypothèse : à comparer l'écriture
du manuscrit de Jassy avec une page du *Codex Sinaïticus graecus*
204 (Leningrade),[21] on constate de suite l'identité de l'écriture
et de la notation musicale (voir en ce sens les exemples de la
page 12/13). Sur la planche publiée par Egon Wellesz (rangées I
et II de gauche) se trouvent les versets 26–28 de l'Evangile
selon St. Jean, chap. I. Si l'on compare ces versets à ceux du
manuscrit de Jassy (2e Evangile, du Lundi de Pâques, partie
finale, pp. 17r–18r), on observe que les lettres en sont identique-
ment calligraphiées, les incises de la notation sont pareilles,
à cette différence près, néanmoins, que sur la planche du Codex
Sinaïticus, au-dessus du mot ἵνα se trouve un oxia, tandis que
dans le manuscrit de Jassy il y a une syrmatiki. De même dans
la seconde rangée du Codex Sinaïticus, on trouve les mots
ὅπου ἦν qui ont des varia simples, alors que dans le manuscrit
de Jassy ils ont des varia doubles. On ne peut que regretter que
le manuscrit de Jassy ne contienne pas le passage selon St. Luc
(24, 12–15) afin d'y pouvoir établir une comparaison avec
celui du Codex Sinaïticus.

[21] Voir V. Benechević, *Monumenta Sinaitica II. Tafel 39.* La planche est publiée
par E. Wellesz dans *Byz. Musik* (Breslau, 1927), p. 86.

S'il est vrai que la planche appartienne au dixième siècle, le manuscrit de Jassy peut aussi bien, dans ce cas, être attribué au même siècle, au point de vue de la calligraphie. Il se pourrait que ce soit une copie écrite au dixième siècle d'après un manuscrit des huitième ou neuvième siècles. N'ayant pas eu à notre disposition le second volume de V. Benechević, ainsi que d'autres manuscrits ecphonétiques, pour y comparer aussi d'autres péricopes, nous nous limitons à émettre aussi cette hypothèse qu'il faudra examiner et vérifier à l'avenir.

Par conséquent, à en juger d'après la notation musicale et la calligraphie du texte, le manuscrit de Jassy pourrait être attribué aux 8ᵉ–10ᵉ siècles inclusivement. C'est aussi l'avis de M. Mihai Regleanu, paléographe des Archives de l'Etat, qui pense que pendant ces siècles la calligraphie s'est maintenue plus ou moins la même et que par conséquent on est en droit de situer le manuscrit dans ce cadre historique.

La présentation, bien que sommaire, du manuscrit de Jassy, nous permet cependant de tirer les conclusions suivantes, concernant son importance en tant que très ancien monument de la musique chrétienne:

1. Les signes musicaux du MS de Jassy représentent des sons plus ou moins fixes et non des formules musicales.

2. La lecture de l'Evangile se faisait sur le ton d'un récitatif mélodique simple, qui tenait compte de l'accent des mots, de l'accent principal des phrases et des membres de phrase.

3. Le récitatif évangélique n'était pas laissé à la libre improvisation du moment du lecteur, mais — étant noté — il était réglé par une tradition unitaire de la lecture, établie par écrit, dans le monde chrétien, laquelle donnait au texte l'interprétation musicale répondant au contenu d'idées en cause. De cette manière, la lecture émouvait les auditeurs, parce que la notation même indiquait au lecteur le caractère d'émotivité du texte.

4. Le cadre dans lequel se mouvait le récitatif était la quinte *sol-re'*. A titre d'exception, il touchait au *mi'* comme broderie du *re'* et dans le registre grave atteignait le *sol* et le *fa*.

5. La grande importance du manuscrit de Jassy réside dans le fait qu'il nous donne, indirectement, une idée de la manière dont on récitait les prières, les ecphonises, les ecthénies, et tous

les récitatifs, pendant le 8ᵉ–10ᵉ siècles, tant à Byzance que probablement aussi dans nos contrées.

Nous donnons en transcription occidentale le début et la fin de l'Evangile du Dimanche de Pâques (f. 5r, 5v et f. 11v) (Jean, chap. I, 1–4 et 17). (Voir p. 140).

Nous mentionnons par ailleurs que certains mots du texte original ne disposent pas des esprits et des accents adéquats, et ni du iota écrit au-dessous, parce que — à notre avis — il s'agit d'une écriture onciale.

NOTE

Though the essay on the Jaşi Evangelion has already been published in a musical journal in the author's country we have included it in the present volume because it raises an important question which is indicated in the title by the words 'a new interpretation'. G. Panţiru sees in the ekphonetic signs indications of melodic formulae of fixed pitch, because today the solemn reading of the lessons is done in a kind of recitative with added melodic phrases and, occasionally, of richly developed melismata. We must state, however, that even today no uniformity exists of singing the same chant to the same ekphonetic signs, nor did such a uniformity exist in the great days of Byzantine liturgy. From the investigations into the ekphonetic notation by Papadopoulos-Kerameus in *Μαυροκορδάτειος βιβλιοθήκη* (1884) p. 50, by J.-B. Thibaut in 'Le chant ekphonétique' in *B.Z.* VIII (1899) pp. 122–47 and *Origine Byzantine de la Notation Neumatique de l'Église Latine* (1907) pp. 17–32, by O. Fleischer in *Neumen-Studien* I (1895) pp. 25–75, it can be seen that all scholars agree about the origin of the ekphonetic notation. They state that the signs derived from the prosodic system of the Greek grammarians. Their purpose was to remind the Anagnostes, the Reader, which phrase had to be treated as a simple narration, which words had to be emphasized, and finally to indicate the end of the lesson.

Had the melodic line been shown as clearly by the ekphonetic signs as G. Panţiru assumes it was, the setting of the signs to a phrase of the lesson would have had to be identical in all the Evangelia, but that is not the case: C. Høeg has given in his *La Notation Ekphonétique, M.M.B. Subsidia I. 2*, pp. 86–94 the lesson from Matth. 18: 10–20, based on the collation of approximately two hundred Evangelia from the eighth to the fourteenth centuries. It emerges from the study of the text and the *apparatus criticus* that the variants in the ekphonetic groupings are so extensive that they do not permit us to interpret the signs musically. This statement, however, does not mean that the lessons were not chanted, i.e. produced in elated speech, but it rules out the suggestion that the ekphonetic signs were indicating definite melodic formulae. G. Panţiru refers, as a proof of his theory, to the table from the Prophetologion Sinaiticus 8 which C. Høeg published on p. 21 of his *Notation Ekphonétique*. At first glance it seems that the table of ekphonetic signs with superimposed 'palaeobyzantine notation' would support the theory of fixed melodic note value, but Høeg found difficulties in adapting the musical notation even approximately to the words. A decisive factor against Panţiru's theory is Høeg's statement that among the vast number of manuscripts which he examined he did not find even two identical ones; there are, in fact, too many variants and exceptions in the notation to build up a strict system of rules. We must content ourselves with professing that we cannot go further than to accept a number of monastic versions of cantillation based on oral tradition. The present melodic way of *lectio solemnis* is generally regarded as a fairly late development which came into use after the fourteenth century when the meaning of the ekphonetic signs had become obsolete.

Based on Gheorgiu's investigation, the author ascribes the Evangelion to the time of the iconoclastic controversy, i.e. to the eighth century or the ninth. Dating of Uncial Codices is not an easy task, particularly in the case of richly produced and bound Evangelia. From the photographs it can be seen that the Codex is written in that kind of archaizing script for which V. Gardthausen used the term 'Prunkunciale' or, more exactly 'Liturgical Uncial'. The term is applied to manuscripts of the 'ninth, tenth, and eleventh centuries in which the old Uncial of the fifth and sixth centuries is imitated, in order to enhance the importance of the Codex. In copying from an older manuscript the scribe was often forced to change at the end of a line the shape of the letters, originally written in circles and squares = ○ and □, into 〇 and 〼. This gives a clue to a later date, and so does e.g. the form of 'P with a long stem and that of X, treated in the same way. We must look at the cross-bars of ℗, marked by pendent triangular strokes, and horizontal strokes of ΓΔΤΎ. All these peculiarities point to the last stage of uncial writing before it was superseded by minuscules. The neumator, i.e. the monk who added the signs for the Ekphonesis, set them in a coarser type than that which is generally found in ninth and tenth-century codices; they have the shape known as 'Slavonic' (cf. New Palaeogr. Soc. Fasc. I) or 'Praeslavonic' (V. Gardthausen, *Griech. Palaeographie*[2], p. 151) which can be immediately observed in the two pages of the eleventh-century Kuprianovski Evangelion published by R. Palikarova Verdeil in *La Musique Byzantine chez les Bulgares et les Russes, M.M.B. Subsidia VIII*, plates VIII and IX.

E. WELLESZ.

9

Christos Patrinelis

ATHENS, GREECE

Protopsaltae, Lampadarii, and Domestikoi of the Great Church during the post-Byzantine Period (1453–1821)[1]

THIS paper is a part of a larger study on the officials of the Great Church during the post-Byzantine period and deals specifically with the Protopsaltae, the Lampadarii, and the Domestikoi of the Great Church, i.e. the officials who served in the two choirs of the patriarchal church of Constantinople from 1453 to 1821.[2] Although these officials did not play a particularly significant role in the administration of the Patriarchate, they are of great interest to the students of Byzantine music, because they were as a group the most important composers of their time and the primary continuators—and often reformers—of the Byzantine musical tradition. Together they have left an impressive body of musical work, which represents the largest and best part of the post-Byzantine musical output in the Eastern Church. The examination of their musical work as such, however, falls outside the scope of this paper. Our main purpose is to present a list of persons who held the offices in question, and to determine the exact period of time during which each one served in the

---

[1] The present paper is a revision of one published in Greek under the title 'Συμβολαὶ εἰς τὴν ἱστορίαν τοῦ Οἰκουμενικοῦ Πατριαρχείου. Α', Πρωτοψάλται, Λαμπαδάριοι καὶ Δομέστικοι τῆς Μεγάλης Ἐκκλησίας (1453-1821)', *Mnemosyne*, ii (Athens, 1969), pp. 64-93+4 plates.

[2] One need hardly explain why 1453 was chosen as an early limit of the period covered by this paper. The year 1821, used here as the other time limit, was again a turning point in the history of Byzantine music; by this time the so-called Chrysanthine reform of the musical notation was completed and signalled the beginning of a new period.

respective office. Thus, our research is of historical rather than musicological character. The usefulness of such research is apparent: the reliable dating of these dominant representatives of the Byzantine musical tradition provides musicologists with an indispensable historical framework within which the development of Byzantine music must be studied.

Our study also has a direct bearing on musical palaeography, because the dating of the musicians provides a sound basis for the dating and evaluation of the musical manuscripts. Obviously, any manuscript containing the works of a given composer must have been written either during his lifetime or later. This simple observation acquires considerable importance in view of the fact that a host of musical manuscripts are dated incorrectly. In the process of research for this paper it became apparent, at least to this author, that very frequently manuscripts have been dated one or even two centuries earlier than the lifetime of the composers whose works they contain! One hardly needs to say that such erroneous dating can mislead (and indeed has often misled) students of the history of Byzantine music.

It is useful also to state here the method followed and the limits set for our study. No attempt is made to give a full biography of the officials concerned, a task that in many instances would have been impossible. The data sought and listed are the following: the correct name of each official, the office or offices which he held, the time of his appointment, and the duration of his tenure of the office(s).

The bibliography concerning each person is also given, but only information pertinent to the points listed above is utilized. I have used only those sources that seemed to me more reliable, and from such sources I have extracted passages which help establish one or more of the points that concern this paper. Corroborating evidence from other sources is deliberately left out. A second source is cited only in cases where it offers information additional to that in the first source.

A separate section is devoted to each official. His name is printed at the top of the relevant section, and is followed by the dates of his earliest and latest mention in the sources as holder of the office. These dates do not therefore necessarily coincide with the beginning and end of his tenure of the office.

The main sources for this study were patriarchal documents, which are occasionally signed also by one or more of the officials examined here, collections of letters from scholars and church dignitaries of the time, old 'Books of Accounts' of the Ecumenical Patriarchate, and most frequently the descriptions of musical manuscripts of the fifteenth to early nineteenth centuries. The dated manuscripts from those centuries were particularly useful, because they supply a secure *terminus ante quem* concerning the composers whose works they contain. Furthermore, several manuscripts bear the *ex libris* or other notes by the officials examined here, who appear to have been also the primary collectors and copyists of musical manuscripts throughout the period studied.

A very useful source of information was also the monumental Θεωρητικὸν Μέγα τῆς Μουσικῆς by Chrysanthos of Madytos (d. 1843), written in 1818–19 and printed at Trieste in 1832 (hereafter referred to as Chrysanthos, *Theoretikon*). In the second part of this book (paginated with Roman numerals) Chrysanthos provides brief biographical notes on the important musicians of the Eastern Church. For the period 1780–1818 his book can be treated as a contemporary source, because Chrysanthos either knew personally the officials concerned or had the benefit of his teacher's (Petros Byzantios) acquaintance with them. It is noteworthy that Chrysanthos' work has been the main if not the only source for all later scholars who have dealt with the history of Byzantine music after the fall of Constantinople. Of these scholars the following ones are worthy of special note:

Manuel Gedeon published several studies on particular problems (see the references below in the footnotes) and also a list of the protopsaltae of the Great Church from 1453 on.[3] The list merely gives the names of thirteen protopsaltae; the names of the first four of them, however, must be eliminated,[4] since we do not have the slightest evidence that they were ever protopsaltae of the Great Church. As to the rest, Gedeon gives more or less approximate dates, without specifying

---

[3] M. Gedeon, 'Πρωτοψάλται τοῦ πατριαρχικοῦ ναοῦ', *Ecclesiastike Aletheia*, iv (1884), pp. 644-5.
[4] Namely Xenos Korones, Gregorios Bounes Alyates, Gerasimos and Georgios, who supposedly covered the period 1453-80.

the length of their tenure in the office,[5] and without citing sources.

The book of G. Papadopoulos, Συμβολαὶ εἰς τὴν ἱστορίαν τῆς παρ'ἡμῖν ἐκκλησιαστικῆς μουσικῆς (Athens, 1890), contains abundant material which, however, the author did not manage to handle critically. Hence it is of dubious usefulness today. His biographical information on post-Byzantine musicians is partly of legendary character and often incorrect, particularly with respect to composers who lived prior to the middle of the eighteenth century.[6] Papadopoulos's book, however, has been the standard reference work for the students of post-Byzantine musicians and musical manuscripts, and has often misled several scholars into confusion and errors.[7]

Sophronios Eustratiades compiled a lengthy list of ecclesiastical composers with references (often incorrect) to Athos manuscripts containing their works, but he did not attempt to give dates.[8]

C. M. Ralles published three short articles on the offices of protopsaltes, lampadarios, and domestikos respectively,[9] which, however, are studied from a canonical rather than a historical aspect.

[5] E.g. for Georgios Raedestinos, Gedeon notes: 'of uncertain time'; for Ioannes Trapezountios he simply remarks that 'he flourished about 1750', whereas, as will be shown below, Trapezountios had been an active singer of the Great Church from at least 1727 to 1769.

[6] He confuses, e.g. the fifteenth-century lampadarios Manuel Chrysaphes with Chrysaphes the New, whose activity is placed by Papadopoulos around 1600, i.e. two generations earlier than the time he really lived (c. 1660); Georgios Raedestinos is dated to 1680, while it is known that he was a teacher of Chrysaphes the New; Chalatzoglou is said to have died in 1748, while he must have died in or before 1736.

[7] See e.g. A. Gastoué, Catalogue des manuscrits de musique byzantine (Paris, 1907), p. 3, where the time of activity of Chrysaphes the New is placed in the sixteenth century (instead of mid-seventeenth); ibid., p. 68, Georgios Raedestinos is dated 'vers 1680'; also see L. Tardo, L'antica melurgia bizantina (Grottaferrata, 1938), p. 104: 'Crisafi [the New] visse nel 1600.'

[8] S. Eustratiades, ''Εκκλησιαστικοὶ Μελογράφοι', published as an appendix to the work by Spyridon Lavriotes and S. Eustratiades, Catalogue of the Greek Manuscripts in the Library of the Lavra on Mount Athos (Harvard Theological Studies, xii) (Cambridge, Mass., 1925).

[9] K. M. Ralles, 'Περὶ τοῦ ἐκκλησιαστικοῦ ἀξιώματος τοῦ πρωτοψάλτου', Praktika (= Proceedings) of the Academy of Athens, xi (1936), pp. 66-9; also his 'Περὶ τοῦ ἐκκλησιαστικοῦ ἀξιώματος τοῦ λαμπαδαρίου', ibid., ix (1934), pp. 259-61; also his 'Περὶ τοῦ ἐκκλησιαστικοῦ ἀξιώματος τοῦ δομεστίκου', ibid., xii (1937), pp. 294-6.

Finally, A. Boudoures published a lengthy study on the choirs of the Great Church[10] with special emphasis on the liturgical duties of each singer. At the end of his work Boudoures appended name-lists of the protopsaltae, lampadarii, and domestikoi of the Great Church from 1453 on. These lists make no reference to sources, but it is obvious that they are based on Chrysanthos' *Theoretikon* and on the writings of Gedeon and of Papadopoulos (whose errors are repeated).

In treating the particular persons and problems in the pages which follow, I do not usually try to refute the errors that occur in older bibliography, except in cases that they have enough plausibility to mislead scholars or when they have been more or less accepted as valid.[11]

The Choirs of the Great Church during the post-Byzantine Period

The composition of the choirs of the Great Church (i.e. St. Sophia) during the Byzantine period is not adequately known. An interesting but neglected bit of information on this question is provided by Pseudo-Kodinos, who undoubtedly refers to the practice of the mid-fourteenth century: . . . οὐδὲ πρωτοψάλτην ἔχει ἡ [Great] ἐκκλησία, ἀλλὰ δομέστικον, ὁ δὲ βασιλικὸς κλῆρος καὶ ἀμφοτέρους. Καὶ ὁ μὲν πρωτοψάλτης τοῦ βασιλικοῦ ἔξαρχος κλήρου, ὁ δὲ γε δομέστικος τοῦ δεσποινικοῦ· καὶ ποτὲ μὲν ἔχει καὶ ἡ ἐκκλησία ἕτερον δομέστικον παρὰ τὸν δεσποινικόν, ποτὲ δὲ ὁ αὐτὸς καὶ ἀμφοτέροις τοῖς κλήροις ὑπηρετεῖ.[12]

Indeed, it seems that, contrary to what is generally believed, there were no protopsaltae and lampadarii among the singers of the Great Church in Byzantine times.[13] In musical manu-

---

[10] A. Boudoures, Οἱ μουσικοὶ χοροὶ τῆς Μεγάλης τοῦ Χριστοῦ Ἐκκλησίας κατὰ τοὺς κάτω χρόνους, in two parts (Constantinople, 1935-7); it was originally published in sections in *Orthodoxia*, ix (1934) and xii (1937).

[11] A few entries, enclosed in square brackets, are included to aid the discussion of some major cases of well-rooted errors, such as those concerning the pseudo-protopsaltae Gregorios Bounes Alyates and Alexios Eulogemenos as well as Manuel Chrysaphes, who has been wrongly considered a lampadarios of the Great Church.

[12] J. Verpeaux, *Pseudo-Kodinos, Traité des offices* (Paris, 1966), p. 265, line 20ff.

[13] These two offices appear in a list of the offices of the Great Church inserted in Pseudo-Kodinos text in older editions. This list, however, has proved to be a spurious compilation of the sixteenth century (see Verpeaux, op. cit., p. 25). Some other later catalogues of the offices of the Great Church (reproduced in the Bonn edition of Pseudo-Kodinos, pp. 114-15) are equally misleading, since they depend on this spurious list.

scripts we often come across composers referred to as protopsaltae or lampadarii, but these were either singers of parochial or provincial churches—where such offices existed[14]—or they belonged to the so-called 'Royal Clergy', i.e. they were members of the palatine choirs.[15] Nevertheless, in later musical manuscripts several well-known Byzantine composers are explicitly mentioned as protopsaltae or lampadarii of St. Sophia. As a rule, however, these manuscripts do not antedate the seventeenth century, and consequently are not reliable sources of information with regard to the composition of the choirs of the Great Church. This error of the later scribes of musical manuscripts must be obviously attributed to confusion of the provincial or palatine singers with those of St. Sophia.[16]

[14] A document of 1085 is signed by Κωνσταντῖνος πρωτοψάλτης of the bishopric of Hierissos (see J. Bompaire, *Actes de Xéropotamou* (Paris, 1964), pp. 66-7); a certain Νικηφόρος ἀναγνώστης καὶ πρωτοψάλτης of an unknown church is reported in the eleventh century (see H. Omont, 'Notes sur les manuscrits grecs du British Museum', *Bibliothèque de l'École des Chartes*, xlv (1884), p. 36 of the off-print); another Ἰωάννης πρωτοψάλτης τῆς μητροπόλεως Ῥόδου ὁ Κασιανὸς is mentioned in 1223 (see M. Vogel and V. Gardthausen, *Die griechischen Schreiber des Mittelalters und der Renaissance* (Leipzig, 1909), p. 173). For later mentions of provincial protopsaltae see K. Ralles, 'Περὶ τοῦ ἀξιώματος τοῦ πρωτοψάλτου', pp. 67-8. The composition of the choirs of the Byzantine provincial churches is described in a fourteenth-century report on the ecclesiastical offices, published by G. Ralles and M. Potles, Σύνταγμα θείων καὶ ἱερῶν κανόνων, v (Athens, 1855), pp. 536-7: Οἱ δύο δομέστικοι στέκουσι ἐν τοῖς δυσὶ χοροῖς καί ψάλλουσι μετὰ τοῦ πρωτοψάλτου . . . Οἱ δύο πριμικήριοι ἵστανται καὶ αὐτοὶ ἐπάνω τῶν ἱεροδιακόνων [leg. ὑποδιακόνων] καὶ ψάλλουσι μετὰ τοῦ πρωτοψάλτου. Ὁ πρωτοψάλτης ἵσταται ἐν μέσῳ τῆς ἐκκλησίας καὶ ἄρχεται πρῶτος τῆς ψαλμῳδίας καὶ μετὰ τοῦτον οἱ δομέστικοι καὶ πριμικήριοι.

[15] On the singers of the Royal Clergy see Verpeaux, op. cit., pp. 37, 39; Ioannes Cantacuzeni, *Historiarum libri iv*, vol. i (Bonn, 1828), p. 199, lines 18-23; DuCange, *Glossarium* (Lyons, 1688), s.v. ψάλτης; cf. H.-G. Beck, *Kirche und theologische Literatur im byzantinischen Reich* (Munich, 1959), p. 119.

[16] Thus, the renowned Byzantine musician Xenos Korones is often mentioned as protopsaltes of the Great Church, whereas he was protopsaltes of the Royal Clergy, as is explicitly stated in the fifteenth-century Athens MS 885 (see I. Sakkelion, Κατάλογος τῶν χειρογράφων τῆς Ἐθνικῆς Βιβλιοθήκης τῆς Ἑλλάδος (Athens, 1892), p. 160). Also the prolific Byzantine composer Ioannes Kladas is usually called lampadarios of St. Sophia, though he was really lampadarios of the Royal Clergy, as it is attested by Athens MS 2406, written in 1453 (see M. Velimirović, 'Byzantine Composers in MS Athens 2406', *Essays Presented to Egon Wellesz* (Oxford, 1966), p. 16) and by MS 46 of Vlattadon monastery, written in 1591 (see S. Eustratiades, Κατάλογος τῶν ἐν τῇ μονῇ Βλαττέων ἀποκειμένων κωδίκων (Thessalonica, 1918, p. 75).

It must be added that a lampadarios did serve in the Great Church, but his duties were 'to clean the candles', etc., in other words he had nothing to do with music (see Ralles-Potles, op. cit., v, p. 536).

With respect to the singers of the Great Church, what we know with certainty is that in late Byzantine times the choir-leader of St. Sophia was called domestikos, and that sometimes he was also a member of the palatine choir.[17]

For a period of over a century following the Turkish conquest (1453) there is no information concerning the names of the singers or the structure of the choirs of the Great Church, as the Ecumenical Patriarchate continued to be called. It is as late as the 1570s that the first known protopsaltae and lampadarii of the Great Church appear in the sources as leaders of the right and of the left choir of the patriarchal church respectively. Their assistants, the two domestikoi, are mentioned for the first time much later, in the early eighteenth century.

It is worth noting that the offices of the protokanonarchos and of the primikerios—reserved for church singers in the Byzantine period—reappeared in the hierarchy of the Great Church in the sixteenth century, but as offices involving administrative duties. Simple kanonarchoi, however, are reported as secondary members of the choirs of the patriarchal church in the early nineteenth century.[18]

At any rate, Chrysanthos of Madytos, referring to the composition of the choirs of the Great Church, mentions only three kinds of church-singers: the protopsaltes, the lampadarios, and the two domestikoi (distinguished into first and second domestikos, or domestikos of the right and domestikos of the left choir).[19]

Finally, it is worth noting that all the known holders of these

[17] See the Pseudo-Kodinos passage cited above. In earlier times, however, there were two or even four domestikoi of the Great Church (see Philotheos' *Cletorologion*, ed. by J. Bury, *The Imperial Administrative System in Ninth Century with Revised Text of the Kletorologion of Philotheos* (London, 1911), pp. 160, line 12; 163, lines 20 and 35).

[18] See K. Psachos, 'Σημειώματα Κωνσταντίνου τοῦ πρωτοψάλτου', *Phorminx*, 2nd period, vol. iii, No. 16-18 (November-December, 1907), p. 9, where an unnamed kanonarchos of the Great Church is mentioned in 1810.

[19] Chrysanthos, *Theoretikon*, p. 111, n. a: ʿΟ μὲν δεξιὸς πρῶτος ψάλτης ἔχει τὸ ὀφφίκιον νὰ ὀνομάζηται πρωτοψάλτης· ὁ δὲ ἀριστερόθεν πρῶτος ψάλτης ἔχει τὸ ὀφφίκιον νά ὀνομάζηται λαμπαδάριος· οἱ δὲ δεύτεροι ψάλται τοῦ δεξιοῦ καὶ ἀριστεροῦ χοροῦ ἐπονομάζονται δομέστικοι. Cf. the letter of patriarch Paisios to the patriarch of Moscow Nicon, dating from 1655 (published by K. Delikanes, Πατριαρχικὰ ἔγγραφα, iii (Constantinople, 1905), p. 56): Λαμπαδάριος δέ ἐστιν ὁ πρῶτος ψάλτης τοῦ <ἀριστεροῦ> χοροῦ; cf. also Chrysanthos of Jerusalem, Συνταγμάτιον περὶ τῶν ὀφφικίων, Tirgoviste 1715, p. 62: ὁ σήμερον λεγόμενος λαμπαδάριος εἶναι ψάλτης τοῦ ἀριστεροῦ χοροῦ.

three offices were laymen, with the unique exception of the first known protopsaltes, Theophanes Karykes, who was a monk at that time.

PROTOPSALTAE

⟦GREGORIOS BOUNES ALYATES

Chrysanthos was the first to note (*Theoretikon*, p. xxxv and n. 1) that Γρηγόριος ἱερομόναχος Βούνης ὁ 'Αλυάτης . . . ὑπῆρχε πρωτοψάλτης τῆς Μεγάλης 'Εκκλησίας ἐπὶ ἁλώσεως τῆς Κωνσταντινουπόλεως. This bit of information has been often repeated ever since, but it has not been corroborated so far by any older source. What is certain is that a composer and monk named Gregorios Alyates—sometimes also referred to as Gregorios Bounes Alyates—lived a little before the fall of Constantinople. Musical works of his are contained in MS Hierosol. 31, written in 1439/40 (see Papadopoulos Kerameus, 'Ιεροσολυμιτικὴ Βιβλιοθήκη (referred to hereafter as *Hierosol. Bibl.*), v, p. 353; see also Velimirović, *op. cit.*, pp. 13 and 15). In all likelihood he is the same person as the monk of Mount Athos Gregorios Alyates, who copied liturgical and musical manuscripts between the years 1433 and 1447 (see Vladimir, *Sistematičeskoe opisanie rukopisej Moskovskoj Sinodal'noj Biblioteki. I. Rukopisi grečeskija* (Moscow, 1894), p. 593, and Papadopoulos Kerameus in *Vizantijskij Vremennik*, vii (1900), p. 676).⟧

⟦ALEXIOS EULOGEMENOS

In Athos-Vatoped. MS 1085 there is the following note, published by S. Eustratiades and Arcadios Vatopedinos, *Catalogue of the Greek Manuscripts in the Library of the Monastery of Vatopedi on Mount Athos* (hereafter cited as Eustratiades-Arcadios, *Catalogue of MSS. of Vatopedi*) (Cambridge, 1924), p. 191: Θεοῦ τὸ δῶρον καὶ πόνος 'Αλεξίου πρωτοψάλτου καὶ νομοφύλακος τοῦ εὐλογημένου ἐν τῷ πατριαρχικῷ ναῷ Κωνσταντινουπόλεως ἐν μηνὶ νοεμβρίῳ τοῦ ἔτους ͵ϛϡϞβ' [=1483] ἰνδικτιῶνος β'. Eustratiades (in his 'Θρᾶκες μουσικοί', *Epeteris Het. Byzant. Spoudon*, xii (1936), p. 73, n. 1), misinterpreted this note, and thought that Alexios was a protopsaltes of the Great Church (supposedly the first one of the post-Byzantine era) and mistook the word εὐλογημένος as a mere adjective. Nevertheless,

Alexios Eulogemenos is a rather well-known person: he copied several manuscripts between the years 1458 and 1466, and signed them as 'protopsaltes of Arta' in Epirus. Furthermore, a new reading of the note of Vatoped. MS 1085 revealed that after the word πρωτοψάλτης the same hand has added in the margin: "Ἄρτης (see L. Polites, 'Eine Schreiberschule im Kloster τῶν 'Ὁδηγῶν', Byzant. Zeit., li (1958), p. 277; for the activity of Alexios as a scribe see ibid.).]

THEOPHANES KARYKES   1 October 1577–before March 1578

The well-known German pastor Stefan Gerlach has noted in his *Tagebuch* that on 1 and 19 October 1577 he visited the Ecumenical Patriarchate, where he made the acquaintance of several patriarchal officials including the '*Vorsinger . . . mit Nahmen Kariteus von Athene*'.[20] It is evident that Gerlach means Theophanes Karykes of Athens, the well-known musician and subsequently ecumenical patriarch.

In a later entry in his *Tagebuch*, under the date 3 March 1578, Gerlach referred to Theophanes Karykes as ex-protopsaltes: '. . . *der Monch Theophanes welcher bissher* πρωτοψάλτης *oder Vorsinger im Patriarchat*'.[21]

NIKOLAOS OURSINOS DOUKATARES   1586/7

The prominent Greek prelate Gabriel Severos, writing to someone residing in Constantinople, expressed his indignation against the 'tenant' of the patriarchal see, deacon Nikephoros, who, among his other wrongdoings, favoured a certain Nikolaos Oursinos Doukatares: τὰ δὲ περὶ τὸν Δουκατάρην τίς ἂν ἐξαρκέσειε χρόνος ἐξειπεῖν, ὃς πάντων μὲν κρατέειν ἐθέλει, πάντεσσι δ' ἀνάσσειν . . . (lacuna) . . . Οὐρσῖνον καβαλιέρην, ἱππότην, πρωτο-ψάλτην πατριαρχικὸν ἀποκαλεῖν ἀέκοντα ἑκόντα ἐπαναγκάζων.[22]

[20] Stefan Gerlachs, *Des Aelteren Türckisches Tagebuch, aus seinen eigenhändig auf-gesetzten und nachgelassenen Schriften herfürgegeben durch seinen Enkel M. Samuel Gerlach* (Frankfurt am Main, 1674), pp. 389 and 393; also A. Papadopoulos Kerameus, 'Περὶ Θεοφάνους Καρύκη, τοῦ γεγονότος οἰκουμενικοῦ πατριάρχου, ἐπιστολιμαία διατριβὴ' in D. Kambouroglou, *Μνημεῖα τῆς ἱστορίας τῶν 'Ἀθηναίων*, ii (Athens, 1890), pp. 194-5.

[21] Gerlach, op. cit., p. 462.

[22] This letter was published by J. Lamius, *Deliciae eruditorum: Gabrielis Severi et aliorum Grecorum recentiorum epistolae* (Florence, 1744), p. 69; it was republished and commented by X. Siderides, 'Γαβριὴλ Σεβήρου ἱστορικὴ ἐπιστολή', *Ecclesiastikos Pharos*, xi (1913), p. 9.

It seems that Doukatares was named 'patriarchal protopsaltes'
by Nikephoros himself during the time of his vicariate, i.e.
between April or May 1586 and the spring of 1587.[23] Severos'
letter bears no date, but we surmise from internal evidence that
it must have been written in the last months of 1586 or the
beginning of 1587.[24]

GEORGIOS RAEDESTINOS   October 1611–21 February 1638

Athos-Lavra MS 1007 (Θ 145), written in October 1611,
contains musical compositions by protopsaltes Georgios
Raedestinos.[25]

A document dated 21 February 1638 is signed by several
prelates and officials of the Great Church including the
'protopsaltes Georgios',[26] evidently our Raedestinos.

Finally, Chrysaphes the New, in a long note (cited in the
following entry) refers to his 'teacher, kyr Georgios Raedestinos,
protopsaltes of the Great Church of Christ'.

CHRYSAPHES THE NEW   April 1655–1665 or 1680?

Concluding the copying of the musical manuscript Hierosol.
(Patriarchal Library) 4, in April 1655, the protopsaltes of the
Great Church Chrysaphes[27] added the following interesting

---

[23] Dates concerning patriarchs of Constantinople are generally based on the
excellent work of the bishop of Sardeis, Germanos, Συμβολὴ εἰς τοὺς πατρι-
αρχικοὺς καταλόγους Κωνσταντινουπόλεως ἀπὸ τῆς ῾Αλώσεως καὶ ἑξῆς
(Constantinople, 1935). For dates concerning other Greek clergymen I relied
on the relevant articles published in Thrēskeutikē kai Ēthikē Enkyklopaedia, vols.
1-12 (Athens, 1962-8) unless it is otherwise indicated.

[24] Siderides, op. cit., pp. 7-9.

[25] Spyridon Lavriotes and S. Eustratiades, Catalogue of the Greek Manuscripts in the
Library of the Lavra on Mount Athos (hereafter referred to as Spyridon-Eustratiades,
Catalogue of Mss. of Lavra) (Cambridge, Mass., 1925), pp. 155 and 447.

[26] Published in D. Kambouroglou, Μνημεῖα ἱστορίας τῶν ᾿Αθηναίων, ii, p. 170.

[27] It is not clear whether the name Chrysaphes was a family name or a given
name or even a pseudonym assumed by our protopsaltes in his desire to prove
himself equal to the old Chrysaphes (cf. the similar case of several post-Byzantine
musicians called Koukouzeles the New; see Eustratiades in Epeteris Het. Byzant.
Spoudon, xiv (1938), p. 25, n. 2). In connection with Chrysaphes' name Mr.
Markos Dragoumis has kindly informed me that in ms. Bodleian. Canonic.
Gr. 25 (fols. 82r and 94r), written in 1729, the name of Chrysaphes appears as
Panayiotes Chrysaphes the New. One should not hesitate to accept this as the
fuller name of Chrysaphes, if this bit of evidence was corroborated by an older
source. In any case, what is certain is that Chrysaphes the New was not named
Manuel, as he is often called even by recent authors, who evidently confuse him

note (fols. 395v–396r): *Τέλος τῶν καθ'ἤχων καθισμάτων καὶ τῷ Θεῷ δόξα. Εἴληφε τέλος ἡ παροῦσα ἀσματομελη<mark>ρ</mark>ρυτόφθογγος βίβλος ἐν ἔτη ἀπὸ μὲν τῆς κοσμοποιίας ,ζρξγ΄, ἀπὸ δὲ τῆς ἐνσάρκου οἰκονομίας τοῦ Κυρίου καὶ Θεοῦ καὶ Σωτῆρος ἡμῶν Ἰησοῦ Χριστοῦ ,αχνέ΄, μηνὶ Ἀπριλίῳ, ἰνδικτιῶνος η΄, συγγραφεῖσα καὶ ἐκπονηθεῖσα παρ'ἐμοῦ τοῦ εὐτελοῦς καὶ ἐλαχίστου καὶ ἀμαθοῦς, ἁμαρτωλοῦ τε ὑπὲρ πάντας Χρυσάφου δῆθεν καὶ πρωτοψάλτου τῆς Μεγάλης τοῦ Χριστοῦ Ἐκκλησίας, προθύμῳ τῇ ἐπιμελείᾳ καὶ δαπάνῃ καὶ πόνῳ οὐ σμικρῷ συντεθεῖσα καὶ αὐτογραφεῖσα ἐκ παλαιοῦ Στιχιραρίου καὶ ἰδιοχείρου γράμματος τοῦ παλαιοῦ κὺρ Χρυσάφου, τοῦ Ἐμμανουὴλ καὶ λαμπαδαρίου τοῦ εὐαγοῦς καὶ βασιλικοῦ κλήρου, οὐ μέντοι κατὰ τὸ κείμενον τοῦ αὐτοῦ βιβλίου ἐκτονισθεῖσα, ἀλλ'ἐν καινῷ τινι καλλωπισμῷ καὶ μελιρρυτοφθόγγοις νεοφανέσι θέσεσι, καθάπερ τανῦν ἀσματολογεῖται τοῖς μελωδοῦσιν ἐν Κωνσταντινουπόλει. Τοῦτο τοίνυν ὅσον τὸ κατεμὲ ἐφικτὸν παρ'ἐμαυτοῦ γέγονε, κατὰ τὴν ἣν παρέλαβον εἰσήγησιν παρὰ τοῦ ἐμοῦ διδασκάλου κὺρ Γεωργίου τοῦ Ραιδεστινοῦ καὶ πρωτοψάλτου τῆς τοῦ Χριστοῦ Μεγάλης Ἐκκλησίας ἐκτεθηκὼς καὶ τονίσας . . .* [28]

Lesbos-Leimonos monastery MS 260, copied in 1676, contains several musical texts including a *Πανηγυρικὸν Χρυσάφου εἰς τὸν Ἱεροσολύμων Νεκτάριον*,[29] which certainly must have been composed after Nektarios' appointment as patriarch of Jerusalem, i.e. January 1661.

The scribe of the musical manuscript Patmos 930, Germanos, bishop of Neae Patrae and a well-known composer, inserted in the manuscript (fols. 425v–426r) a long note of his own, dated August 1665; in this note Germanos refers to Chrysaphes as his teacher and as still active protopsaltes of the Great Church: . . . *τούτου χάριν κἀγὼ ὁ ἐν ἀρχιερεῦσι ταπεινὸς Νέων Πατρῶν Γερμανὸς . . . συνέγραψα ἐκ πολλῶν πρωτοτύπων, παλαιῶν τε καὶ νέων ἀναλεξάμενος· ἔνια καὶ παρ'ἐμαυτοῦ ἔστιν, ἃ προσθεὶς καλλονῆς ἕνεκα οἷα που πρὸς τῶν ἐμοῦ καθηγητῶν, προκρίτως δὲ πρὸς τοῦ λογιοτάτου καὶ μουσικοτάτου κυρίου Χρυσάφου πρωτοψάλτου τῆς Μεγάλης Ἐκκλησίας ἐδιδάχθην . . . χρόνος τοίγαρ τοὶ καθὸν ἀπὸ*

---

with the fifteenth-century lampadarios Manuel Chrysaphes, i.e. the old (on this see A. Papadopoulos Kerameus, *Μανουὴλ Χρυσάφης, λαμπαδάριος τοῦ βασιλικοῦ κλήρου*', *Vizantijskij Vremennik*, viii (1901), p. 526f.).

[28] Papadopoulos Kerameus, *Hierosol. Bibl.*, v, pp. 325-6.

[29] Papadopoulos Kerameus, *Μαυρογορδάτειος Βιβλιοθήκη*, i (Constantinople, 1884), p. 121.

μὲν τοῦ κόσμου γεννεσίας ͵ζϱ′ [leg. ͵ζϱογ′], ἀπὸ δὲ τῆς τοῦ Θεοῦ
Λόγου ἐνανθρωπήσεως ͵αχξε′ [= 1665] μηνὶ αὐγούστῳ . . .³⁰

Finally, the musical Athens-National Library MS 947
contains the following note: Τὸ παρὸν βιβλίον ἐγράφη παρ᾽ἐμοῦ
τοῦ εὐτελοῦς Χρυσάφου ἐν ἔτει ͵αχπ′ [= 1680], μηνὶ ἰουλίῳ κε′ διὰ
ἐπιμελείας Δημητρίου τοῦ ἐξ ᾽Αθηνῶν.³¹ Although the Chrysaphes
in this note does not refer to himself as an official, it is
reasonable to assume that this scribe is the same person as
Chrysaphes, the protopsaltes of the Great Church; the absence
of his title in the note may indicate that he had resigned from
his office by that time.³²

PANAYIOTES CHALATZOGLOU   1728

In his treatise on Arabic-Persian music, written in 1728,
Panayiotes Chalatzoglou styles himself 'protopsaltes of the
Great Church'.³³

---

³⁰ A. Kominis, Πίνακες χρονολογημένων πατμιακῶν κωδίκων (Athens, 1968),
pp. 49-50.
³¹ I. Sakkelion, Κατάλογος χειρογράφων ᾽Εθν. Βιβλιοθήκης τῆς ῾Ελλάδος
(Athens 1892), p. 171.
³² It seems puzzling that Lesbos-Leimonos monastery MS 249 (written in 1777)
contains some Πολυχρονισμοὶ Χρυσάφου τοῦ Νέου εἰς τὸν ῾Ιεροσολύμων
Χρύσανθον καὶ τὸν Μυτιλήνης ῎Ανθιμον (see Papadopoulos Kerameus,
Μαυρογορδάτειος Βιβλιοθήκη, i, p. 118); also Hierosol.-Abraham monastery
MS 129 (eighteenth century) contains an 'Encomium' of Chrysaphes the New
to the patriarch of Jerusalem Chrysanthos and a 'Polychronion' of his to
Paisios of Nicomedia (see Papadopoulos Kerameus, Hierosol. Bibl., v, p. 455). It
seems very improbable, however, that Chrysaphes was still alive in 1707, when
Chrysanthos became patriarch of Jerusalem, and it is impossible to believe
that he lived until the time of Paisios of Nicomedia (1721-6) and of Anthimos
of Mytilene (1746-67). It seems that Chrysaphes had composed 'Polychronia'
and 'Encomia' to several prominent prelates of his time (such as the above-
mentioned Nektarios of Jerusalem) which later scribes used to glorify clergymen
of their time such as Paisios and Anthimos.
³³ The treatise of Chalatzoglou was published by Iakovos Naupliotes in the
Ergasiai (Proceedings) of the Ecclesiastical Musical Association of Constantinople,
No. 2 (June 1, 1900), pp. 68-75.
    The musical MS 212 of the Olympiotissa monastery in Thessaly bears the
title ᾽Ανθολόγιον . . . διορθωθὲν παρὰ τοῦ ἐντιμωτάτου κὺρ Παναγιώτου καὶ
πρωτοψάλτου τῆς Μεγάλης ᾽Εκκλησίας, μικρὸν δὲ καὶ παρὰ τοῦ ἀρχιερέως
κὺρ Γερμανοῦ Νέων Πατρῶν (see E. Skouvaras, ᾽Ολυμπιώτισσα (Athens,
1967), pp. 410-11). Since this manuscript was written in June 1724, we might
infer that Chalatzoglou was already protopsaltes at that time. An ana-
chronism, however, as well as some palaeographical irregularities which
appear in this title make it suspect. More specifically, examining the facsimile
of the title page (published by Skouvaras, op. cit., p. 383) one may observe
a) that after the name Παναγιώτου there is a blank space resulting from the

Cf. below Panayiotes Chalatzoglou, lampadarios and domestikos.

IOANNES TRAPEZOUNTIOS 1736–June 1769

He was a pupil of Panayiotes Chalatzoglou and his successor in the office of protopsaltes.[34]

In a letter of Makarios Kalogeras of Patmos to Ioannes, the latter is addressed as protopsaltes of the Great Church: Ἐντιμότατε καὶ μουσικώτατε πρωτοψάλτα τῆς Μεγάλης Ἐκκλησίας κύριε Ἰωάννη . . .[35] This letter bears no date, but since it is known that Makarios died on 17 January 1737, we may conclude that Ioannes had been appointed protopsaltes before that date.

---

erasure of one or two words; unintelligible traces of these words, however, are still showing; b) Germanos of Neae Patrae (mentioned in the title above) is known from scores of manuscripts to have revised the Anthology of Chrysaphes the New; c) there is no other evidence that Chalatzoglou compiled an Anthology; d) Germanos is reported as bishop of Neae Patrae around 1665 (for chronological data on him see K. Sathas in *Attikon Hēmerologion* (Athens, 1869), p. 197ff.; Alexandros Lavriotes in *Ecclesiastike Aletheia*, xxiii, 1903, p. 420; D. Zakythinos in *Hellēnika*, ii (1928), p. 166; S. Eustratiades in *Hellēnika*, iii (1929), p. 55). Consequently, it would be impossible for him to revise the works of Chalatzoglou, who was active around 1728. The above considerations lead us to the conclusion that the title of the Olympiotissa monastery manuscript must have been partly falsified: the name Παναγιώτου replaced another name, probably that of Chrysaphes the New.

[34] Chrysanthos, *Theoretikon*, p. xxvii, n. 3: Τραπεζούντιος ἦν οὗτος ὁ Ἰωάννης, χρυσοχόος τὸ κατ᾽ἀρχὰς γενόμενος· εἶτα τῷ Παναγιώτῃ μαθητεύσας καὶ ἅπαντα τὰ τότε σωζόμενα μουσικὰ ποιήματα ἐκδιδαχθεὶς ὑπ᾽αὐτοῦ, καὶ ἱκανῶς ἐπιδοὺς εἰς τὴν μουσικὴν ἐψηφίσθη λαμπαδάριος τῷ διδασκάλῳ συμψάλλων· ὃν καὶ μετὰ τὸν θάνατον αὐτοῦ διεδέξατο πρωτοψάλτης γενόμενος.

[35] Published by M. Gedeon, 'Πρωτοψάλται', *Ecclesiastike Aletheia*, iv (1884), p. 645. Gedeon says vaguely that the edition of the letter is based on a manuscript of the Iveron monastery. Certainly, he means Athos-Iveron MS 136 (see Sp. Lambros, *Catalogue of the Greek Manuscripts on Mount Athos*, ii (Cambridge, 1900), p. 28). It is rather strange that this letter of Makarios to Ioannes is almost identical with an undated letter of the same Makarios to protopsaltes Panayiotes Chalatzoglou (published along with two other letters of Makarios to Chalatzoglou by G. Papadopoulos in the *Ergasiai* (Proceedings) of the Ecclesiastical Musical Association of Constantinople, No. 4 (1 November 1901), pp. 42-6). It is worth noting here that the Iveron manuscript mentioned above also contains a letter of Ioannes to a certain George (published by Gedeon in *Ecclesiastike Aletheia*, ix (1889), p. 327). As we may assume from the contents of the letter Ioannes was then a youth and a student at the Patmos school; hence his connection with Makarios, then principal of the school. The same letter informs us that Ioannes originated from Tripolis of Pontos, close to Trebizond, hence his surname Trapezountios.

L

The name of protopsaltes Ioannes occurs several times in a manuscript containing the correspondence of Silvester, patriarch of Antioch. From a letter of Silvester dated November 1752 to the ecumenical patriarch Cyrillos we learn that Ioannes had earlier served as *kapikechayia* of the patriarch of Constantinople.[36] This bit of evidence permits us to identify Ioannes with an unnamed official who is mentioned in a document of 1742 as being protopsaltes and at the same time *kapikechayia*.[37]

The musical manuscript Meteora-St. Stephanos MS 52 was copied by protopsaltes Ioannes in March 1743; its colophon reads: Ἐτελειώθη ἡ παροῦσα ἀσματομελιρρυτόφθογγος βίβλος, ἥ καὶ παπαδικὴ τοῖς ἀρχαίοις κέκληται, διὰ χειρὸς ἐμοῦ Ἰωάννου πρωτοψάλτου ἐν ἔτει ͵αψμγ´ μαρτίῳ.[38]

The last mention of Ioannes as protopsaltes occurs in Athos-Iveron MS 1157, also copied by him and concluded with the following colophon: Ἐγράφησαν ὑπὸ Ἰωάννου πρωτοψάλτου τῆς Μεγάλης Ἐκκλησίας ἐν ἔτει ͵αψξθ´ [= 1769] μηνὶ Ἰουνίῳ.[39]

The exact time of his death is not known. Chrysanthos, however, says that right after the death of Ioannes, lampadarios Daniel was promoted to protopsaltes, while the vacant office of lampadarios was given to Petros Peloponnesios, who then took Petros Byzantios as his assistant, i.e. second domestikos.[40] Since it is known that this Petros Byzantios was already second domestikos in November 1773,[41] it follows that the death of Ioannes, which occasioned all these promotions, took place before that date and certainly after June 1769, when Ioannes was still alive.

Cf. below Ioannes Trapezountios lampadarios (1728–34) and domestikos (1727).

---

[36] This letter is published by the bishop of Helioupolis Gennadios [Arabatzoglou], Φωτίειος Βιβλιοθήκη, ii (Constantinople, 1935), p. 173. Part of the correspondence between Silvester and Ioannes is published ibid., pp. 174-8 and 180-4; cf. ibid., pp. 53, 55, 58, 63-7.

[37] M. Gedeon, "Ἀμοιβαὶ μουσικῶν', Ecclesiastike Aletheia, xxv (1905), pp. 59-60. For details about the annual salary of Ioannes between the years 1742 and 1753 see ibid.

[38] This manuscript is described in the forthcoming second volume of N. Bees, Τὰ χειρόγραφα τῶν Μετεώρων.

[39] Lambros, Catalogue of Mss. of Mt. Athos, ii, p. 254.

[40] Chrysanthos, Theoretikon, p. xl, n. 2. See also below the entry Petros Peloponnesios, lampadarios.

[41] See below the entry Petros Byzantios, domestikos.

DANIEL   *c.* 1771–died 23 December 1789

He was the immediate successor to protopsaltes Ioannes Trapezountios,[42] who died *c.* 1771 (between June 1769 and November 1773).

Daniel is mentioned explicitly as protopsaltes in 1774; in the musical manuscript Hierosol. 597, fol. 12, there is the following note: Τὸ παρὸν ἐγράφη παρ᾽ἐμοῦ Σταυρῆ ‹μαθητοῦ› τοῦ πρωτο-ψάλτου κὺρ Δανιὴλ ἐν ἔτει ͵αψοδ' [= 1774].[43]

When a school of ecclesiastical music was founded at the Patriarchate in 1776, ὑπεσχέθησαν τῷ πρωτοψάλτῃ Δανιὴλ γρόσια *400* τὸν χρόνον διὰ νὰ παραδίδῃ μαθηματάρι.[44]

Athos-Lavra MS 1016 (Θ 154), written in May 1786, contains several compositions including some τοῦ νῦν πρωτοψάλτου κὺρ Δανιὴλ.[45]

According to Chrysanthos, Δανιὴλ ὁ πρωτοψάλτης, ἡ μελῳδικὴ σάλπιγξ τοῦ ἡμετέρου αἰῶνος, κατήγετο ἀπὸ τὸν Τούρναβον κατὰ τὴν Λάρισαν, περὶ δὲ τὸ ͵αψπθ' [= 1789] ἔτος, Δεκεμβρίου κγ', ἡμέρᾳ Σαββάτῳ εἰς τὰς *12* ὥρας ἔδωκε τὸ κοινὸν χρέος.[46]

Cf. below Daniel lampadarios (1740–*c.* 1771) and domestikos (1734).

IAKOVOS PELOPONNESIOS   5 March 1790–d. 23 April 1800

He was the immediate successor to protopsaltes Daniel,[47] who died on 23 December 1789.

His first mention in the sources is on 5 March 1790, when he signed a patriarchal letter as πρωτοψάλτης ᾽Ιακωβάκης.[48]

[42] Chrysanthos, *Theoretikon*, p. xl, n. 2.
[43] Papadopoulos Kerameus, *Hierol. Bibl.*, i, p. 484. I have emended this note after similar colophons written by the same Stavres (see below the entry Stavres or Stavrakes, domestikos).
[44] Athanasios Comnenos Hypsilantis, Τὰ μετὰ τὴν "Αλωσιν, ed. G. Aphthonides (Constantinople, 1870), p. 555.
[45] Spyridon-Eustratiadis, *Catalogue of Lavra Mss.*, p. 157.
[46] Chrysanthos, *Theoretikon*, p. xxxv, n. 3.   [47] Ibid.
[48] M. Gedeon, ᾽Εκκλησίαι βυζαντιναὶ ἐξακριβούμεναι (Constantinople, 1900), p. 146. The musical manuscript Lesbos-Leimonos monastery 243, however, written in June 1787, according to Papadopoulos Kerameus, contains a Πολυέλεος . . . συντεθὲν νεωστὶ παρὰ τοῦ πρωτοψάλτου κὺρ ᾽Ιακώβου διὰ προτροπῆς τοῦ παναγιωτάτου πατριάρχου κυρίου Νεοφύτου (see Papadopoulos Kerameus, Μαυρογορδάτειος Βιβλιοθήκη, i, p. 116). Since it is beyond doubt that Neophytos became patriarch on 1 May 1789, we may assume that the date of the manuscript was read (or written) wrongly, and therefore it cannot be taken into consideration here.

L*

With regard to his income we know that he received an annual salary of 600 piastres, plus 400 piastres annually assigned to him by patriarch Neophytos VII on 1 December 1791 for his teaching at the patriarchal school of music.[49] Besides, we are informed by a letter of the same patriarch—dated 28 June 1799—that Iakovos had been appointed exarch (i.e. he received the fees) of the Zerbitsa monastery in Laconia.[50] A note written in Athens-Historike Ethnolog. Hetaireia MS 89, fol. 6r, informs us that Iakovos died on 23 April 1800: *1800 Ἀπριλίου κγʹ ὁ μουσικολογιώτατος κύριος Ἰάκωβος, ὁ τῆς Χριστοῦ Μεγάλης Ἐκκλησίας πρωτοψάλτης ἀπῆλθεν εἰς τὰς αἰωνίους μονάς· ἄνδρας ἐν φρονήσει τε καὶ μαθήσει θεοσεβὴς, ὀρθόδοξος, φιλακόλουθος καὶ τέλειος τῆς χριστιανικῆς πολιτείας . . .*[51] Cf. below Iakovos Peloponnesios lampadarios (1784–9) and domestikos (1764–76).

PETROS BYZANTIOS   end of April 1800–*c.* 1805

He succeeded Iakovos Peloponnesios,[52] who died on 23 April 1800.

Ankara-Hellenikos Philol. Syllogos of Constantinople MS 112, written in April 1803, contains compositions by various musicians including some of *Πέτρου πρωτοψάλτου τοῦ Βυζαντίου.*[53]

According to Chrysanthos, Petros Byzantios *ἦν Κωνσταντινουπολίτης, καὶ ἐπαιδεύθη τὴν μουσικὴν ὑπὸ Πέτρου τοῦ Λακεδαίμονος . . . ἐπὶ δὲ τῆς πρώτης πατριαρχείας Καλλινίκου τοῦ ἀπὸ Νικαίας* [17 June 1801–22 September 1806] *διά τινα σφάλματα ἐξώσθη τοῦ κλήρου καὶ ἔφυγεν εἰς Χερσόναν· κἀκεῖθεν εἰς Υἰάσι τῆς Μολδαβίας, καὶ πολλὰ ἐπὶ τῆς ἀλλοδαπῆς ἀναξιοπαθήσας τὸν βίον μετήλλαξε κατὰ τὸ ͵αωηʹ ἔτη ἀπὸ Χριστοῦ.*[54] For this reason Petros is often called 'Phygas', i.e. fugitive.

Cf. below Petros Byzantios lampadarios (1789–1800) and domestikos (*c.* 1771–89).

---

[49] M. Gedeon, *Παιδεία καὶ πτωχεία παρ'ἡμῖν* (Constantinople, 1893), pp. 59-65; and same author's, "*Η παρ'ἡμῖν διδασκαλία τῆς ἐκκλησιαστικῆς μουσικῆς*', *Ecclesiastike Aletheia*, viii (1888), p. 36.

[50] Th. Simopoulos, '*Η ἱερὰ μονὴ Ζερμπίτσης* (Athens, 1966), pp. 44-5.

[51] Sp. Lambros, "*Ἐνθυμήσεων συλλογή*', *Neos Hellēnomnēmon*, vii (1910), p. 253.

[52] Chrysanthos, *Theoretikon*, p. liii.

[53] D. Sarros, '*Κατάλογος χειρογράφων τοῦ ἐν Κωνσταντινουπόλει Ἑλλην. Φιλολ. Συλλόγου*', *Epeteris Het. Byzant. Spoudon*, ix (1932), p. 151.

[54] Chrysanthos, *Theoretikon*, pp. xl-xli, and n. 1.

MANUEL BYZANTIOS   *c.* 1805–d. 21 June 1819

He succeeded Petros Byzantios during the first patriarchate of Kallinikos IV,[55] i.e. before September 1806.

He is explicitly referred to as protopsaltes in 1808: Hierosol. MS 597, fol. 126r, contains a musical composition with the title: Μακάριος ἀνήρ, ὅπερ συνετέθη παρὰ τοῦ κῦρ Ἐμμανουὴλ πρωτοψάλτου τῆς τοῦ Χριστοῦ Μεγάλης Ἐκκλησίας ἐπὶ τῆς πατρι- αρχείας τοῦ κῦρ Γρηγορίου τοῦ Πελοποννησίου τῇ αὐτοῦ ζητήσει. ͵αωη΄[56] (i.e. before September 1808, when Gregory V resigned from the patriarchal throne).

According to Chrysanthos,[57] Manuel died on 21 June 1819.

GREGORIOS   end of June 1819–d. 23 December 1821

He succeeded protopsaltes Manuel Byzantios,[58] who died on 21 June 1819. Gregorios was one of the three 'inventors of the new musical method'[59] and was nicknamed 'Levites'. He died on 23 December 1821.[60]

Cf. below Gregorios lampadarios (1813–19).

CONSTANTINOS BYZANTIOS   24 December 1821–1855

He was appointed protopsaltes on 24 December 1821[61] and held this office until 1855. He died on 30 June 1862.[62]

Cf. below Constantinos Byzantios domestikos (1800–8).

LAMPADARII

〖MANUEL DOUKAS CHRYSAPHES   1440–July 1463

He was not a lampadarios of the Great Church, as he is

---

[55] Ibid., p. lv.   [56] Papadopoulos Kerameus, *Hierosol. Bibl.*, i, p. 484.
[57] Chrysanthos, *Theoretikon*, p. liv.
[58] Ibid., p. 6 of the Preface of the editor, Panayiotes Pelopides, a former pupil of Gregorios. Strangely enough Gregorios is mentioned as protopsaltes in a list of subscribers which is attached at the end of a book (the *Geographia* by Dionysios Pyrros) published at Venice in 1818. We may suppose that the printing of this book did start in 1818, as it is indicated on its title-page, but it was probably completed much later, i.e. after June 1819, when Gregorios had become protopsaltes.
[59] Chrysanthos, *Theoretikon*, p. 6 of the Preface, note.
[60] Th. Aristokleous, Κωνσταντίου Α΄τοῦ ἀπὸ Σιναίου βιογραφία καὶ συγγραφαὶ αἱ ἐλάσσονες (Constantinople, 1866), p. 65.
[61] Ibid.; also Chrysanthos, *Theoretikon*, p. 6 of the Preface, note.
[62] Aristokleous, op. cit., pp. 64-6.

often called, but lampadarios of the 'Royal Clergy' (see A. Papadopoulos Kerameus, '*Μανουὴλ Χρυσάφης, λαμπαδάριος τοῦ βασιλικοῦ κλήρου*', *Vizantijskij Vremennik*, viii (1901), pp. 526–33). As such he is mentioned for the first time in Hierosol. MS 31, written in 1439/40 (see Papadopoulos Kerameus, *Hierosol. Bibl.*, v, pp. 351–3).

Athos-Iveron MS 1120, written by Chrysaphes himself in July 1458, bears the following colophon: '*Ἐτελειώθη τὸ παρὸν βιβλίον, αἱ ἀκολουθίαι πᾶσαι τῆς ψαλτικῆς, διὰ χειρὸς Μανουὴλ Δούκα λαμπαδαρίου τοῦ Χρυσάφη ἐν ἔτει ,ϛϡξϛ' ἰνδικτιῶνος ϛ' ἰουλλίου* . . . (see Lambros, *Catalogue of MSS of Mt. Athos*, ii, p. 252; also A. Dmitrievski in *Vizantijskij Vremennik*, i (1894), p. 585).

Chrysaphes was still living on 29 July 1463, when he finished the writing of and signed Constantinople-Topkapu Seraglio MS 15 (see A. Deissmann, *Forschungen und Funde im Serai, mit einem Verzeichnis der nichtislamischen Handschriften im Topkapu Serai zu Istanbul* (Berlin-Leipzig 1933), p. 59).

It seems that after the Turkish conquest of Constantinople—probably after 1463—Chrysaphes fled to Crete, for the Jerusalem manuscript mentioned above (in an additional folio of the sixteenth century) contains musical compositions entitled: *Ποιήματα ταῦτα πάντα τοῦ κὺρ Μανουὴλ λαμπαδαρίου τοῦ Χρυσάφη· ἐποίησε δὲ ταῦτα ἐν τῇ νήσῳ Κρήτῃ*. His stay in Crete may be confirmed by the well-known scholar Michael Apostolis, also a resident of Crete from 1455 on, who addressed a letter to an 'Emmanuel Chrysaphes' described by Apostolis as Constantinopolitan (see this letter in E. Legrand, *Bibliographie hellénique, XV–XVI siècles*, ii (Paris, 1885), p. 239; cf. H. Noiret, *Lettres inédites de Michel Apostolis* (Paris, 1889), pp. 59 and 30). It is also known that Chrysaphes had spent some time in Serbia: Meteora-Metamorphosis MS 479 (seventeenth century), fol. 265r, contains a piece by *κὺρ Μανουὴλ τοῦ Χρυσάφη, ὅπερ ἐποιήθη ἐν τῇ Σερβίᾳ* (see N. Bees, *Τὰ χειρόγραφα τῶν Μετεώρων*, i, p. 482; also M. Velimirović, "*Ιωακεὶμ μοναχὸς τοῦ Χαρσιανίτου καὶ δομέστικος Σερβίας*', *Zbornik Radova*, viii (Mélanges G. Ostrogorsky), No. 2, 1964, pp. 451–4). Finally, it is worth noting that several manuscripts preserve Chrysaphes' melodies composed *δι'ὁρισμοῦ τοῦ ἀοιδίμου καὶ μακαρίου βασιλέως Κωνσταντίνου τοῦ Παλαιολόγου*, which certainly corroborates the view that Chrysaphes belonged to the 'Royal Clergy' (see such manuscripts in Papadopoulos Kerameus, *Hierosol. Bibl.*, v, p. 454, and Bees, *op. cit.*, pp. 125 and 344).]]

PHOCAS   March 1575–1578

Athens-National Library MS 24, copied by lampadarios Phocas, bears the following colophon: *Τουτὶ τό βιβλίον, ὅ τὰς προφητείας τῶν προφητῶν περιέχει, ὑπάρχει τοῦ Φιλίππου, δούλου καὶ πιστοῦ οἰκέτου τοῦ εὐγενεστάτου καὶ τιμιωτάτου ἄρχοντος κυρίου Μιχαήλου Καντακουζηνοῦ, ὑπὸ τοῦ τῆς Μεγάλης Ἐκκλησίας λαμπαδαρίου τοῦ κεκλημένου Φωκᾶ γραφὲν ἐπιμελῶς καὶ σπουδαίως, ἐν ἔτει ͵ζπγ´* [= 1575] *μηνὶ μαρτίῳ, ἰνδικτιῶνος ι´.*[63]

The name of lampadarios Phocas also figures in a list of important personalities that Stephan Gerlach met in Constantinople in 1578.[64]

GEORGIOS   before October 1616–after 1620

Lamius published a letter signed by 'George lampadarios of the Great Church' and addressed to the metropolitan of Philadelphia, Gabriel Severos.[65] The letter is undated, but it must have been written before October 1616, when Severos died.

An also undated letter of the patriarch of Alexandria, Gerasimos Spartaliotes is addressed *Τῷ κυρίῳ Γεωργίῳ λαμπαδαρίῳ τῆς Μεγάλης Ἐκκλησίας.*[66] Given that Gerasimos was patriarch of Alexandria from 1620 to 1636, it follows that Georgios' service in the office of lampadarios lasted at least until 1620.

[63] Sakkelion, *Κατάλογος χειρογράφων τῆς Ἐθνικῆς Βιβλιοθήκης*, p. 4.

[64] See Martini Crusii, *Turcograecia* (Basel, 1584), p. 507. In an undated letter, published ibid., p. 292, the ecumenical patriarch Hieremias II spoke of the *ἐντιμότατος λαμπαδάριος τῆς καθ᾽ ἡμᾶς ἐκκλησίας κύριος Φωκᾶς*. It seems that Phocas was among the officials who escorted patriarch Hieremias in his historic trip to Moscow (1588-9). That is what may be inferred from an entry in Crusius Diary (quoted by B. Mystakides in *Epirotika Chronika*, iv, 1929, p. 93) under the date 7 February 1589. Referring to a patriarchal letter of recommendation which was handed to him by a certain Greek, Crusius noted there that: *Ait τὸ συστατικὸν esse scriptum ὑπὸ λαμπαδαρίου, a lambadario, qui cum Patr. Hieremia sit in Moscovia.*

[65] J. Lamius, *Deliciae eruditorum: Gabrielis Severi . . . epistolae*, p. 25.

[66] N. Tomadakis, 'Δύο Κρῆτες πατριάρχαι Ἀλεξανδρείας συγχεόμενοι. Γεράσιμος Α´ Σπαρταλιώτης καὶ Γεράσιμος Β´ Παλλαδᾶς', *Crētika Chronika*, iii (1949), p. 175.

He did not hold this office, however, in 1629, when another lampadarios, Michael, is reported.

MICHAEL   15 June 1629

His name and title appear among the signatories of a patriarchal document dated 15 June 1629.[67]

PANAYIOTES CHALATZOGLOU   before 1728

Melodies of 'lampadarios Panayiotes Chalatzoglou' are contained in Athens-National Library MS 893 (eighteenth century).[68]

[67] K. Mertzios, Πατριαρχικά, in the series Pragmateiae of the Academy of Athens, No. 15 (Athens, 1951), p. 57; published in E. Hurmuzaki, Documente, iv, part 2, p. 429.

[68] Sakkelion, op. cit., p. 162; cf. Olympiotissa MS 208 (in Skouvaras, 'Ολυμπιώτισσα, p. 398), and Patmos MS 499 (I. Sakkelion, Πατμιακὴ Βιβλιοθήκη, Athens 1890, p. 217). According to Chrysanthos (Theoretikon, p. xxxix, n. 5), Panayiotes Chalatzoglou studied Byzantine music with the hieromonachos Damianos Vatopedinos on Mount Athos, διότι κατ᾽ἐκεῖνον τὸν καιρὸν ἐξέλιπον ἐν Κωνσταντινουπόλει εἰδήμονες ψαλμῳδοί. The time of Chalatzoglou's musical studies with Damianos should be placed in the last decades of the seventeenth century; hieromonachos Damianos Vatopedinos from Beroea is known as a musician and as the scribe of the musical manuscripts Athos-Vatoped. 1473, and Athos-Lavra 478 (E.16), dated by him 1679 and 1680 respectively (see Eustratiades-Arcadios, Catalogue of Mss. of Vatopedi, p. 232, and Spyridon-Eustratiades, Catalogue of Lavra Mss., p. 76). Compositions of Damianos are contained in several MSS, but one must be careful not to confuse him with another hieromonachos Damianos Vatopedinos from Athens, who is also reported as a musician and copyist of musical manuscripts c. 1633 (see Sp. Lambros, "Αθηναῖοι βιβλιογράφοι', Epeteris Parnassou, vi (1902), p. 203). As to Chrysanthos' assertion that at the time of Chalatzoglou's youth there were no masters in Constantinople able to teach Byzantine music, it seems to be partly true. Indeed, it is strange that not a single protopsaltes, lampadarios or domestikos of the Great Church is reported during the period from 1665 (or possibly 1680) to about 1720, i.e. between Chrysaphes the New and Chalatzoglou. Thus, Chalatzoglou would appear not to have been exactly a continuator of the old Constantinopolitan musical tradition, but an introducer of the Byzantine music as it was sung in the monasteries of Mount Athos. However, we can hardly speak of a break in the musical tradition of Constantinople, since we do know that in this very period of silence two outstanding musicians and prolific composers lived in Constantinople: the priest Balasios (active between the years 1663 and at least 1701; see Papadopoulos Kerameus in Hurmuzaki, Documente..., xiii, p. 356, and also Lambros, Catalogue of Mss. of Mt. Athos, ii, p. 246) and Petros Bereketes, protopsaltes at the church of St. Constantine of Psamathia in Constantinople. Bereketes composed an Encomium which he addressed to Tzar Peter the Great (1682-1725), and from this fact we may infer that he was still living in the first decades of the eighteenth century (for this Encomium see Papadopoulos Kerameus, Hierosol. Bibl., i, p. 249; also see Meteora-Metamorphosis MS 444, antedating 1732, which contains several musical pieces by

Cf. Panayiotes Chalatzoglou protopsaltes (1728) and domestikos.

IOANNES TRAPEZOUNTIOS   16 October 1728–January 1734

The musical manuscript Athos-Lavra 1784 (M 93) was copied by lampadarios Ioannes, who added the following colophon (fol. 422v): Εἴληφε πέρας ἡ παροῦσα ἀσματομελιρρυτόφθογγος βίβλος, ἥτις παπαδικὴ τοῖς ἀρχαίοις κέκληται, παρ'ἐμοῦ λαμπαδαρίου Ἰωάννου . . . ἐν ἔτει ͵αψκη ͵ὀκτωβρίου ις'.[69]

The same lampadarios Ioannes is the scribe of Hierosol. MS 323, which bears the note: Ἡ παροῦσα βίβλος ἐγράφη παρ'ἐμοῦ Ἰωάννου λαμπαδαρίου ἐν ἔτει ͵αψλδ' ἰαννουαρίῳ.[70] No doubt this lampadarios Ioannes is no other than Ioannes Trapezountios, later protopsaltes (1736–69) and formerly domestikos (1727).

DANIEL   5 September 1740–c. 1771

A letter dated 5 September 1740, and addressed to the bishop of Litza and Agrapha, Constantios (1739–48), is signed by the λαμπαδάριος τῆς τοῦ Χριστοῦ Μεγάλης Ἐκκλησίας Δανιήλ.[71]

The same lampadarios Daniel signed as a witness in a document dated 6 August 1766.[72]

According to Chrysanthos,[73] Daniel was promoted to protopsaltes right after the death of protopsaltes Ioannes

---

Bereketes; Bees, Τὰ χειρόγραφα τῶν Μετεώρων, p. 452). Therefore, the oft-repeated view that Bereketes lived around 1768 is not correct (see e.g. G. Papadopoulos, Συμβολαὶ εἰς] τὴν ἱστορίαν τῆς παρ'ἡμῖν ἐκκλησιαστικῆς μουσικῆς, p. 311, and A. Gastoué, Catalogue des manuscrits de musique byzantine, p. 69).

[69] Spyridon-Eustratiades, Catalogue of Lavra Mss., p. 319; cf. Eustratiades in Epeteris Het. Byzant. Spoudon, xii (1936), p. 67, who states incorrectly that the manuscript was written in 1721. This MS once belonged to the eminent student of Byzantine music, C. Psachos, who has written a note at the beginning of the manuscript asserting that the hand-writing of this manuscript is that of Ioannes Trapezountios (see Spyridon-Eustratiades, Catalogue of Lavra Mss., p. 319, and C. Psachos, Παρασημαντικὴ (Athens, 1917), p. 36, n. 42).

[70] Papadopoulos Kerameus, Hierosol. Bibl., i, p. 371. At the top of a composition included in this manuscript, Ioannes has written the following title: Παναγιώτου πρωτοψάλτου, ἡμετέρου διδασκάλου, i.e. Chalatzoglou.

[71] It is published by Ch. Chatzithanos, Διονυσίου ἱερομονάχου κῶδιξ τῆς ἱερᾶς μονῆς Ζωοδόχου Πηγῆς τοῦ Φουρνᾶ τῶν Ἀγράφων (Athens, 1963), pp. 50-1.

[72] It is published by K. Delikanes, Ἔγγραφα τοῦ Οἰκουμενικοῦ πατριαρχείου, ii (Constantinople, 1904), pp. 209-10.

[73] Chrysanthos, Theoretikon, p. xl, n. 2.

Trapezountios, *c.* 1771, or more precisely between June 1769 and November 1773.

Several entries in an old 'Book of Accounts' of the Patriarchate show that Daniel received an annual salary of 133 piastres in 1741. At the same time Daniel served as Γραμματικὸς τοῦ Κοινοῦ. In 1745 he received 120 piastres plus 12 piastres διὰ τὴν τσόχαν του, while in 1753 his salary was raised to 150 piastres.[74]

Cf. Daniel protopsaltes (*c.* 1771–89) and domestikos (1734).

PETROS PELOPONNESIOS   *c.* 1771–8

According to Chrysanthos, Petros, using unfair methods, managed to supplant the first domestikos Iakovos and was appointed lampadarios: Ὅτε ἐπλήρωσε τὸ κοινὸν χρέος ὁ πρωτοψάλτης Ἰωάννης καὶ ἔγινε πρωτοψάλτης ὁ Δανιήλ, ἔπρεπε μὲν νὰ γίνῃ λαμπαδάριος ὁ Ἰάκωβος, ὡς δεξιὸς δομέστικος, ὁ δὲ Πέτρος [being second domestikos] διὰ μεσιτείας δυνατωτέρων παραβὰς τὴν τάξιν, ἔγινε λαμπαδάριος καὶ ἐπῆρε δομέστικόν του [i.e. second] τὸν Βυζάντιον Πέτρον.[75] As we have already seen, this happened around 1771, or more specifically between June 1769 and November 1773.

The next mention of lampadarios Petros Peloponnesios in the sources appears in 1774: the musical manuscript Hierosol. 597, written in that year, contains Καταβασίαι τῶν δεσποτικῶν καὶ θεομητορικῶν ἑορτῶν συντεθεῖσαι κατὰ τὸ ὕφος τῆς Μεγάλης Ἐκκλησίας παρὰ τοῦ μουσικολογιωτάτου κὺρ Πέτρου λαμπαδαρίου τοῦ Πελοποννησίου.[76]

In 1776 Petros was among the teaching staff of the newly founded patriarchal school of music.[77]

His service in the office of lampadarios was brief, but his musical production was really astonishing both in terms of quality and of quantity. As Chrysanthos remarked, Petros ἐποίησε ταῦτα πάντα ἐν ὀλίγῳ διαστήματι καιροῦ, διότι λαμπαδάριος ἔτι ὢν τὸν βίον μετήλλαξε, λοιμοῦ παρανάλωμα γενόμενος.[78] The exact time of his death is not known. The traditional and generally accepted view that he died in 1777 is not sufficiently

[74] Gedeon, ''Ἀμοιβαὶ μουσικῶν', Ecclesiastike Aletheia, xxv (1905), pp. 59-60.
[75] Chrysanthos, Theoretikon, p. xl, n. 2.
[76] Papadopoulos Kerameus, Hierosol. Bibl., i, p. 484.
[77] Comnenos Hypselantis, op. cit., p. 555.
[78] Chrysanthos, Theoretikon, p. xl, n. 2.

documented. Nevertheless, the detail provided by Chrysanthos that Petros died in a plague epidemic leads us to the year 1778, when such an epidemic did afflict Constantinople.[79] At any rate it is certain that in June 1784 Petros Peloponnesios was not alive, for at this time the office of lampadarios was occupied by Iakovos Peloponnesios.

Cf. Petros Peloponnesios, domestikos (1764–c. 1771).

IAKOVOS PELOPONNESIOS   22 June 1784–end of December 1789

He was the successor of Petros Peloponnesios in the office of lampadarios, and as such he signed a patriarchal document dated 22 June 1784.[80]

He held that office until he was promoted to protopsaltes right after the death of Daniel[81] (23 December 1789).

Cf. Iakovos Peloponnesios protopsaltes (1790–1800) and domestikos (1764–76).

PETROS BYZANTIOS   end of December 1789–end of April 1800

He was appointed lampadarios in succession of Iakovos, when the latter was promoted to protopsaltes after the death of Daniel (23 December 1789).[82]

An act of patriarch Neophytos VII, dated December 1791, granted Petros Byzantios an annual salary of 400 piastres for

---

[79] See a note on Athos-Pantel. MS 203; Lambros, *Catalogue of Mss. of Mt. Athos*, ii, p. 323.

On this renowned composer, Petros Peloponnesios, see the article of P. Georgiou in *Thrēskeutikē kai Ēthikē Enkyklopaedia*, x, pp. 375-6, where the relevant bibliography is cited. To his entries the following works should be added: C. Papademetriou, '*Τὰ προβλήματα τῆς βυζαντινῆς μουσικῆς καὶ αἱ σύγχρονοι ἔρευναι*', *Praktika* (Proceedings) of the Academy of Athens, vi (1931), pp. 53-8; D. Stefanović and M. Velimirović, 'Peter Lampadarios and Metropolitan Serafim of Bosnia', *Studies in Eastern Chant*, i, pp. 67-88. Some uncertain information about Petros' origin is given by D. Philippopoulos, '*Πέτρος ὁ Λακεδαιμόνιος ἢ Πελοποννήσιος*', *Spartiatika Chronika*, i (1937), No. 5, pp. 15-16. Nevertheless, his Laconian origin is attested by an epigram which is written at the end of the musical manuscript Hierosol. 347, copied by his pupil Petros Byzantios: *Πέτρου τοῦ μελῳδοῦ τοῦ Λάκωνος ἐξέφυν | χειρὸς δ'ἐγεγράφην Πέτρου τοῦ Βυζαντίου | κτῆμά τε πέφυκα τῷ ἐκ Τενέδου | Μητροφάνει, ᾧ τῷ τέχνῃ ᾄδειν ἔρως | 1809 Φευρ.* 10 (see Papadopoulos Kerameus, *Hierosol. Bibl.*, i, p. 381).

[80] Delikanes, op. cit., iii, p. 704.

[81] Chrysanthos, *Theoretikon*, p. xxxv, n. 3.

[82] Ibid. It is worth adding that Paris. suppl. Gr. MS 1332 was copied and signed by Petros Byzantios, while a lampadarios, on 3 April 1791 (see C. Astruc and M.-L. Concasty, *Bibliothèque Nationale. Catalogue des manuscrits grecs. Le supplément grec*, iii (Paris, 1960), p. 635).

his teaching at the patriarchal school of music. His regular salary as lampadarios was 520 piastres annually.[83]

A note in a musical manuscript of the Psachos collection, informs us that it was copied by Petros Byzantios in June 1797:
. . . ἐγράφη δὲ παρ'ἐμοῦ λαμπαδαρίου Πέτρου τοῦ Βυζαντίου ἐν ἔτει 1797 ἐν μηνὶ 'Ιουνίῳ.[84]

Petros Byzantios was promoted to protopsaltes immediately after the death of Iakovos Peloponnesios (23 April 1800).

Cf. Petros Byzantios protopsaltes (1800–c. 1805) and domestikos (c. 1771–89).

GREGORIOS   1813–end of June 1819

The musical manuscript of Soumela monastery 65, written in 1813, contains various liturgical melodies including some τοῦ νῦν λαμπαδαρίου Γρηγορίου.[85]

Hierosol. (Metochion in Constantinople) MS 754 was written by Gregorios himself in June 1818: . . . ἐξηγηθεῖσα γοῦν καὶ ἡ βίβλος αὕτη παρ'ἐμοῦ Γρηγορίου λαμπαδαρίου τῆς τοῦ Χριστοῦ Μεγάλης 'Εκκλησίας, εἴληφε πέρας τὸ 1818 κατὰ μῆνα 'Ιούνιον.[86]

According to Panayiotes Pelopides, Gregorios' former pupil and editor of Chrysanthos' Theoretikon, Gregorios was promoted to protopsaltes right after the death of Manuel Byzantios (21 June 1819).[87]

Cf. Gregorios protopsaltes (1819–21).

DOMESTIKOI

PANAYIOTES [CHALATZOGLOU]   before 1728

Lesbos-Leimonos monastery MS 230 (eighteenth century) contains several ecclesiastical melodies including some pieces

[83] Gedeon, "Ἡ παρ'ἡμῖν διδασκαλία τῆς ἐκκλησιαστικῆς μουσικῆς', Ecclesiastike Aletheia, viii (1888), p. 36.
[84] C. Psachos, 'Πέτρος ὁ Βυζάντιος, πρωτοψάλτης τῆς Μεγάλης τοῦ Χριστοῦ 'Εκκλησίας, καὶ τὰ σωζόμενα ἰδιόχειρα αὐτοῦ χειρόγραφα', Phorminx, 2nd period, vi, No. 13-14 (January 1911), p. 3; a specimen of Petros hand-writing is published ibid., p. 4.
[85] Papadopoulos Kerameus, "Ἑλληνικοὶ κώδικες ἐν τῇ βιβλιοθήκῃ τῆς μονῆς Σουμελᾶ', Vizantijskij Vremennik, xix (1912), p. 301.
[86] Papadopoulos Kerameus, Hierosol. Bibl., v, pp. 255-6.
[87] Chrysanthos, Theoretikon, p. 6 of the Preface.

attributed to 'domestikos Panayiotes'.[88] He may be identified with Panayiotes Chalatzoglou, since no other composer is known to have had that name.

Cf. Panayiotes Chalatzoglou protopsaltes (1728).

IOANNES TRAPEZOUNTIOS   1727

In 1727, patriarch Païsios issued a document by which *ὁ ἐντιμώτατος δομέστικος κυρίτζης Ἰωαννάκης* was appointed teacher at the newly established musical school with an annual salary of 200 piastres.[89] It is evident that this domestikos Ioannes is no other than Ioannes Trapezountios, subsequently lampadarios (1728–34) and protopsaltes (1736–*c*. 1771).

DANIEL   February 1734

A synodical letter of patriarch Seraphim, issued in February 1734, is signed by several officials of the Great Church including *Δανιὴλ δομέστικος*.[90]

Cf. Daniel lampadarios (1740–*c*. 1771) and protopsaltes (*c*. 1771–89).

IAKOVOS PELOPONNESIOS   first domestikos, 1764–76

An entry in an old 'Book of Accounts' of the Patriarchate informs us that in 1764 Iakovos was already first domestikos with an annual salary of 120 piastres, which was raised to 240 in 1768.[91]

Furthermore, Iakovos is reported in various sources simply as domestikos on 26 June 1764,[92] 14 December 1765,[93] and 6 August 1768.[94] He was still holding the same office in 1776,

[88] Papadopoulos Kerameus, *Μαυρογορδάτειος Βιβλιοθήκη*, i, p. 113.
[89] Gedeon, op. cit., pp. 35-6.
[90] Papadopoulos Kerameus, '*Μᾶρκος ὁ Εὐγενικός*', *Byzantinische Zeitschrift*, xi (1902), pp. 66-7; and same author's '*Δύο κώδικες τῆς βιβλιοθήκης Νικολάου Καρατζᾶ*', *Epeteris Parnassou*, viii (1904), p. 18.
[91] Gedeon, op. cit., p. 36 and n. 5. Gedeon is obviously wrong when he states in the same article that four years later, in 1768, Iakovos bore the dignity of second domestikos (which would imply a strange demotion) while Petros Peloponnesios was first domestikos (an office which Petros never held).
[92] D. Zakythenos, '*Πατριαρχικὰ ἔγγραφα*', *Hellēnika*, iii (1930), p. 446.
[93] P. Sokolov, '*Ἐπαρχιακὰ Ἐκκλησίας Κωνσταντινουπόλεως*' (title also in Russian) (St. Petersburg, 1915), p. 5 of the Appendix.
[94] Delikanes, op. cit., ii, pp. 209-10.

when he was invited to teach at the patriarchal school of music established in that year.[95]

Cf. Iakovos Peloponnesios lampadarios (1784–9) and protopsaltes (1790–1800).

PETROS PELOPONNESIOS   second domestikos 1764–c. 1771

According to an entry in the 'Book of Accounts' of the Patriarchate, Petros Peloponnesios was second domestikos in 1764 and received a salary of 100 piastres annually.[96]

He held the same office until he was promoted to lampadarios c. 1771 (or more specifically, between June 1769 and November 1773).

Cf. Petros Peloponnesios lampadarios (c. 1771–8).

PETROS BYZANTIOS   c. 1771–end of December 1789

When Petros Peloponnesios was appointed lampadarios c. 1771, ἐπῆρε δομέστικόν του τὸν Βυζάντιον Πέτρον,[97] i.e. second domestikos.

Petros Byzantios still held the same office on 25 November 1773, when he finished the copying of the musical MS 13 (olim 4) of the Gritsanes collection, in which he wrote the following colophon: Χεὶρ ἁμαρτωλοῦ Πέτρου δομεστίκου μικροῦ ... ͵αψογ΄ [= 1773] νοεμβρίου κε΄.[98]

Petros Byzantios was most probably promoted to first domestikos immediately after the death of his master, Petros Peloponnesios (1778) and he remained in that office until his promotion to lampadarios soon after 23 December 1789.

He signed simply as Πέτρος δομέστικος τῆς τοῦ Χριστοῦ Μεγάλης Ἐκκλησίας in Paris. suppl. Gr. MS 1139, which was copied by him in 1782.[99]

Cf. Petros Byzantios lampadarios (1789–1800) and protopsaltes (1800–c. 1805).

[95] Comnenos Hypsilantis, op. cit., p. 555.
[96] Gedeon, op. cit., p. 36 and n. 5; cf. above n. 91.
[97] Chrysanthos, Theoretikon, p. xl, n. 2.
[98] M. Adamis, 'Κατάλογος τῶν χειρογράφων τῆς βιβλιοθήκης Παναγιώτου Γριτσάνη, ἀποκειμένης νῦν ἐν τῇ ἱερᾷ μητροπόλει Ζακύνθου', Epeteris Het. Byzant. Spoudon, xxxv (1966-7), p. 331.
[99] H. Omont, 'Manuscrits grecs datés récemment acquis par la Bibliothèque Nationale', Revue des Bibliothèques, viii (1898), p. 360; cf. A. Gastoué, Catalogue des manuscrits de musique byzantine de la Bibliothèque Nationale de Paris (Paris, 1907), pp. 67 and 92; and C. Astruc and M.-L. Concasty, Le supplément grec, p. 271.

ATHANASIOS [PHOTINOS?] PELOPONNESIOS second domestikos
September 1784–1 December 1785

In the following two manuscripts, copied by him in September
1784 and on 1 December 1785 respectively, he signed himself
as domestikos of the Great Church: Athos-Vatoped. 1256:
Εἴληφε τέλος τὸ παρὸν διὰ χειρὸς ἐμοῦ ᾿Αθανασίου ἁμαρτωλοῦ
δομεστίκου τῆς τοῦΧριστοῦ Μεγάλης ᾿Εκκλησίας τοῦΠελοποννησίου·
͵αψπδ' [= 1784] σεπτεμβρίῳ;[100] and Athos-Pantel. 979: Εἴληφε
τέλος τὸ παρὸν ἀσματομελίρρυτον εἱρμολόγιον διὰ χειρὸς ἐμοῦ
᾿Αθανασίου Πελοποννησίου καὶ δομεστίκου τῆς τοῦ Χριστοῦ Μεγάλης
᾿Εκκλησίας ἐν ἔτει ͵αψπε' [= 1785] ἐν μηνὶ δεκεμβρίῳ α'.[101]
He was apparently second domestikos, for we know that the
office of the first domestikos during the years 1778–90 was held
by Petros Byzantios.

In Hierosol. (Metochion in Constantinople) MS 756 there is
the following note (fol. 154r): Γέγραπται ἡ παροῦσα μουσικὴ
βίβλος διὰ χειρὸς ἐμοῦ ἐλαχίστου ᾿Αθανασίου Πελοποννησίου,
ἰατροῦ . . . ἐν ἔτει σωτηρίῳ ͵αψπε' [=1785] ἰανουαρίου ὀκτώ.[102]
Although this Athanasios Peloponnesios is not described here
as holder of any office, it seems that he is no other than the
homonymous domestikos. If so, the detail that he was also a
physician permits us to identify him with Athanasios Photinos
Peloponnesios, the physician of Sultan Abdul Hamid I (1774–
89) and a well-known student of Byzantine music.[103]

ANASTASIOS PROIKONESIOS for two years between May 1789
and March 1794

He copied the musical manuscript Paris. suppl. Gr. 1046, in
which he added the following note (fol. 242r): ᾿Εγράφθη διὰ
χειρὸς ἐμοῦ ᾿Αναστασίου δομεστίκου Προικονησίου, οὗ καὶ μέμνησθε
οἱ ἐντυγχάνοντες τῇ βίβλῳ ταύτῃ, ἐν ἔτει ͵αψϟε' [= 1795] μαΐου
κθ'.[104]

---

[100] Eustratiadis-Arcadios, *Catalogue of the Mss. of Vatopedi*, p. 209.
[101] Lambros, *Catalogue of the Mss. of Mt. Athos*, ii, p. 458.
[102] Papadopoulos Kerameus, *Hierosol. Bibl.*, v, p. 256.
[103] See N. Svoronos, "῾Ο Διονύσιος Φωτεινὸς καὶ τὸ ἱστορικὸν ἔργον αὐτοῦ',
Hellenika, x (1938), p. 137; V. Papacostea, 'Date nouă despre viaţa şi opera
lui Dionisie Fotino', *Balcania*, vii (1944), p. 318, and D. Oikonomides, "᾿Απὸ
τὰς ἑλληνορουμανικὰς ἐκκλησιαστικὰς σχέσεις', *Epeteris Het. Byzantinon Spoudon*,
xxiii (1953), p. 462.
[104] H. Omont, 'Les manuscrits grecs datés', p. 87; cf. Astruc-Concasty, *Le
Supplément grec*, p. 163.

More details about his service in the office of domestikos are
provided by another note that he wrote in MS 17 (olim 22) of
the Gritsanes collection, also copied by him a little after 15
October 1795: Ἀντεγράφη ἐξ αὐτοῦ τοῦ πρωτοτύπου παρ'ἐμοῦ
Ἀναστασίου Προικονησίου τοῦ καὶ δομεστίκου προχειρισθέντος ἐπὶ
τῆς πατριαρχίας κὺρ Νεοφύτου, καὶ μετὰ διετίαν οὐκ οἶδ'ὅπως,
φθόνῳ τοῦ μισοκάλου ἀπερισκέπτως παρὰ τοῦ ἰδίου παρεκβληθέντος·
μέμνησθε δέ μου πρὸς Θεὸν οἱ ἐντρυφῶντες τῷ παρόντι.[105] The
Neophytos in this note became patriarch twice: from 1 May
1789 until 1 March 1794, and from December 1798 until
June 1801. It is apparent that the note cited above refers to
Neophytos' first term in the patriarchal See, since we know that
Anastasios was already domestikos in May 1795 (see above).
It seems, however, that even after his dismissal from the office,
Anastasios continued to style himself domestikos.

STAVRES OR STAVRAKES   c. 1795

In several manuscripts that he copied between 1760 and 1774
he describes himself simply as 'pupil and secretary of Daniel',
the lampadarios and subsequently protopsaltes of the Great
Church.[106] Therefore, one may surmise that Stavres did not
hold any office before 1774.

In a note that he wrote in the musical manuscript Athos-
Vatoped. 1416, which he copied evidently after 1774, he refers
to himself as domestikos.[107] However, since this manuscript is
not dated, we cannot determine the exact time of his appointment to this office. In any case, it seems that he had not
become domestikos at least prior to 1785, for we know that
until this year the office of the second domestikos had been
occupied by Athanasios Peloponnesios, while the office of the
first domestikos had been held by Petros Byzantios until 1789.

[105] Adamis, op. cit., p. 335.
[106] In 1760 he copied Athos-Xeropot. MS 324 (see Lambros, *Catalogue of Mss. of
Mt. Athos*, i, p. 232); in 1774 he copied Hierosol. MS 597 (see Papadopoulos
Kerameus, *Hierosol. Bibl.*, i, p. 484; cf. above the entry Daniel protopsaltes);
he is also the scribe of Lesbos-Mandamados school MS 13 (see Papadopoulos
Kerameus, *Μαυρογορδάτειος Βιβλιοθήκη*, i, p. 165). In the second of these
manuscripts as well as in the above-mentioned Athos-Vatoped. MS 1416 he
has signed himself as Σταυρῆς, whereas in the two other MSS he calls
himself Σταυράκης, diminutive form of Stavres.
[107] Eustratiades-Arcadios, *Catalogue of Mss. of Vatopedi*, p. 224, where this manuscript is wrongly dated in the seventeenth century.

According to G. Papadopoulos (who cites no sources), Stavrakes had served as domestikos while Manuel was protopsaltes,[108] i.e. between *c.* 1805 and 1819. Stavrakes, however, must have been about 20 years old (if not older) in 1760, when he appears for the first time as a scribe of musical manuscripts; therefore, he would have been in his late sixties when he was supposedly appointed domestikos sometime after 1805, and an appointment at that age is rather improbable. Consequently, it is more plausible to place the time of his service as domestikos in the last decade of the eighteenth century.

CONSTANTINOS BYZANTIOS   second domestikos, 23 April 1800; first domestikos, 1808

He was appointed second domestikos on 23 April 1800.[109]

A liturgical manuscript of the Psachos collection bears the following note: *1808, ἐπὶ πατριαρχείας δευτέρας κυρίου κὺρ Γρηγορίου. Τυπικὸν περιέχον ὅλην τὴν τάξιν τῆς ἀκολουθίας τοῦ ἐνιαυτοῦ. Κ. α′ Δ.* According to Psachos' astute decipherment, the abbreviation at the end of the note means *Κωνσταντῖνος α′ Δομέστικος.* Furthermore, Psachos, an expert in musical palaeography, asserted that the handwriting of this manuscript is that of Constantinos Byzantios.[110]

Cf. Constantinos Byzantios protopsaltes (1821–55).

CHRONOLOGICAL LIST OF SINGERS OF THE GREAT CHURCH

Protopsaltae

Theophanes Karykes, 1 October 1577–before March 1578
Nikolaos Oursinos Doukatares, 1586/7
Georgios Raedestinos, October 1611–21 February 1638
Chrysaphes the New, April 1655–1665 or 1680?
Panayiotes Chalatzoglou, 1728
Ioannes Trapezountios, 1736–June 1769

[108] G. Papadopoulos, *Συμβολαὶ . . .*, p. 318.
[109] Th. Aristokleous, *Κωνσταντίου Α′ βιογραφία καὶ συγγραφαὶ*, p. 65. Aristokles was a friend of Constantinos Byzantios. His information, however, about the subsequent promotions of Constantinos is not always accurate.
[110] Psachos, 'Σημειώματα Κωνσταντίνου τοῦ πρωτοψάλτου', *Phorminx*, 2nd period, ii, No. 16-18 (November-December 1907), p. 9.

Daniel, *c.* 1771–d. 23 December 1789
Iakovos Peloponnesios, 5 March 1790–d. 23 April 1800
Petros Byzantios, end of April 1800–*c.* 1805
Manuel Byzantios, *c.* 1805–d. 21 June 1819
Gregorios, end of June 1819–d. 23 December 1821
Constantinos Byzantios, 24 December 1821–1855

Lampadarii

Phocas, March 1575–1578
Georgios, before 1616–after 1620
Michael, 15 June 1629
Panayiotes Chalatzoglou, before 1728
Ioannes Trapezountios, 16 October 1728–January 1734
Daniel, 5 September 1740–*c.* 1771
Petros Peloponnesios, *c.* 1771–1778
Iakovos Peloponnesios, 22 June 1784–end of December 1789
Petros Byzantios, end of December 1789–end of April 1800
Gregorios, 1813–end of June 1819

Domestikoi

Panayiotes Chalatzoglou, before 1728
Ioannes Trapezountios, 1727
Daniel, February 1734
Iakovos Peloponnesios (first domestikos), 1764–76
Petros Peloponnesios (second domestikos), 1764–*c.* 1771
Petros Byzantios
     (second domestikos), *c.* 1771–25 November 1773
     (first domestikos), –end of December 1789
Athanasios [Photinos?] Peloponnesios (second domestikos),
     September 1784–1 December 1785
Anastasios Proikonesios, for two years between May 1789 and
     March 1794
Stavres or Stavrakes, *c.* 1795
Constantinos Byzantios (second domestikos), 23 April 1800
                         (first domestikos), 1808

IO

Jørgen Raasted

ROSKILDE

Voice and Verse in a Troparion of Cassia

In her recent monograph on Cassia[1] Ilse Rochow points out that 'ein wichtiges Problem in Zusammenhang mit der Edition der liturgischen Dichtungen ist auch ihre musikalische Seite, also die Feststellung ihrer Melodien, die im Fall der Kassia fast sämtlich von ihr komponiert sind'.[2] In this connection she refers to one of Tillyard's earliest articles, *A Musical Study of the Hymns of Casia*[3] and to transcriptions in Wellesz's *History of Byzantine Music and Hymnography* and in the *Transcripta* series of the *Monumenta Musicae Byzantinae*.[4]

I should like to discuss some melodic details of Cassia's most famous liturgical poem, the Doxastikon Κύριε ἡ ἐν πολλαῖς ἁμαρτίαις (Plagios Tetartos) for the morning service on Wednesday of Holy Week. I do not propose to carry out an investigation into the original shape of this melody or of its modifications through the centuries; such an investigation must be based on the collation of a great number of manuscripts. For the present purpose a sufficient base is provided by a Palaeobyzantine manuscript, the Stikherarion Ohrid 53, dating from the eleventh century,[5] and by three dated Stikheraria in Round notation: Sinai 1218 (A.D. 1177, which makes it one of

---

[1] *Studien zu der Person, den Werken und dem Nachleben der Dichterin Kassia, Berliner Byzantinistische Arbeiten*, Band 38 (Berlin, 1967).

[2] Rochow, p. 34.

[3] *Byzantinische Zeitschrift*, 20 (1911), pp. 420-85.

[4] Rochow, p. 34, n. 247-50.

[5] For Ohrid 53, see Oliver Strunk, *Specimina Notationum Antiquiorum* (*MMB VII*, 1966), p. 22, n. 50 and p. 24; plates 94 and 95.

our earliest sources in Round notation), Vienna Theol. Gr. 181
(A.D. 1217 or 1221; our Troparion was transcribed from this
manuscript by Egon Wellesz in his *History* (second edition,
pp. 395–7, cf. first edition, pp. 312–14)), and Sinai 1230 (A.D.
1365).[6] Despite minor differences between these four versions,
the general picture of the phenomena to be discussed comes out
clearly enough. To simplify the presentation of the musical
phrases, I shall refer the reader to the transcription in either
edition of Wellesz's *History* (from the Vienna Stikherarion,
siglum 'D').

Following the *MMB* practice, Wellesz prints his transcription
as a prose text, without indication of any verse structure; but
in the chapter on 'Words and Music'[7] the poetical text is given
in extenso, divided into 31 short-verses that make up 16 long-
verses. A different structure of the poem is given in C. A.
Trypanis's anthology *Medieval and Modern Greek Poetry* (No. 6).
Here, based on the metrical scheme in Christ-Paranikas'
Anthologia Graeca (1871) p. 104, the text is given in 20 verses of
different length, organized in 8 sections; some of the long-
verses are subdivided, with a total of 28 units to be compared
with Wellesz's 31 short-verses.

The discrepancy between these two ways of dividing the
poetical text obviously has something to do with the musical
structure. It would be unjust to blame Trypanis for having
reproduced in 1949 (the date of his Preface) the 1872 setting
without paying due attention to the structure as revealed by
the melody; for Wellesz's *History* was published in the very same

[6] The Stikherarion Sinai 1218, the Psaltikon Patmos 221, and the Typikon Patmos
265 are written by the same scribe, Nikephoros, between 1162 and 1179,
probably in Bithynia—cf. Christian Thodberg, *Der byzantinische Alleluiarionzyklus*
(*MMB Subsidia VIII*, 1966), pp. 20-1. In my *Intonation Formulas* (*MMB Subsidia
VII*, 1966) Sinai 1218 is frequently quoted, see Index of Manuscripts, p. 218.

Vienna Theol. Gr. 181—the codex Dalasseni—has been studied in more detail
than most other MSS of Byzantine music, especially since 1935 when it was
published as vol. i of the Série principale of the *MMB*. Many of its palaeographical and codicological peculiarities are discussed in my *Intonation Formulas*,
see Index of Manuscripts, p. 222.

Sinai 1230, written in Trebizond A.D. 1365, is rightly praised for its accuracy
by Heinrich Husmann in his 'Modulation und Transposition in den bi- und
trimodalen Stichera', *Archiv für Musikwissenschaft* xxvii, 1970, p. 8. In his complementary report to Wellesz's 'Melody Construction in Byzantine Chant',
Actes du XIIᵉ congrès international d'études byzantines, Ohrid 1961, I (Belgrade, 1963),
p. 369, Oliver Strunk has some remarks on its place in the tradition.

[7] In the *History* (1st ed., p. 278; 2nd ed., p. 353).

year (1949)—and Tillyard's old article in the *Byzantinische
Zeitschrift* from 1911 numbers the lines according to the
Anthologia from 1872 and is, besides, written in the period when
Tillyard still believed in Riemann's rhythmical theories about
'a musical 2-bar phrase in common time' as the main unit of
rhythm.[8] My point is simply to show that the medieval melody
of a Troparion—that is, of a monostrophic text without any
fixed metrical pattern—has so much to tell us about the
structure of the poetical text, that an editor of the latter must
consult the former; otherwise he may distort the metre of the
text.

The setting in Trypanis's *Anthology* (T) is as follows:

Κύριε, ἡ ἐν πολλαῖς ἁμαρτίαις περιπεσοῦσα γυνή,
   τὴν σὴν αἰσθομένη θεότητα,
   μυροφόρου ἀναλαβοῦσα τάξιν,
   ὀδυρομένη μύρον σοι   πρὸ τοῦ ἐνταφιασμοῦ κομίζει·
5 οἴμοι! λέγουσα,   ὅτι νύξ μοι ὑπάρχει,
   οἶστρος ἀκολασίας   ζοφώδης τε καὶ ἀσέληνος,
   ἔρως τῆς ἁμαρτίας·
   δέξαι μου τὰς πηγὰς τῶν δακρύων
   ὁ νεφέλαις διεξάγων   τῆς θαλάσσης τὸ ὕδωρ·
10 κάμφθητί μοι   πρὸς τοὺς στεναγμοὺς τῆς καρδίας
   ὁ κλίνας τοὺς οὐρανοὺς   τῇ ἀφράστῳ σου κενώσει·
   καταφιλήσω τοὺς ἀχράντους σου πόδας,
   ἀποσμήξω τούτους δὲ πάλιν
   τοῖς τῆς κεφαλῆς μου βοστρύχοις·
15 ὧν ἐν τῷ παραδείσῳ Εὔα τὸ δειλινὸν
   κρότον τοῖς ὠσὶν ἠχηθεῖσα   τῷ φόβῳ ἐκρύβη·
   ἁμαρτιῶν μου τὰ πλήθη   καὶ κριμάτων σου ἀβύσσους
   τίς ἐξιχνιάσει, ψυχοσῶστα σωτήρ μου;
   Μή με τὴν σὴν δούλην παρίδῃς
20 ὁ ἀμέτρητον ἔχων τὸ ἔλεος.

This setting differs from Wellesz's short-verse arrangement (W)
in several places:

LINE 1 is given as one continuous long-verse in T, as two
short-verses in W—with a stop after ἁμαρτίαις. This stop is not

---

[8] *Byzantinische Zeitschrift*, 20 (1911), pp. 438-40. The melody is transcribed pp·
461ff.

M

174 STUDIES IN EASTERN CHANT

melodically marked, and W's subdivision is evidently made to avoid an oversized verse. In any short-verse arrangement of a Byzantine Troparion we may run into similar cases. Evidently not every long-verse is made up of shorter units, although this seems to be far more common than an unsplittable long-verse.

After Κύριε Ohrid 53 and Sinai 1218 set a dot, and a minor stop is also indicated by a lengthening of the note on (Κύρι)ε in all sources. Similar treatment of the first word or words of a poem—or one of its main sections, or even of a long-verse—is so frequently found that it is to be considered an important element of the musical style.[9]

LINES 5–7: In the beginning of line 5, the words οἴμοι λέγουσα are similarly set apart from the following, and there are punctuation dots in all four manuscripts. This short-verse introduces a whole section, and is not only the first half of one long-verse. In the following there is musical evidence to show that the peculiar and unbalanced setting in T is wrong; the melody clearly suggests an arrangement in two subdivided long-verses:

ὅτι νύξ μοι ὑπάρχει   οἶστρος ἀκολασίας

ζοφώδης τε καὶ ἀσέληνος ἔρως τῆς ἁμαρτίας.

This structure, which is corroborated by the rhyme, is suggested by the following details in the melody:

1) There is no marked stop after ὑπάρχει; the melody goes on like that of line 1. (Punctuation dot only in Ohrid 53.)

2) Cadential ending on ἀκολασίας. Its last note carries an Apoderma which has a leading-on function, cf. the parallel in line 1, γυνή. (All four manuscripts punctuate after ἀκολασίας.)

3) The beginning of the second of these long-verses (ζοφώδης τε) is set to a melody, elements of which are used later on for similar beginnings of long-verses (8 δέξαι μου, 9 ὀνεφέλαις, 12 καταφιλήσω, 19 μή με). That the melisma on τε ($\overset{?}{c}\ \overset{?}{b}\ \overset{\prime}{c}_d$) serves the same purpose as the bcc-groups in most of these instances is seen, too, from the

---

[9] Jørgen Raasted, 'Some Reflections on Byzantine Musical Style', *Studies in Eastern Chant*, I (1966), pp. 57-60.

red Xeron Klasma which is added as a subsidiary sign in
Sinai 1230 (〉 〉 ⁄ .). The cbcd-melisma is used with
the same implication in Pentecostarium, Hymn 59, lines
7, 8, and 10 (*MMB Transcripta VII*, p. 76).

4) The formula on *καὶ ἀσέληνος* is used at the same place
within the long-verse in line 4, (*ὀδυρο*)*μένη μύρον σοι*.

LINE 15 is printed in T as one continuous verse, whereas W
divides after *παραδείσῳ*, in accordance with the punctuation of
D (and, e.g., Sinai 1230). In this case only a comparison with
other manuscripts reveals that Cassia's own melody goes against
this textual structure; for in the three other manuscripts the
word *ενα* carries the end of the 'Anastama' aEFED, a common
cadential formula in this mode:

1230:	ων	εν	τω	πα	ρα	δει	σω·	ευ	α	
	a	G	F	E	GF	G a	E	FE	D	

1218:	a	G	F	E?	F	G a	E	F	D	10

53:	a	G	F	E	F	G a	E	F	D	

D:	a	G	G	G	G	a b	G	bc	a	11

Whether we read *τὸ δειλινόν* or *τὸν δειλινόν*, the *word ενα*
belongs to the following text, whereas the *melody* of this word is
directly coupled together with that of the preceding *παραδείσῳ*.

A more striking case of 'melodic enjambement' is found earlier
in the Troparion, in the transition from line 9 to line 10. The
textual stop after *τὸ ὕδωρ* is considerable, but the melody goes on
without any break at all and does not rest until after *καμφθητί
μοι*.[12]

---

[10] Sinai 1218 has a punctuation dot after *ενα*; in the same manuscript, the Ison
over the first syllable of *παραδεισω* is wrong: an Apostrophos is needed, cf.
Ohrid 53.

[11] The note on the last syllable of *παραδεισω* is *not* lengthened in the Vienna
manuscript.

[12] A parallel case is discussed in my article in *SEC* I (see above, note 9), pp. 60-2.

A minor conflict between syntactical structure and melody can be observed already in line 4, where μύρον σοι belongs *textually* to the following (as does Εὔα in line 15), but *melodically* to the preceding ὀδυρομένη.

I shall return to the implications of these observations later on. But before I leave Cassia's Troparion, I should like to comment on a couple of details in Tillyard's article in the *Byzantinische Zeitschrift* from 1911. In his analysis of its structure (pp. 464–5) Tillyard makes use of

1) the 'division-marks' (i.e. the punctuation) of Brit. Mus. Add. 27865;
2) 'the obvious parallelism of the words in many places';
3) the martyriae (medial signatures) of Athens 883;
4) Riemann's rhythmical theories.[13]

He concludes as follows: 'It will be seen that the sense and, with the single exception already mentioned, the martyriae support the scheme of division that I give, and which, I venture to believe, makes the hymn easier to understand as a work of art' (p. 465). The 'single exception already mentioned' is a medial signature which in the Athens manuscript is given after κάμφθητί μοι in line 10. On this signature Tillyard remarks: 'The martyria in the middle of line 10 obviously cannot be the end of a sentence, but is merely a help to the singer' (p. 464). We have already seen that this place is certainly not the end of a sentence—in fact, the imperative is placed at the beginning of a couple of lines, corresponding to δέξαι in line 8—but at the same time we have seen that we are at the end of a musical phrase. As I see it, a medial intonation sung at this place would further underline the musical enjambement; it is not merely to be understood as 'a help to the singer'.[14]

Another detail worth mentioning is Tillyard's remark on the structure of line 13, one of the few places where he deviates from the punctuation of Brit. Mus. 27865: 'line 13 undivided, although 12 is divided. This is certainly a great improvement; a weak phrase like τούτους δὲ πάλιν is much better not made into a separate colon.' The argument is here based on the meaning, the sense.

---

[13] Cf. above, note 8.
[14] There are medial signatures at this place in Sinai 1218, D, and Sinai 1230. For the notion of medial signatures as symbols of a more or less *ad libitum* singing of the corresponding intonations, see my *Intonation Formulas*, p. 162. Parallels to the habit of intercalating such medial intonations after the first word or words of a hymn (or a section or a long-verse) are easily found, see e.g. ibid., pp. 99 (Ex. 8 and n. 32), 128 (Ex. 29), and 145 (Ex. 41).

Tillyard has nothing to say about the unusual position of δέ, a particle which is normally put second in its clause. In a Troparion where no fixed rhythmical or metrical scheme can possibly have influenced the word order,[15] Cassia might easily have written τούτους δὲ πάλιν ἀποσμήξω or some other smooth construction. It is possible, therefore, that Cassia's actual wording is another instance of a device which we have already observed in many verses of her Troparion: the setting apart, by some suitable means, of their *initium*, as in:

1	Κύριε	9	ὁ νεφέλαις
2	τὴν σήν	10	κάμφθητί μοι
3	μυροφόρου	12	καταφιλήσω
6	ζοφώδης τε	13	ἀποσμήξω
8	δέξαι μου	19	μή με.

To maintain this explanation, two conditions must be fulfilled: the text *and* music of the Troparion should have been 'composed' simultaneously, and the manuscript sources of the eleventh–fourteenth centuries have preserved Cassia's original melody of the ninth century, at least in respect of these punctuating melismas and groupettos. To the best of my knowledge, neither condition is open to serious doubt.

We have now seen how the melody can help in establishing the textual structure of a Troparion. The famous Τροπάριον τῆς Κασσιανῆς was chosen as a suitable starting point, but any monostrophic and non-melismatic hymn could have served the purpose; for although each case may have peculiarities of its own, the underlying principles remain the same. Evidently, then, joint investigation of the poetical *and* the musical structure of these pieces of hymnography are likely to lead to results which neither a literary nor a musical analysis alone can obtain.

We have of course no guarantee that the neumatic tradition of the manuscripts has preserved all details of the melody which the poet had in mind; since generally several centuries of oral tradition precede the oldest written sources, and even in the best period of written tradition the melodies are not absolutely stable. Quite apart from these well-known factors of uncertainty, which are caused by the very nature of oral and written παράδοσις, there are other obstacles to a mechanical application of the 'combined poetico-musical analysis'. As I see it, some of

[15] J. D. Denniston, *The Greek Particles* (2nd ed., Oxford, 1954), pp. 187-9.

these obstacles are connected with precisely those subtleties of style for which we admire the Troparia, the interplay of resting and leading-on cadences[16] and the phenomena of *enjambement*.

In 1959, when my first article on these problems was printed,[17] I was able to observe that 'cadences . . . can be found at unexpected places or are missing where you would expect them', but at the time I did not go beyond this bare statement, nor was I able to define such situations as cases of *enjambement*— musical (as we have seen in the above analysis of Cassia's Troparion) or textual. The phenomena of *enjambement* are among those features of style which deserve to be studied more thoroughly. At present, however, they have been mentioned only as factors of uncertainty which must be borne in mind when a combined poetico-musical analysis is applied to the Byzantine Troparia.

[16] Jørgen Raasted, 'Some Reflections . . .' (*SEC* I, 1966), p. 59; *Intonation Formulas*, pp. 60-3.
[17] 'The Structure of the Stichera in Byzantine Rite', *Byzantion* 28 (1958), pp. 529-41, especially pp. 532-3.

II

Miloš Velimirović

MADISON, WISCONSIN

'Persian Music' in Byzantium?

IT is not an unknown occurrence while browsing through a manuscript to stumble upon some puzzle which raises a number of knotty questions and remains unsolved. Such an example is presented here in the hope that other scholars may help to determine the nature of an unusual piece of music encountered in a Byzantine musical manuscript.

In a rather large anthology of Byzantine chants, Athens MS 2401, in the National Library in Athens, on the lower half of folio 122v there is a musical composition which is not related to the contents. Judging by the ink and handwriting, it would appear that this piece was added, at the latest, shortly after the completion of the manuscript. Paleographical evidence as well as the paper suggest that the manuscript may have been written not later than the middle of the fifteenth century. The composition is entitled 'persikon' which seems to mean 'Persian [piece of music]'! The text is written in Greek letters and is fairly legible. The thought that the text itself may be Persian might suggest itself, yet a consultation with an expert in this field, Professor Firuz Kazemzadeh of Yale University, discarded this possibility. Since in the fifteenth century it was already a well-established practice in Byzantium to sing 'tererisms' which did not contain any text but only nonsense syllables, the next possibility might be that these were nonsense syllables. Or to carry the question even further—is it a scribal joke?

The piece is notated with Middle Byzantine neumes, in mode IV and mode IV Plagal, with very clear signatures of these two modes. The piece even contains certain musical phrases which are repeated and some of the patterns resemble

179

those which are encountered in some of the more extravagant kalophonic Byzantine examples. Since Byzantine neumatic notation indicates only musical intervals without indication of their size, it may appear at first as a piece in a diatonic transcription, as presented here. Yet one could be tempted to transcribe at least some of the melodic phrases using chromatically modified intervals. If this were done the opening phrase for instance would appear quite 'oriental' in sound, indeed. But it must be noted that to achieve such an effect one would have to disregard the norms already accepted for transcribing the Middle Byzantine neumatic notation.

A copy of the transcription of this piece was also submitted to Professor Bruno Nettl of the University of Illinois, who recently spent a year in Iran. He was kind enough to examine the piece and suggested that if this were an example of dance music the use of nonsense syllables might conceivably be appropriate. As for the music itself, Professor Nettl suggested that some melodic segments, especially some of passages with successive seconds in downward motion (e.g. B–A, A–G, G–F) are similar to the type of melodic cells which are indeed known in Persian music. Even the repeated notes on the same pitch (see line 10) may be found in dances (if performed in a fast tempo) or in classical vocal or instrumental music (if performed slowly). Professor Nettl's conclusion (for which I am deeply grateful to him) is that while there is nothing in this piece that would definitely mark it as of Persian origin, there are nevertheless some features which indicate that this possibility is not to be discarded. In short, this mysterious addition in a Byzantine musical manuscript still awaits an explanation and any suggestions and comments concerning it on the basis of the appended transcription are invited.

Athens 2401, f. 122v. 'πέρσικον'

Index 1

Byzantine Musicians

Index 2

Byzantine Musical Manuscripts Cited